CARROLL & GRAF PUBLISHERS
NEW YORK

Step Right Up
Stories of Carnivals, Sideshows, and the Circus

Carroll & Graf Publishers
An Imprint of Avalon Publishing Group Inc.
245 West 17th Street
New York, NY 10011

First Carroll & Graf edition 2004

Library of Congress Cataloging-in-Publication Data is available.

ISBN: 0-7867-1332-1

Printed in the United States of America
Interior design by Simon M. Sullivan
Distributed by Publishers Group West

For Karl Francis Knaebel

CONTENTS

ACKNOWLEDGMENTS

There are far too many people to thank, really, so I'll keep this short and sort it out later. Thanks to all of my colleagues at the Avalon Publishing Group especially Tina Pohlman, Dan O'Connor, Will Balliett, Shawneric Hachey, Simon Sullivan, Jennifer Steffey, Philip Turner, Mike O'Connor, Keith Wallman, Paul Paddock, and Leslie Miller. I'd also like to thank the following people for their suggestions and advice: Karl Hendricks, Josh Leeman, Carolyn Nash, Lisa Podemski, and Audrey Wasser. And the Knaebel family for their support. Once more with feeling, thanks.

INTRODUCTION

Dog-boy, atlas, half-man, the geeks, the hired hands
There was not one among them that did not cast an eye behind
In the hope that the carny would return to his own kind

—Nick Cave, "The Carny"

TRUTH BE TOLD, NICK Cave's snarling, sleazy, scheming carny is at best creative hyperbole, if not altogether nonexistent. In reality, many of today's carnival workers, something of a dying breed unfortunately, are as hard-working, industrious, and, well, normal (relatively speaking, I suppose) as any other American entrepreneur. As one young carny pointed out in the recent *Rolling Stone* article "I Was a Teenage Freak," "Not everyone's mom is the bearded lady." And to a certain extent it's always been that way. Arthur H. Lewis's 1970 exposé *Carnival* is filled with characters that are at best nothing more than blue-collar eccentrics. Of course that's not much fun now, is it? HBO's hit series *Carnivàle* wouldn't be nearly as popular or intriguing if it followed the exploits of a clan of diligent clean-cut normals trekking through the dust bowl, and, admit it, Siegfried & Roy became a hell of a lot more interesting after Roy Horn almost got his head torn off by one of his tigers.

There's something strange, and, shall we say, not quite right about carnivals, sideshows, and the circus, and it is as much this festering peculiarness that draws us to the midway as it is a tightrope act or the chance to win a plush rabbit. It is that odd, not-quite-right milieu found in what is otherwise old-fashioned entertainment that this collection of stories seeks to capture. To put it another way, I'm not interested in Cirque du Soleil or a genteel church fair, whether it has a Tilt-A-Whirl or not. In fact, the very spirit that this collection attempts to embody may in fact exist only in the realm of myth. But why debunk myth, especially when it's so alluring?

This of course begs the question, what exactly do we find so alluring about these unusual displays? It can't possibly be pure entertainment. There's more than enough high-resolution entertainment out there to run the circus right out of town. Yet they persist. This certainly isn't the golden age of the carnival or the sideshow, but they're not dead yet either (been to Coney Island lately?). What is it, then? Do they validate our precarious understanding of our own normalcy, or do they offer a splendid, sordid inside-out look at our own twisted inner workings? Are we on some level attracted to the peripatetic anywhere-I-lay-my-head lifestyle? Or is it simply that we just want to look at a bearded lady and a Lobster Boy because frankly it's not something you see every day? Edward Hoagland seems to think so. In his wonderful essay "Circus Music," he argues, "In a circus you didn't have to—weren't supposed to—avert your eyes, and that may have been its ultimate kick."

There are plenty of freaks to gaze upon in this collection, from Katherine Dunn's Binewski clan to Eudora Welty's outcast Indian maiden. And although perhaps not a freak in the "gabba gabba" sense, Mabel Stark routinely stuck her head between the jaws of man-eating (or at least man-maiming) tigers, and that, to say the least, is freakish. In one way or another, everyone found on the pages of this collection is a freak, an oddity, an outcast—even the normals. And they all find solace at the circus or on the midway. Perhaps that's it right there, as banal as it sounds. If one is willing to accept that on some level we're all freaks—a sentiment echoed in many of these selections—the carnival's very existence is a comforting thought. If they're willing to offer a home to the 400-pound man, a frog boy, a sword swallower, and a gas-huffing ex-con, then surely they've got a place for you and me.

Nathaniel Knaebel
New York City, N.Y.

CIRCUS MUSIC: FOR CLOWNS, LIONS, AND SOLO TRAPEZE

Edward Hoagland

—Essayist and former carnival worker Edward Hoagland is the author of seventeen books. This piece first appeared in the February 2002 issue of Harper's *and was selected for inclusion in* The Best American Essays 2003.

A CIRCUS IS BOTH ACROBATIC and elephantine, wholesome but freakish, and that is partly why we like it so—because we are two-headed, too. A showgirl in the center ring displays her pretty legs to daddy while his children are engrossed in watching a palomino stallion dance to the band's tempo. But that, of course, is an illusion. The bandmaster, flourishing his silver cornet, is actually following the horse's mannered, jerky prance, not vice versa, which in turn is being cued by the same short-skirted lady's cracking whip. And in the old days the sideshow used to be called "The Ten-in-One" because it had "Ten Different Freaks Under One Tent for Only One Dollar! Can you beat that, folks?" as the barkers yelled. Only, I suppose, by looking inside oneself. People too fat or too small, too thin or too tall, remind us of a certain unwieldy, weird, but shrinking-violet personage whom we know all too well—as does the Knife-Thrower, the Escape Artist or Contortionist, the Tattooed or Albino Lady, hefting a boa constrictor, perhaps, and the knuckle-walking Wild Man, bearded all over, or the Living Skeleton, and the kinky but outwardly clean-cut gentleman who is wed to the swords and fireballs that he swallows a dozen times a day for our entertainment. Why is it entertainment, if we're not gawking at a caricature of ourselves?

In the big top everybody wears a spiffy uniform, but if yours isn't a one-night stand and they stay until tomorrow, you'll see some of the circus people sleeping in the horse straw on the ground. And when the costumes come off, baby, don't imagine they'll remember you, no matter how hard you may think you clapped. Behind the greasepaint is quite a different sort of face and person. You wouldn't necessarily trust one of the clowns or animal handlers who give such intense pleasure to tens of thousands of children with the downright raising of even a couple; they might already have abandoned a family. Like actors only more so, circus performers are expected to be manic and depressive, and we accept the paradox that a real genius at making little kids laugh, like Danny Kaye or Charlie Chaplin, could verge on frightening them as a father. The funniness is vertiginous, and the hippodrome food is too sweet. Too much is going on in the rings to absorb it all, and the physical stunts sometimes edge toward the suicidal. Maybe the grisly part of the bargain is that we, the "lot lice," the Elmers, rubes, towners, hayseeds, hicks, yokels, are paying green money to watch the star troupers risk their lives. If a trapeze artist falls and hits the ground, he'll lie in front of a grandstand of utter strangers, whimpering, jactitating, and dying alone.

A circus is high and low, piccolos and trombones. The edgy tiger roars and charges, but then licks her trainer at the end, as if they had been friends all along. A clown meanly tricks his chum, dunks him treacherously in a barrel of water, and gloats for the crowd, but then the high-wire walker steals all his thunder as soon as the whistle blows. The ringmaster, though he seems the boss, is curiously not the star; the saddest puss gets the biggest laugh; and the innocence is raunchy (those leggy girls who strut their stuff alongside a whiteface Bozo so that dad has his own reasons to snicker). The clowns teach most memorably that if you trust anybody he will betray you.

We want circus people to be different from us—homeless and garish, heedless and tawdry (otherwise why pay to watch?)—yet to connect with us in deeper currents that we share. Our fear of heights and ridicule, our complicated fascination with animals (whips, but kindness), our love of grace and agility, of stylish vanity and splendid boasting, of dressing in spangles yet living in tents and trailers. As an element of rooting our children in a stable home, we nourish them with this annual spectacle of the elaborately raffish and picaresque. Therefore, we want the show people to be outlandish but never outrageous, to hide from us their perverse, larcenous, or alcoholic tendencies that may accompany the tramping life. A guy who just got out of the county jail (we hope not the Big House) for doing whatever (and we don't want to know whatever) and then hit the road because his wife didn't want him is coiling and flinging the ropes around that keep the aerialists' rigging up; and somehow it has become the kind of responsibility he can handle. And without quite articulating it, we want our offspring to be flexible and adventurous as well as predictable, tolerant as well as ethical, capable of flights of delight as well as down-to-earth. Also, we want circus people to know us better than we know them, in a sense: to be wise beyond their education and social status should officially warrant in gauging human nature, and cater to and inspire our children, even though we have come to watch some of them risk breaking their necks—which is base of us—and even if they can't always manage their own private behavior. People are juggling themselves, hand-to-mouth, in brassy penury, in the circus, not just tossing torches or chancing an awful clawing. Then they'll live in back-street rented rooms during the winter until they can take to the road again.

It's no coincidence that circus music is often identical to the sort of marches that soldiers used to go off to die to. The stakes are high. Bravery, resourcefulness, pinpoint concentration, and self-containment are what make it work, and one reason why so many losers and handicapped souls have found their footing in the circus may be because they see in the crowds how thin a veneer conventional society paints upon our basic greed, inertia, and callousness. So why worry that you're an oddball and have to move somewhere new every other day to keep your haywire impulses under control and sublimate them into stunts? Like rich people, you have that privilege. New audience, new town, never seen you before, never'll see you again. It's anesthetic. If you screw up one of the acts today, you'll get it right tomorrow—so, no sweat, you get it right today.

"We have the fattest woman in the world, and the tallest man, and a girl who has no arms or legs, and midgets who are married! Have you ever seen a camel spit, or seals play catch, or elephants stand on their heads? A man with reptile's scales, who was once just like you! And the Good Lord made him. Can you finish your ice cream after you have looked at him?" Good question. In the pre-television era, when much of the novel technology related to transportation, not electronics, live entertainment toured between cities by train or motor vehicle. Repertory-stage and opera companies, evangelist preachers, Chautauqua lecturers, freelance physic salesmen, vaudeville magicians, humorists, and strippers, who formerly had gone by riverboat or wagon, would troop through town—as well as the more celebrated Sells-Floto, or Sparks, or Hagenbeck-Wallace, or Sam B. Dill's, or Walter L. Main, or Robbins Bros., and Christy Bros. circuses, not to mention Ringling Bros. and Barnum & Bailey, The Greatest Show on Earth. There was Downie Bros. Wild Animal Circus, The Largest Motor Circus in the World (families and brothers stuck together in business in those days), and the famous Clyde Beatty-Cole Bros. big show, and Col. Tim McCoy & His Indian Village, or his Congress of Rough Riders of the World, and Marcellus' Golden Models (with the men's pectorals as big as the women's breasts), and Tommy Atkins' Military Riding Maids.

Fortunately, we aren't entirely bereft of a visual record of these arcane marvels. A Manhattan banquet photographer named Edward Kelty, whose usual venue was hotel ballrooms and Christmas parties, went out intermittently in the summer from the early-1920s to the mid-1940s, taking panoramic tripod pictures of circus personnel, in what could only have constituted a labor of love. He was expert, anyway, from his bread-and-butter job, at joshing smiles and camaraderie out of disparate collections of people, coaxing them to drape their arms around each other and trust the box's eye. He had begun close at home, at Coney Island freak shows, when the subway was extended out there, and Times Square flea-circus "museums" and variety halls, and the Harlem Amusement Palace. Later, building upon contacts and friendships from those places, he outfitted a truck for darkroom purposes (presumable to sleep in too) and sallied farther to photograph the tented circuses that played on vacant lots in New Jersey, Connecticut, or on Long Island, and gradually beyond. He would pose an ensemble of horse wranglers, canvasmen, ticket takers, candy butchers, teeterboard tumblers, "web-sitters" (the guys who hold the ropes for the ballet girls who climb up them and twirl), and limelight daredevils, or the bosses and moneymen. He took everybody, roustabouts as conscientiously as impresarios, and although he was not artistically very ambitious—and did hawk his prints both to the public and to the troupers, at "6 for $5"—in his consuming hobby he surely aspired to document this vivid, disreputable demimonde obsessively, thoroughly: which is his gift to us. (An exhibition and a book are planned.)

More of these guys may have been camera-shy than publicity hounds, but Kelty's rubber-chicken award ceremonies and industrial photo shoots must have taught him how to relax jumpy people for the few minutes required. With his Broadway pinstripes and a newsman's bent fedora, as proprietor of Century Flashlight Photographers, in the West Forties, he must have become a trusted presence in the "Backyard" and "Clown Alley." He knew show-business and street touts, bookies and scalpers—but also how to flirt with a marquee star. Because his personal life seems to have been a bit of a train wreck, I think of him more as a hatcheck girl's swain, yet he knew how to let the sangfroid sing from some of these faces, or simple good rolling-stone mischief, while doing justice to the ragged stringbeans, ranked in another line. These zany tribes of showboaters must have amused him, after the wintertime's chore of recording for posterity some forty-year drudge receiving a gold watch. Other faces look muddled with inchoate emotions, however, as if the man indeed had just gotten out of the penitentiary, or were mentally retarded, or could already feel the dreadful undertow of an illness like epilepsy, schizophrenia, pedophilia, kleptomania, tuberculosis, or diabetic collapse that had choked off so many fresh starts he had attempted before. You wouldn't see him in a hotel ballroom, even as a waiter.

The ushers, the prop men and riggers, the cookhouse crew, the elephant men and cat men, the showgirls arrayed in white bathing suits in a tightly chaperoned, winsome line, the hoboes who had put the tent up and, in the wee hours, would tear it down, and the bosses whose body language, with arms akimbo and swaggering legs, tells us something of who they were: These collective images telegraph the complexity of the circus hierarchy, with stars at the top, winos at the bottom. Except that still below the winos were the "jigs," or Negroes, whom you may notice in uneasily angular positions as they perch semi-perilously on a wagon roof behind everybody else, up in "nigger heaven" (as expressed in movie-house terms), signifying their loose-balloon moorings in this segregated world, based on the mores of winter quarters, which were usually down South. There may even be two bands in the picture, a black one and a white one, that might have sounded better playing together.

While arranging corporate personnel in the phony bonhomie of an office get-together for a company's annual report, Kelty must have longed for summer, when he would be snapping "Congresses" of mugging clowns, fugueing freaks, rodeo sharpshooters, plus the train crews known as "razorbacks" (Raise your backs!), who loaded and unloaded the wagons from railroad flatcars at midnight and dawn. That was the way a chug-a-lug bar fighter might wind up, in this era when "rootless" was a pejorative word, like "hedonistic" or "atheistic," and a new face in town was cause for suspicion. These ladies toted pythons, strolling around the hippodrome track, and didn't wear enough clothes; and some of the men looked as bathless as the guys from a hobo jungle who would steal your wife's apple pie that she'd left to cool on the kitchen windowsill, yet had skills you hadn't imagined. Circuses flouted convention as part of their pitch—flaunted and cashed in on the romance of outlawry, like Old World gypsies. If there hadn't been a crime wave when the show was in town, everybody had sure expected one. And the exotic physiognomies, strangely cut clothes, and oddly focused, disciplined bodies were almost as disturbing—"Near Eastern," whatever Near Eastern meant (it somehow sounded weirder than "Middle Eastern" or "Far Eastern"), bedouin Arabs, Turks and Persians, or Pygmies, Zulus, people cicatrized, "platter-lipped," or nose-split. That was the point. They came from all over the known world to parade on gaudy ten-hitch wagons or caparisoned elephants down Main Street, and then, like the animals in the cages, you wanted them to leave town. Yet if you were a farmer who thought a bear that had killed a pig was scary to come to grips with, try managing half a dozen snarling lions! Or maybe you had screwed up your nerve recently to reroof the barn? Try walking the high wire, fifty feet up, with just your wife standing underneath you in case of a slip.

When it rained, the rest of us went indoors, but show folk didn't have an indoors. They were negotiating with the mud in order to hit the road. The seat men folded thousands of chairs and "bibles," or souvenir programs. The "bull hands," the elephant men, controlled the pachyderms with a club with a hook on the end as the animals pulled out the quarter poles and the center poles and any wagons that got stuck. The transience of the circus jibed better with wild nature than the closely trimmed lawns at home—and willy-nilly a circus rolled. People with survival skills pitched in to fill the gaps. The whole grew bigger than the parts, though close to nature meant close to scandal too, as they intersect in such a phrase as "Nature calls." Nature is randy as well as rainy, smelly as well as sunny. Circus Day was uncivilized like the Fourth of July, with candied apples, cotton candy, fireworks, and special dispensation for skimpy costumes, public lust, trials of strength, breakneck stunts, colossal crowds. "It was a circus," we'll still say when some ordinary scene bursts out of control. And if your blouse stuck out farther than the next girl's, that cage boy loafing over there might decide to persuade the hippopotamus to gape her mouth for you and poke his hand inside and scratch her gums the way she liked, to make you ooh and aah at how heroic he was.

I was such a cage boy myself, with Ringling Bros. and Barnum & Bailey in 1951 and 1952, and would also pet the menagerie leopards for the right admirer. I worked for two dollars per sixteen-hour day and slept two to a bunk, three bunks high, on the train, or else could rattle through the night outside on a flatcar. The faces of the drifters I was with sometimes looked as grim and bitter as a WANTED poster, and quite at their wit's end, not having had much wit to begin with, and what they might have had perhaps dispelled in prison. They'd slammed around, with their hats pulled down over their eyes, every mother-in-law's nightmare, and knew how to jump on a moving train without saying goodbye to anybody—knew the Front Range of the Rockies, and the Tex-Mex border. And not even our rumpled banquets guy with the windblown tie—a theater-district barfly and Coney Island dime-museum habitue, who scarcely saw his own sons after they were toddlers—could have coaxed a trustful look out of them.

Up on that giddy wire or the trapeze bar—or in the Iron Jaw act, spinning relentlessly by their teeth people did things they shouldn't reasonably do, with no ostensible purpose but showing off, while the tuba oompahed, the trombone slalomed, the clarinet climbed a rope, and the comet hit the canvas's peak line. "Flyers" and slack-wire artists and "risley" foot-jugglers and whiteface or "auguste" clowns hoarded and pruned their skills, like the humble juggler of legend, who during the night tiptoed into the empty cathedral on the Madonna's feast day after the wealthier citizens had long since delivered their heavy gifts, genuflected before her statue, and gone comfortably home. Alone and barefoot, he performed for her with whatever grace and dexterity he could muster. And for the first time in all of history, tears welled up in her stone eyes.

That's what we try to do, isn't it? Keep rolling, keep juggling and strutting our stuff, honoring our gods; then take a bow and exit smiling? But magic seldom happens unless a structure has been erected—whether a church or a tent—that is hospitable to it. Art is fragile, and a windless silence helps. Then depart just as the applause crests, leaving some emotion for the next act, because the thrust of the circus never stops, whether in mud or sunshine, whether the tickets have sold out or not. High stakes. The aerialist Lillian Leitzel, the most mesmerizing female performer ever, fell to her death in 1931, and afterward Alfredo Codona, her husband and male counterpart, at least on the trapeze, married an aerialist/equestrienne, but injured himself while doing a triple somersault in 1933 and never flew again. Grotesquely, he became his wife's hostler on the Tom Mix Circus—until, estranged, he shot both her and himself in her divorce lawyer's office.

Karl Wallenda, the greatest wire-walker and another compulsive, fell twelve stories off a cable strung 750 feet between two hotels in 1978, at seventy-three. But for some of these plain old Okies, Arkies, Hoosiers, and Wisconsin Cheeseheads and Georgia Crackers who got the show to run on time and then maybe drove a trailer truck all night, the gamble was compelling, too. Their trajectory ran toward alcohol and the jitters of oblivion, even though they had a seaman's way with ropes. And several gaze at Kelty's camera as if reminded of a police-station booking room, whereas the performers pose in a row in profile with their biceps bulged, or ponytail pert. "Is your body as trim as mine?" they seem to ask. "I'll stand on one hand—or one finger! I'll do a back flip from one horse to another and then lie down on the ground and let the elephant put her foot on my nose, but because we're all a family she won't crush it. Instead she'll lift me onto her shoulders and we'll chase that clown until he drops his red bloomers."

The moneymen, gimlet-eyed, with peremptory chests, let their suits, cufflinks and stickpins, their oxblood shoes and railroad men's timepieces, speak for them. They owned the tents and trucks and railroad cars, of course, but also often the lions too, despite the trainer's intimacy with them. He could be fired and have to pack his kit and never see those particular cats again. Similarly, the acrobats were not terribly suited to busking for spare change on the subway. They needed complicated rigging and a spread of canvas overhead—the whole apparatus—to gather an audience sufficient to justify risking their lives, without being clinically crazy. And a run-of-the-mill hobo, who was used to sneaking across the hazardous, lightless bustle of a railroad yard to boost himself into a moving boxcar without being detected, had probably found a raison d'etre with Ringling Bros., called by show people "the Big One." In my time, if he was fired with the dreaded words "No Rehire" scribbled on his pink slip to go into the company's records, it might take the little wind that he had out of his sails. The performance, the crowds and ovations, though not directly for him, had centered and justified his shaky life.

The center poles and brocaded, bejeweled elephant howdahs might be bedecked with the Stars and Stripes, and yet one knew that the entire spectacle, unlike July 4, wasn't quite American. The men and women holding hands in the center ring to take a bow after manipulating their bodies on the teeterboard were probably foreigners, and might not even be married to each other—and God knows where they slept. They had somehow gelled their flightiness for professional purposes, but the idea of a new town tomorrow, a new town the next day, and consorting in a business way with freaks whose very livelihood was exhibiting their disfigurements like fakirs in an Asian marketplace (freaks inherently were un-American) was not like the Home of the Brave. What demons in themselves were they trying to anesthetize by harboring values so different from ours? We, the Elmers, the hicks, the towners, the hayshakers, had just put down good money to watch somebody shoot himself out of a cannon on the assurance that it was going to be genuine and he might really die before our eyes. But he landed succinctly on his back in the L-shaped net, swung to the ground, acknowledged our claps—and didn't then thank his lucky stars and settle down to a productive existence like ours. Eat your heart out, rube, was part of his message. We'll be gone tomorrow. We'll see Chicago. We'll be in Florida. You stay here and milk your cows!

To "the Strange People," misshapen on their little stages in the sideshow and peddling ten-cent likenesses of their deformities to the public, the conventional response would be, "There but for the grace of God go I." But why had He withheld His mercy when constructing them? Did their burden, as suggested by ancient superstitions, express a spiritual canker? Was external ugliness a punishment laid on the erring soul? My own feeling, while working next to them in Madison Square Garden and other arenas half a century ago, was that the object lesson ran deeper still. People were fascinated not just because of morbid curiosity and schadenfreude but because we saw ourselves incarnate in the Knife-Thrower, the Living Skeleton (or "Pincushion," or "Picture Gallery"), the Human Pretzel, the Fat Lady, the lame and wheezing Giant, and were encouraged to stare without being rude. The foxfire flicker of ferocity and awful insecurity that so frequently subverted our genial veneer lay out there exposed—much as the bum, the coward, the fussbudget and spoilsport whom we knew all too well was embodied in some of the skits the clowns performed. (Our Knife-Thrower really got to people when, as a piece de resistance, he "horse-whipped" pretty women who volunteered from the crowd.)

A clown or Santa Claus costume, in my experience of the individuals who wear them, can conceal a multitude of sins. But so does the attire that the rest of us hide in, using blandness to mask our shamefaced failures and maladjustments. We, too, have flat feet and big asses, chalky faces and weepy tendencies when frightened of our shadows or searching through the tanbark for a nickel we have lost, a button that popped off, or a pebble that was in our shoe—we took it out but now we miss it. In the smaller tent shows the Fat Lady in the baby-doll nightie might even show it all in a curtained-off area, if you paid an extra four bits (and it was said you could insert them). In a circus you didn't have to—weren't supposed to—avert your eyes, and that may have been its ultimate kick. The guy might die, but without muttering the piety "Oh, I can't watch," we simply did.

Uzbeks rode on saddled camels. Elephants sashayed. A sway-pole acrobat almost seemed to touch the ground on each backswing, then locked his feet and slid down headfirst. A lovely woman with blonde hair hanging to her coccyx adjusted her shoulder straps, kicked off her silver slippers, and gripped a knotted rope to ascend for the Cloud Swing. Over at one side, we might not notice a self-effacing clown—not bizarrely loud now to attract attention—pulling her up with considerable care, then standing underneath in case of a mishap. But if you were observant, you realized there might be some people who had a love life after all.

The black-maned lion roared with bestial fury yet soon lapsed into contented amiability, as if he might be willing to settle in our burg. And the Albino Girl and Snake Charmer and other troupers were said to have bought cough medicine, underpants, and other personal stuff in the local stores. But just when we thought they really liked us and had been converted to our home-sweet-home values, they up and did a disappearing act. Overnight, the magic cavalcade vanished to another state, another climate. We have the gimpy, haywire gene as well, the one that makes you want to hit the road each spring while you last—a hail-fellow who knows that nothing is for keeps. You do your thing, to just whatever tattoo of music and battery of lights are available to you, survive today, sleep it off, and get up on that wire again tomorrow.

FROM SOMETHING WICKED THIS WAY COMES

Ray Bradbury

—Master sci-fi writer Ray Bradbury is the author of over thirty books. This passage from his novel Something Wicked This Way Comes *(1962) describes the giddy anticipation and wistful longing that precedes the arrival of a supernatural carnival.*

WILL STOPPED. WILL LOOKED at the Friday night town. It seemed when the first stroke of nine banged from the big courthouse clock all the lights were on and business humming in the shops. But by the time the last stroke of nine shook everyone's fillings in his teeth, the barbers had yanked off the sheets, powdered the customers, trotted them forth; the druggist's fount had stopped fizzing like a nest of snakes, the insect neons everywhere had ceased buzzing, and the vast glittering acreage of the dime store with its ten billion metal, glass and paper oddments waiting to be fished over, suddenly blacked out. Shades slithered, doors boomed, keys rattled their bones in locks, people fled with hordes of torn newspaper mice nibbling their heels.

Bang! they were gone!

"Boy!" yelled Will. "Folks run like they thought the storm was here!"

"It is!" shouted Jim. "*Us!*"

They stomp-pound-thundered over iron grates, steel trapdoors, past a dozen unlit shops, a dozen half-lit, a dozen dying dark. The city was dead as they rounded the United Cigar Store corner to see a wooden Cherokee glide in darkness, by himself.

"Hey!"

Mr. Tetley, the proprietor, peered over the Indian's shoulder.

"Scare you, boys?"

"Naw!"

But Will shivered, feeling cold tidal waves of strange rain moving down the prairie as on a deserted shore. When the lightning nailed the town, he wanted to be layered under sixteen blankets and a pillow.

"Mr. Tetley?" said Will, quietly.

For now there were two wooden Indians upright in ripe tobacco darkness. Mr. Tetley, amidst his jest, had frozen, mouth open, listening.

"Mr. Tetley?"

He heard something far away on the wind, but couldn't say what it was.

The boys backed off.

He did not see them. He did not move. He only listened.

They left him. They ran.

In the fourth empty block from the library, the boys came upon a third wooden Indian.

Mr. Crosetti, in front of his barber shop, his door key in his trembling fingers, did not see them stop.

What had stopped them?

A teardrop.

It moved shining down Mr. Crosetti's left cheek. He breathed heavily.

"Crosetti, you fool! *Something* happens, *nothing* happens, you cry like a baby!"

Mr. Crosetti took a trembling breath, snuffing. "Don't you *smell* it?"

Jim and Will sniffed.

"Licorice!"

"Heck, no. Cotton candy!"

"I haven't smelled that in years," said Mr. Crosetti.

Jim snorted. "It's around."

"Yes, but who notices? When? Now, my nose tells me, breathe!

And I'm crying. Why? Because I remember how a long time ago, boys ate that stuff. Why haven't I stopped to think and smell the last thirty years?"

"You're busy, Mr. Crosetti," Will said. "You haven't got time."

"Time, time." Mr. Crosetti wiped his eyes. "Where does that smell come from? There's no place in town sells cotton candy. Only circuses."

"Hey," said Will. "That's right!"

"Well, Crosetti is done crying." The barber blew his nose and turned to lock his shop door. As he did this, Will watched the barber pole whirl its red serpentine up out of nothing, leading his gaze around, rising to vanish into more nothing. On countless noons Will had stood here trying to unravel that ribbon, watch it come, go, end without ending.

Mr. Crosetti put his hand to the light switch under the spinning pole.

"Don't," said Will. Then, murmuring, "Don't turn it off."

Mr. Crosetti looked at the pole, as if freshly aware of its miraculous properties. He nodded, gently, his eyes soft. "Where does it come from, where does it go, eh? Who knows? Not you, not him, not me. Oh, the mysteries, by God. So. We'll leave it on!"

It's good to know, thought Will, it'll be running until dawn, winding up from nothing, winding away to nothing, while we sleep.

"Good night!"

"Good night."

And they left him behind in a wind that very faintly smelled of licorice and cotton candy.

Charles Halloway put his hand to the saloon's double swing doors, hesitant, as if the gray hairs on the back of his hand, like antennae, had felt something beyond slide by in the October night. Perhaps great fires burned somewhere and their furnace blasts warned him not to step forth. Or another Ice Age had loomed across the land, its freezing bulk might already have laid waste a billion people in the hour. Perhaps Time itself was draining off down an immense glass, with powdered darkness falling after to bury all.

Or maybe it was only that man in a dark suit, seen through the saloon window, across the street. Great paper rolls under one arm, a brush and bucket in his free hand, the man was whistling a tune, very far away.

It was a tune from another season, one that never ceased making Charles Halloway sad when he heard it. The song was incongruous for October, but immensely moving, overwhelming, no matter what day or what month it was sung:

I heard the bells on Christmas Day
Their old, familiar carols play,
And wild and sweet
Their words repeat
Of peace on earth, good will to men!

Charles Halloway shivered. Suddenly there was the old sense of terrified elation, of wanting to laugh and cry together when he saw the innocents of the earth wandering the snowy streets the day before Christmas among all the tired men and women whose faces were dirty with guilt, unwashed of sin, and smashed like small windows by life that hit without warning, ran, hid, came back and hit again.

Then pealed the bells more loud and deep:
"God is not dead, nor doth He sleep!
The Wrong shall fail,
The Right prevail,
With peace on earth, good will to men!"

The whistling died.

Charles Halloway stepped out. Far up ahead, the man who had whistled the tune was motioning his arms by a telegraph pole, silently working. Now he vanished into the open door of a shop.

Charles Halloway, not knowing why, crossed the street to watch the man pasting up one of the posters inside the unrented and empty store.

Now the man stepped out the door with his brush, his paste

bucket, his rolled papers. His eyes, a fierce and lustful shine, fixed on Charles Halloway. Smiling, he gestured an open hand.

Halloway stared.

The palm of that hand was covered with fine black silken hair. It looked like—

The hand clenched, tight. It waved. The man swept around the corner. Charles Halloway, stunned, flushed with sudden summer heat, swayed, then turned to gaze into the empty shop.

Two sawhorses stood parallel to each other under a single spotlight.

Placed over these two sawhorses like a funeral of snow and crystal was a block of ice six feet long. It shone dimly with its own effulgence, and its color was light green-blue. It was a great cool gem resting there in the dark.

On a little white placard at one side near the window the following calligraphic message could be read by lamplight:

Cooger & Dark's Pandemonium Shadow Show—
Fantoccini, Marionette Circus, and Your
Plain Meadow Carnival. Arriving
Immediately! Here on Display, one of
our many attractions:

THE MOST BEAUTIFUL WOMAN IN THE WORLD!

Halloway's eyes leaped to the poster on the inside of the window.

THE MOST BEAUTIFUL WOMAN IN THE WORLD!

And back to the cold long block of ice.

It was such a block of ice as he remembered from traveling magician's shows when he was a boy, when the local ice company contributed a chunk of winter in which, for 12 hours on end, frost maidens lay embedded, on display while people watched and comedies toppled down the raw white screen and coming attractions came and went and at last the pale ladies slid forth all rimed, chipped free by perspiring sorcerers to be led off smiling into the dark behind the curtains.

THE MOST BEAUTIFUL WOMAN IN THE WORLD!

And yet this vast chunk of wintry glass held nothing but frozen river water.

No. Not quite empty.

Halloway felt his heart pound one special time.

Within the huge winter gem was there not a special vacuum? a voluptuous hollow, a prolonged emptiness which undulated from tip to toe of the ice? and wasn't this vacuum, this emptiness waiting to be filled with summer flesh, was it not shaped somewhat like a . . . woman?

Yes.

The ice. And the lovely hollows, the horizontal flow of emptiness within the ice. The lovely nothingness. The exquisite flow of an invisible mermaid daring the ice to capture it.

The ice was cold.

The emptiness within the ice was warm.

He wanted to go away from here.

But Charles Halloway stood in the strange night for a long time looking in at the empty shop and the two sawhorses and the cold waiting arctic coffin set there like a vast Star of India in the dark. . . .

Jim Nightshade stopped at the corner of Hickory and Main, breathing easily, his eyes fixed tenderly on the leafy darkness of Hickory Street.

"Will . . . ?"

"No!" Will stopped, surprised at his own violence.

"It's just there. The fifth house. Just *one* minute, Will," Jim pleaded, softly.

"Minute . . . ?" Will glanced down the street.

Which was the street of the Theater.

Until this summer it had been an ordinary street where they stole peaches, plums and apricots, each in its day. But late in August, while they were monkey-climbing for the sourest apples, the "thing" happened which changed the houses, the taste of the fruit, and the very air within the gossiping trees.

"Will! It's waiting. Maybe something's *happening!*" hissed Jim.

Maybe something is. Will swallowed hard, and felt Jim's hand pinch his arm.

For it was no longer the street of the apples or plums or apricots, it was the one house with a window at the side and this window, Jim said, was a stage, with a curtain—the shade, that is—up. And in that room, on that strange stage, were the actors, who spoke mysteries, mouthed wild things, laughed, sighed, murmured so much; so *much* of it was whispers Will did not understand.

"Just one last time, Will."

"You know it won't be last!"

Jim's face was flushed, his cheeks blazing, his eyes green-glass fire. He thought of that night, them picking the apples, Jim suddenly crying softly, "Oh, there!"

And Will, hanging to the limbs of the tree, tight-pressed, terribly excited, staring in at the Theater, that peculiar stage where people, all unknowing, flourished shirts above their heads, let fall clothes to the rug, stood raw and animal-crazy, naked, like shivering horses, hands out to touch each other.

What're they *doing!* thought Will. Why are they laughing? What's wrong with them, what's *wrong!?*

He wished the light would go out.

But he hung tight to the suddenly slippery tree and watched the bright window Theater, heard the laughing, and numb at last let go, slid, fell, lay dazed, then stood in dark gazing up at Jim, who still clung to his high limb. Jim's face, hearth-flushed, cheeks fire-fuzzed, lips parted, stared in. "Jim, Jim, come down!" But Jim did not hear. "Jim!" And when Jim looked down at last he saw Will as a stranger below with some silly request to give off living and come down to earth. So Will ran off, alone, thinking too much, thinking nothing at all, not knowing what to think.

"Will, please . . . "

Will looked at Jim now, with the library books in his hands.

"We been to the library. Ain't that enough?"

Jim shook his head. "Carry these for me."

He handed Will his books and trotted softly off under the hissing whispering trees. Three houses down he called back: "Will? Know what you *are?* A darn old dimwit Episcopal Baptist!"

Then Jim was gone.

Will seized the books tight to his chest. They were wet from his hands.

Don't look back! he thought.

I won't! I won't!

And looking only toward home, he walked that way. Quickly.

Halfway home, Will felt a shadow breathing hard behind him.

"Theater closed?" said Will, not looking back.

Jim walked in silence beside him for a long while and then said, "Nobody home."

"Swell!"

Jim spat. "Darn Baptist preacher, you!"

And around the corner a tumbleweed slithered, a great cotton ball of pale paper which bounced, then clung shivering to Jim's legs.

Will grabbed the paper, laughing, pulled it off, let it fly! He stopped laughing.

The boys, watching the pale throwaway rattle and flit through the trees, were suddenly cold.

"Wait a minute . . ." said Jim, slowly.

All of a sudden they were yelling, running, leaping. "Don't tear it! Careful!"

The paper fluttered like a snare drum in their hands.

"COMING, OCTOBER TWENTY-FOURTH!"

Their lips moved, shadowing the words set in rococo type.

"Cooger and Dark's . . . "

"Carnival!"

"October twenty-fourth! That's tomorrow!"

"It can't be," said Will. "All carnivals stop after Labor Day—"

"Who cares? A thousand and one wonders! See! MEPHISTOPHELE, THE LAVA DRINKER! MR. ELECTRICO! THE MONSTER MONTGOLFIER?"

"Balloon," said Will. "A Montgolfier is a balloon."

"MADEMOISELLE TAROT!" read Jim. "THE DANGLING MAN. THE DEMON GUILLOTINE! THE ILLUSTRATED MAN! Hey!"

"That's just an old guy with tattoos."

"No." Jim breathed warm on the paper. "He's *illustrated.* Special. See! Covered with monsters! A menagerie!" Jim's eyes jumped. "SEE! THE SKELETON! Ain't that fine, Will? Not Thin Man, no, but SKELETON! SEE! THE DUST WITCH! What's a Dust Witch, Will?"

"Dirty old Gypsy—"

"No." Jim squinted off, seeing things. "A Gypsy that was born in the Dust, raised in the Dust, and some day winds up *back* in the Dust Here's more: EGYPTIAN MIRROR MAZE! SEE YOURSELF TEN THOUSAND TIMES! SAINT ANTHONY'S TEMPLE OF TEMPTATION!"

"THE MOST BEAUTIFUL—" read Will.

"—WOMAN IN THE WORLD," finished Jim.

They looked at each other.

"*Can* a carnival have the Most Beautiful Woman on Earth in its side show, Will?"

"You ever *seen* carnival ladies, Jim?"

"Grizzly bears. But how come this handbill claims—"

"Oh, shut up!"

"You mad at me, Will?"

"No, it's just—get it!"

The wind had torn the paper from their hands.

The handbill blew over the trees and away in an idiot caper, gone.

"It's not true, anyway," Will gasped. "Carnivals don't come this late in the year. Silly darn-sounding thing. Who'd *go* to it?"

"Me." Jim stood quiet in the dark.

Me, thought Will, seeing the guillotine flash, the Egyptian mirrors unfold accordions of light, and the sulphur-skinned devil-man sipping lava, like gunpowder tea.

"That music . . ." Jim murmured. "Calliope. Must be coming *tonight!*"

"Carnivals come at sunrise."

"Yeah, but what about the licorice and cotton candy we smelled, close?"

And Will thought of the smells and the sounds flowing on the river of wind from beyond the darkening houses, Mr. Tetley listening by his wooden Indian friend, Mr. Crosetti with the single tear shining down his cheek, and the barber pole sliding its red tongue up and around forever out of nowhere and away to eternity.

Will's teeth chattered.

"Let's go home."

"We *are* home!" cried Jim, surprised.

For, not knowing it, they had reached their separate houses and now moved up separate walks.

On his porch, Jim leaned over and called softly.

"Will. You're not mad?"

"Heck, no."

"We won't go by that street, that house, the Theater, again for a month. A *year!* I swear."

"Sure, Jim, sure."

They stood with their hands on the doorknobs of their houses, and Will looked up at Jim's roof where the lightning rod glittered against the cold stars.

The storm was coming. The storm *wasn't* coming.

No matter which, he was glad Jim had that grand contraption up there.

"Night!"

"Night."

Their separate doors slammed.

Will opened the door and shut it again. Quietly, this time.

"That's better," said his mother's voice.

Framed through the hall door Will saw the only theater he cared for now, the familiar stage where sat his father (home already! he and Jim *must* have run the long way round!) holding a book but reading the empty spaces. In a chair by the fire mother knitted and hummed like a tea-kettle.

He wanted to be near and not near them, he saw them close, he saw them far. Suddenly they were awfully small in too large a room in too big a town and much too huge a world. In this unlocked place they seemed at the mercy of anything that might break in from the night.

Including me, Will thought. Including me.

Suddenly he loved them more for their smallness than he ever had when they seemed tall.

His mother's fingers twitched, her mouth counted, the happiest woman he had ever seen. He remembered a greenhouse on a winter day, pushing aside thick jungle leaves to find a creamy pink hothouse rose poised alone in the wilderness. That was mother, smelling like fresh milk, happy, to herself, in this room.

Happy? But how and why? Here, a few feet off, was the janitor, the library man, the stranger, his uniform gone, but his face still the face of a man happier at night alone in the deep marble vaults, whispering his broom in the drafty corridors.

Will watched, wondering why this woman was so happy and this man so sad.

His father stared deep in the fire, one hand relaxed. Half cupped in that hand lay a crumpled paper ball.

Will blinked.

He remembered the wind blowing the pale handbill skittering in the trees. Now the same color paper lay crushed, its rococo type hidden, in his father's fingers. . . .

"Hey!"

Will stepped into the parlor.

Immediately Mom opened a smile that was like lighting a second fire.

Dad, stricken, looked dismayed, as if caught in a criminal act.

Will wanted to say, "Hey, what'd you think of the handbill . . . ?"

But Dad was cramming the handbill deep in the chair upholstery.

And mother was leafing the library books.

"Oh, these are fine, Willy!"

So Will just stood with Cooger and Dark on his tongue and said:

"Boy, the wind really *flew* us home. Streets full of *paper* blowing."

Dad did not flinch at this.

"Anything new, Dad?"

Dad's hand still lay tucked in the side of the chair. He lifted a gray, slightly worried, very tired gaze to his son:

"Stone lion blew off the library steps. Prowling the town now, looking for Christians. Won't find any. Got the only one in captivity here, and she's a good cook."

"Bosh," said Mom.

Walking upstairs, Will heard what he half expected to hear.

A soft fluming sigh as something fresh was tossed on the fire. In his mind, he saw Dad standing at the hearth looking down as the paper crinkled to ash:

". . . COOGER . . . DARK . . . CARNIVAL . . . WITCH . . . WONDERS . . ."

He wanted to go back down and stand with Dad, hands out, to be warmed by the fire.

Instead he went slowly up to shut the door of his room.

Some nights, abed, Will put his ear to the wall to listen, and if his folks talked things that were right, he stayed, and if not right he turned away. If it was about time and passing years or himself or town or just the general inconclusive way God ran the world, he listened warmly, comfortably, secretly, for it was usually Dad talking. He could not often speak with Dad anywhere in the world, inside or out, but this was different. There was a thing in Dad's voice, up, over, down, easy as a hand winging soft in the air like a white bird describing flight patterns, made the ear want to follow and the mind's eye to see.

And the odd thing in Dad's voice was the sound truth makes being said. The sound of truth, in a wild roving land of city or plain country lies, will spell any boy. Many nights Will drowsed this way, his senses like stopped clocks long before that half-singing voice was still. Dad's voice was a midnight school, teaching deep fathom hours, and the subject was life.

So it was this night, Will's eyes shut, head leaned to the cool plaster. At first Dad's voice, a Congo drum, boomed softly, horizons away. Mother's voice, she used her water-bright soprano in the Baptist choir, did not sing, yet sang back replies. Will imagined Dad sprawled talking to the empty ceiling:

". . . Will . . . makes me feel so *old* . . . a man should play baseball with his son. . . ."

"Not necessary," said the woman's voice, kindly. "You're a good man."

"—in a bad season. Hell, I was forty when he was *born!* And *you.* Who's your *daughter?* people say. God, when you lie down your thoughts turn to mush. Hell!"

Will heard the shift of weight as Dad sat up in the dark. A match was being struck, a pipe was being smoked. The wind rattled the windows.

". . . man with posters under his arm . . ."

". . . carnival . . ." said his mother's voice, ". . . *this* late in the year??"

Will wanted to turn away, but couldn't.

". . . most beautiful . . . woman . . . in the world," Dad's voice murmured.

Mother laughed softly. "You know I'm not."

No! thought Will, that's from the handbill! Why doesn't Dad *tell!!?*

Because, Will answered himself. Something's going on. Oh, something *is* going on!

Will saw that paper frolicked in the trees, its words THE MOST BEAUTIFUL WOMAN, and fever prickled his cheeks. He thought: Jim, the street of the Theater, the naked people in the stage of that Theater window, crazy as Chinese opera, darn odd crazy as old Chinese opera, judo, jujitsu, Indian puzzles, and now his father's voice, dreaming off, sad, sadder, saddest, much too much to understand. And suddenly he was scared because Dad wouldn't talk about the handbill he had secretly burned. Will gazed out the window. There! Like a milkweed plume! White paper danced in the air.

"No," he whispered, "no carnival's coming *this* late. It can't!" He hid under the covers, switched on his flashlight, opened a book. The first picture he saw was a prehistoric reptile trap-drumming a night sky a million years lost.

Heck, he thought, in the rush I got Jim's book, he's got one of mine.

But it was a pretty fine reptile.

And flying toward sleep, he thought he heard his father, restless, below. The front door shut. His father was going back to work late, for no reason, with brooms, or books, downtown, away . . . away. . . .

And mother asleep, content, not knowing he had gone.

Midnight then and the town clocks chiming on toward one and two and then three in the deep morning and the peals of the great clocks shaking dust off old toys in high attics and shedding silver off old mirrors in yet higher attics and stirring up dreams about clocks in all the beds where children slept.

Will heard it.

Muffled away in the prairie lands, the chuffing of an engine, the slow-following dragon-glide of a train.

Will sat up in bed.

Across the way, like a mirror image, Jim sat up, too.

A calliope began to play oh so softly, grieving to itself, a million miles away.

In one single motion, Will leaned from his window, as did Jim. Without a word they gazed over the trembling surf of trees.

Their rooms were high, as boys' rooms should be. From these gaunt windows they could rifle-fire their gaze artillery distances past library, city hall, depot, cow barns, farmlands to empty prairie!

There, on the world's rim, the lovely snail-gleam of the railway tracks ran, flinging wild gesticulations of lemon or cherry-colored semaphore to the stars.

There, on the precipice of earth, a small steam feather uprose like the first of a storm cloud yet to come.

The train itself appeared, link by link, engine, coal-car, and numerous and numbered all-asleep-and-slumbering-dreamfilled cars that followed the firefly-sparked churn, chant, drowsy autumn hearth-fire roar. Hellfires flushed the stunned hills. Even at this remote view, one imagined men with buffalo-haunched arms shoveling black meteor falls of coal into the open boilers of the engine.

The engine!

Both boys vanished, came back to lift binoculars.

"The engine!"

"Civil War! No other stack like that since 1900!"

"The rest of the train, *all* of it's old!"

"The flags! The cages! It's the carnival!"

They listened. At first Will thought he heard the air whistling fast in his nostrils. But no—it was the train, and the calliope sighing, weeping, on that train.

"Sounds like church music!"

"Hell. Why would a carnival play church music?"

"Don't say hell," hissed Will.

"Hell." Jim ferociously leaned out. "I've saved up all day. Everyone's asleep so—hell!"

The music drifted by their windows. Goose pimples rose big as boils on Will's arms.

"That *is* church music. Changed."

"For cri-yi, I'm froze, let's go watch them set up!"

"At three A.M.?"

"At three A.M.!"

Jim vanished.

For a moment, Will watched Jim dance around over there, shirt uplifted, pants going on, while off in night country, panting, churning was this funeral train all black plumed cars, licorice-colored cages, and a sooty calliope clamoring, banging three different hymns mixed and lost, maybe not there at all.

"Here goes nothing!"

Jim slid down the drainpipe on his house, toward the sleeping lawns.

"Jim! Wait!"

Will thrashed into his clothes.

"Jim, don't go *alone!*"

And followed after.

Sometimes you see a kite so high, so wise it almost knows the wind. It travels, then chooses to land in one spot and no other and no matter how you yank, run this way or that, it will simply break its cord, seek its resting place and bring you, blood-mouthed, running.

"Jim! Wait for me!"

So now Jim was the kite, the wild twine cut, and whatever wisdom was his taking him away from Will who could only run, earthbound, after one so high and dark silent and suddenly strange.

"Jim, here I come!"

And running, Will thought, Boy, it's the same old thing. I talk. Jim runs. I tilt stones, Jim grabs the cold junk under the stones and—lickety-split! I climb hills. Jim yells off church steeples. I got a bank account. Jim's got the hair on his head, the yell in his mouth, the shirt on his back and the tennis shoes on his feet. How come I think *he's* richer? Because, Will thought, I sit on a rock in the sun and old Jim, he prickles his arm-hairs by moonlight and dances with hoptoads. I tend cows. Jim tames Gila monsters. Fool! I yell at Jim. Coward! he yells back. And here we—*go!*

And they ran from town, across fields and both froze under a rail bridge with the moon ready beyond the hills and the meadows trembling with a fur of dew.

WHAM!

The carnival train thundered the bridge. The calliope wailed.

"There's no one playing it!" Jim stared up.

"Jim, no jokes!"

"Mother's honor, look!"

Going away, away, the calliope pipes shimmered with star explosions, but no one sat at the high keyboard. The wind, sluicing ice-water air in the pipes, made the music.

The boys ran. The train curved away, gonging its undersea funeral bell, sunk, rusted, green-mossed, tolling, tolling. Then the engine whistle blew a great steam whiff and Will broke out in pearls of ice.

Way late at night Will had heard—how often?—train whistles jetting steam along the rim of sleep, forlorn, alone and far, no matter how near they came. Sometimes he woke to find tears on his cheek, asked why, lay back, listened and thought, Yes! *they* make me cry, going east, going west, the trains of far gone in country deeps they drown in tides of sleep that escape the towns.

Those trains and their grieving sounds were lost forever between stations, not remembering where they had been, not guessing where they might go, exhaling their last pale breaths over the horizon, gone. So it was with all trains, ever.

Yet *this* train's whistle!

The wails of a lifetime were gathered in it from other nights in other slumbering years; the howl of moon-dreamed dogs, the seep of river-cold winds through January porch screens which stopped the blood, a thousand fire sirens weeping, or worse! the outgone shreds of breath, the protests of a billion people dead or dying, not wanting to be dead, their groans, their sighs, burst over the earth!

Tears jumped to Will's eyes. He lurched. He knelt. He pretended to lace one shoe.

But then he saw Jim's hands clap *his* ears, his eyes wet, too. The whistle screamed. Jim screamed against the scream. The whistle shrieked. Will shrieked against the shriek.

Then the billion voices ceased, instantly, as if the train had plunged in a fire storm off the earth.

The train skimmed on softly, slithering, black pennants fluttering, black confetti lost on its own sick-sweet candy wind, down the hill, with the boys pursuing, the air so cold they ate ice cream with each breath.

They climbed a last rise to look down.

"Boy," whispered Jim.

The train had pulled off into Rolfe's moon meadow, so-called because town couples came out to see the moon rise here over a land so wide, so long, it was like an inland sea, filled with grass in spring, or hay in late summer or snow in winter, it was fine walking here along its crisp shore with the moon coming up to tremble in its tides.

Well, the carnival train was crouched there now in the autumn grass on the old rail spur near the woods, and the boys crept and lay down under a bush, waiting.

"It's so quiet," whispered Will.

The train just stood in the middle of the dry autumn field, no one in the locomotive, no one in the tender, no one in any of the cars behind, all black under the moon, and just the small sounds of its metal cooling, ticking on the rails.

"Ssst," said Jim. "I *feel* them *moving* in there."

Will felt the cat fuzz on his body bramble up by the thousands.

"You think they *mind* us watching?"

"Maybe," said Jim, happily.

"Then why the noisy calliope?"

"When I figure that," Jim smiled, "I'll tell you. Look!"

Whisper.

As if exhaling itself straight down from the sky, a vast moss-green balloon touched at the moon.

It hovered two hundred yards above and away, quietly riding the wind.

"The basket under the balloon, someone *in* it!"

But then a tall man stepped down from the train caboose platform like a captain assaying the tidal weathers of this inland sea. All dark suit, shadow-faced, he waded to the center of the meadow, his shirt as black as the gloved hands he now stretched to the sky.

He gestured, once.

And the train came to life.

At first a head lifted in one window, then an arm, then another head like a puppet in a marionette theater. Suddenly two men in black were carrying a dark tent pole out across the hissing grass.

It was the silence that made Will pull back, even as Jim leaned forward, eyes moon-bright.

A carnival should be all growls, roars like timberlands stacked, bundled, rolled and crashed, great explosions of lion dust, men ablaze with working anger, pop bottles jangling, horse buckles shivering, engines and elephants in full stampede through rains of sweat while zebras neighed and trembled like cage trapped in cage.

But this was like old movies, the silent theater haunted with black-and-white ghosts, silvery mouths opening to let moonlight smoke out, gestures made in silence so hushed you could hear the wind fizz the hair on your cheeks.

More shadows rustled from the train, passing the animal cages where darkness prowled with unlit eyes and the calliope stood mute save for the faintest idiot tune the breeze piped wandering up the flues.

The ringmaster stood in the middle of the land. The balloon like a vast moldy green cheese stood fixed to the sky. Then—darkness came.

The last thing Will saw was the balloon swooping down, as clouds covered the moon.

In the night he felt the men rush to unseen tasks. He sensed the balloon, like a great fat spider, fiddling with the lines and poles, rearing a tapestry in the sky.

The clouds arose. The balloon sifted up.

In the meadow stood the skeleton main poles and wires of the main tent, waiting for its canvas skin.

More clouds poured over the white moon. Shadowed, Will shivered. He heard Jim crawling forward, seized his ankle, felt him stiffen.

"Wait!" said Will. "They're bringing out the canvas!"

"No," said Jim. "Oh, no . . ."

For somehow instead, they both knew, the wires high-flung on the poles were catching swift clouds, ripping them free from the wind in streamers which, stitched and sewn by some great monster shadow, made canvas and more canvas as the tent took shape. At last there was the clear-water sound of vast flags blowing.

The motion stopped. The darkness within darkness was still.

Will lay, eyes shut, hearing the beat of great oil-black wings as if a huge, ancient bird had drummed down to live, to breathe, to survive in the night meadow.

The clouds blew away.

The balloon was gone.

The men were gone.

The tents rippled like black rain on their poles.

Suddenly it seemed a long way to town.

Instinctively, Will glanced behind himself.

Nothing but grass and whispers.

Slowly he looked back at the silent, dark, seemingly empty tents.

"I don't like it," he said.

Jim could not tear his eyes away.

"Yeah," he whispered. "Yeah."

Will stood up. Jim lay on the earth.

"Jim!" said Will.

Jim jerked his head as if slapped. He was on his knees, he swayed up. His body turned, but his eyes were fastened to those black flags, the great sideshow signs swarming with unguessed wings, horns, and demon smiles.

A bird screamed.

Jim jumped. Jim gasped.

Cloud shadows panicked them over the hills to the edge of town.

From there, the two boys ran alone.

FROM SUITE FOR CALLIOPE

Ellen Hunnicutt

—This selection from Ellen Hunnicutt's 1987 novel Suite for Calliope *describes the frenzied anticipation of opening day at an Indiana circus, and a near tragedy averted by the power of music.*

THE FIRST OF MAY, a morning of timid sun and cool breezes. Our tent is up, a blazing curtain of red and yellow stripes. Overnight, our hired acts have arrived, outsiders booked for the summer to augment the skills of our elderly performers. The field behind the tent is a sea of trucks and house trailers. Their license plates announce Texas and Oklahoma, Missouri and Florida. The followers and fakers are here too. Their sideshows and vending trailers fill nearly all of the space between the tent and the museum barn. Everyone is welcome. Our residents wander among the new arrivals looking for familiar faces, listening for news. The grounds are fringed with budding locust trees, the beginnings of wild grape and milkweed, a greening assemblage bent on parallel adventure.

I am here to superintend my portable calliope, resplendent now with gold figures on a field of red: eagles and gargoyles, the head of Neptune blowing ropy wreaths of sea spray, winged Roman soldiers with the voluptuous breasts of women, all joined with sensuous, serpentine golden vines, a fanciful coat of arms with a lurid and eclectic past. The calliope has been drawn into position before the big top. I fear jostlers and vandals, but with only this thin sprinkle of early customers, I can circle and wander while standing guard.

It is barely eleven o'clock when the barkers start up:

"Tarantulas, tarantulas, tarantulas! They are here. Boas and anacondas! They're here, too! Don't go home without seeing them! Spiders and snakes! Spiders and snakes! They are here! They're alive. Those giant spiders and snakes! Tarantulas, tarantulas, tarantulas! We are open now! There is time before the big show! They are here! Bring your girlfriend! Bring your boyfriend! Spiders and snakes! Spiders and snakes! They are here! They're alive! Tarantulas, tarantulas, tarantulas!"

"World's smallest horse! No higher than a man's knee! Bring the children to this educational display! It is open now! World's smallest horse! Scientifically bred as a house pet! Featured in the national press! Bring the children to this educational display! World's smallest horse! We are open now! There is time!"

"Popcorn! Funnel cakes! Corn dogs! Cotton candy! Get them before the show! Do not let your pleasure in the performance be interrupted! Popcorn! Funnel cakes! Corn dogs! Cotton candy! Get yours now!"

"Peanuts salted and roasted in the shell! Inside selected packages are wristwatches! Genuine wristwatches! Peanuts salted and roasted in the shell! This gentleman has found a wristwatch in his package! Hold it up, sir! Hold it up high! Peanuts salted and roasted in the shell! Inside selected packages are wristwatches! Peanuts salted and roasted in the shell!"

Fully assembled on opening day, our company is one third Hispanic. The soft accents of Mexico hum through the staging area.

Belle's authentic Italian flyers, who call themselves Luigi and Cosica, are man and wife. They chat quietly together.

"*Se van a fines de la semana que viene.*"

"*Sí. Documentos. Siempre documentos.*"

"*Sí. A fin de cuentas, todo se resolvió sin dificultad.*"

"Too much money. Dollars, never pesos."

Behind the snake show, our high wire man stretches through a series of warm-ups. "What is your name?" asks a roaming early customer, a lady with blue-white hair.

"Wolfgang, madame. I am from the National Circus of Germany."

"Germany! How interesting."

"Sí, madame."

In their holding pen, Teddy MacKay's poodles, coal black, dressed with red ruffles around their necks, yap frantically. Over the winter, they have nearly forgotten the stench of our rented-for-summer animals: a pinto pony, five smallish scruffy dromedaries, and most odorous of all, an elephant.

Belle has left off currying the pony to chat with a group we have not seen before, a family of Vietnamese tumblers. Of the parents, two daughters, and two sons, only the youngest child, a precocious boy of perhaps nine, speaks understandable English.

"Good horse!" he tells Belle, touching the pony's nose, then reaching up to capture its neck in a fervent embrace. He looks like any child yearning to ride a pony, and also like no child I have ever seen. His difference—I am a bit startled—is not in his powerful young body but in his face: eyes that watch everything without seeming to move; a smile dancing out from sinewy cheeks, bringing some message about resolve; yet a supple, spontaneous mouth, merry now with delight over this horse.

Belle has seen it too; her face is alert. "Come up, then!" she commands, patting the pony's bare back. The boy springs; in barely an instant he is astride the horse, shoulders squared, one hand swept out in a theatrical gesture. "Little love!" Belle cries in admiration. "Precious little man!" The boy's parents look on with tentative, courteous smiles; the other children, eager and hopeful, watch the pony.

Joe arrives with the local boy he has hired to keep the boiler on the calliope fired. He lingers, not quite willing to put this gaudy chariot into a stranger's care. Joe started the fire early; it must be continued all day to have steam at the ready. Orange coals flare beneath the tank. A curl of black smoke dances from the stack.

The boy is perhaps fourteen, lean and eager. He looks at the head of Neptune and then at me. "You play this thing, miss?"

"I do."

"I guess you've been with the circus a long time. You fall off of something? Your leg?"

"I guess."

There is something in this interchange that pleases Joe. He looks at the boy with new interest. "What do you do, son?"

"Nothing."

"No," Joe insists, "what do you do?"

"My folks think it's crazy. I mean they like to come and watch the show, but they think it's crazy."

"Tell me what you do."

"I ride pretty well. We have horses. I can do almost anything with a horse. My folks think it's crazy."

"The circus," Joe tells him, "began with the horse. If you take away everything else, that's what you have left—the horse."

"The horse?" the boy asks. He has not expected this news. His face registers surprise, and then pleasure. "The horse," he says again. "I'm not afraid to fall."

"You can break ribs," says Joe, "as many ribs as you like. Only a neck or knee injury is serious, especially for riders."

"The neck," says the boy, "the knee," recording this information, prepared to cast away all of his sound ribs with heroic abandon.

"Keep this boiler going," says Joe, confident now. "Don't let the fire go out."

"I will," says the boy. "I won't. You can depend on me."

Reynard appears in a Gypsy costume provided by Belle. Beside the entrance to the tent, he takes up his fiddle and begins playing Romany airs. On the ground, his open violin case is seeded with two one-dollar bills. But when half an hour of plaintive Hungarian tunes has stirred no interest, he glances down into his case with a practiced eye, and switches to "The Flight of the Bumblebee." Almost immediately, his bills are peppered with a fine sprinkle of silver. He smiles and nods his thanks at his benefactors.

Joe reappears as an Abraham Lincoln clown, a new concept. I had thought it inappropriate, but children squeal with pleasure and recognition at the sight of his tall hat and beard cruising the ticket line. I realize I have no feel for this business after all, no true instinct.

The pace quickens. Joe takes up a stack of circus programs. "Souvenir programs! Circus programs! One dollar! Inside the big top they will be two dollars! Get yours now! Circus programs! Souvenir programs! Illustrated in full color! One dollar!"

Alexander, the Calabrias, and Rick Ross file by in full costume—black pants, red vests, white shirts, and red captain's hats. Shiny black bow ties complete their outfits. The sight of the uniforms stirs excitement. We are building, from tarantulas to the calliope. Alexander gazes at the restored instrument, then sends me a satisfied smile.

I mount the steps to the calliope and insert my earplugs. "The Saints Go Marching In" whistles forth in earsplitting grandeur. The crowd falls back in stupefaction at this miracle of noise. Children shout and clap their hands over their ears. Infants scream.

Customers now hurl themselves into our tent, where they immediately confront Reynard, a red vendor's jacket covering his Gypsy garb, standing beneath a sign that proclaims PREFERRED SEATING, ONLY ONE ADDITIONAL DOLLAR! Bills are torn from pockets and thrust at him. "The Saints" blends into "Dixie," and then "Happy Days Are Here Again." The tarantula man, looking bored, slides a Closed sign across his ticket window. The vendors move inside. "Over the Waves," sings the calliope, and beyond its perimeter, beyond Reynard's shoulder, I see waves of customers scrambling up into the bleachers. En route, they buy popcorn and cotton candy, which have now doubled in price. Arrogant vendors refuse to change ten-dollar bills, and customers, in a panic, make change among themselves in stressful camaraderie. Popcorn and cotton candy are passed down long rows of people, dollar bills are passed back. "In the Good Old Summertime," whistles the calliope, and I see the peanut man's shill hold up a wristwatch. As a second chorus of "Summertime" hurtles to a close, I watch Alexander. Across a sea of hands, he waves his trumpet at me. I dismount and straggle inside, leaving our stoic boiler boy a lonely figure on the nearly deserted grounds.

Rick Ross produces a mighty drumroll. Alexander and the Calabrias, who have also taken up trumpets, play a fanfare. The ringmaster, in tall black hat and red cutaway coat, steps into our circus's single ring. "Ladies and gentlemen! Children of all ages!"

"The tickets were worth every penny of the price," says Reynard, as I slip into the seat he has saved for me. "I'm so glad I could bring my little girl to the circus." He is a courteous but persistent voice-over. "I only wish your mother could have come."

"From the corners of the earth!" intones the ringmaster. "Death-defying acts!"

"Do not be misled if feats seem effortless," Reynard instructs. "The master always makes the difficult appear easy."

"Hush, Reynard."

But a hush is unnecessary. The ringmaster concludes his speech, waves his hat, and folds himself into a deep bow. "The Entry of the Gladiators" thunders from the band, the curtains open, and Belle appears astride the pinto pony to lead the grand processional around the perimeter of the ring. Rouged and feathered, in a brief leather dress, she is an Indian maiden. The bare legs and bare pointed toes that slip gracefully along the horse's flanks are those of a young girl. She is followed by the rented camels, draped in crimson and gold, led by Teddy MacKay, who will work them. On the back of each camel perches a poodle. The dogs are settled now, professionals eager for performance. Teddy MacKay is dressed as a sheik.

After the camels comes Joe, borne by the elephant. In pith helmet and khaki safari garb, he sits just behind the animal's head, saluting the crowd with a trainer's baton. Four of our residents are clowns, their old faces anonymous behind makeup. They are still sprightly in baggy pants and ballooning jesters' suits. I am amazed at how grand our shabby company has become.

Lest our enthusiasm wane for a moment, Alexander's trumpet samples the glorious repertoire of circus music—"Gentry's Grand Triumphal," "Georgia Girl," "The Billboard," "The Thunderer," "Bombasto"—and the performers file by.

The Vietnamese children march sedately behind their parents, all of the family now in billowing lime green shirts. The children are Asian princes and princesses.

The band plays the grand processional out of sight and into the spotlight steps our first act, a girl who performs on a low trapeze. The blue velvet robe and pink boa Belle has provided do not mask her clumsiness. Casting them off, she stands in the circle of light, a straight, wooden figure, graceless and unmuscled. Our budget for hired performers is limited. It will buy us one or two top acts, and a complement of the less skilled. From the trumpet's rich middle range, "Deep Purple" unrolls like satin. But even underwritten by voluptuous music, the girl cannot succeed. With mechanical movements, she hangs upside down, arms thrashing, and then forms a lopsided bird's nest. She skins the cat and does a backward pullover. The trapeze wobbles erratically. But our warm crowd is still caught up in its early frenzy. Excitement will carry them mesmerized through the initial acts. Alexander picks up the tempo and launches "Ecret's Galop" to cover the girl's awkward departure.

The ringmaster introduces the poodles. "No animal," he cries, "enjoys performing so much as the dog!" The poodles bound into the ring, then abruptly stop and arrange themselves in a semicircle. Teddy MacKay skips in after them, glittering now in a suit of silver and blue. One of the riggers flies by him to set up props, inverted tubs in graduated sizes, a set of steps, a frame-mounted hoop. "How Much Is That Doggie in the Window?" asks the band, Daviso's trombone yelping playfully. With barely a flip of his hand, Teddy sends balls of black fur hurtling through the air, somersaulting, leaping, dancing through intricate patterns. The horns have fallen silent. Rick Ross's snare follows the accelerating feet of the dogs as they sail upward; his bass proclaims their safe return to earth. A poodle on its hind legs slowly climbs the steps, and the band remembers "Old Dog Tray." Teddy's modest signals belie his role in all of this geometry, and the self-important poodles claim everything for themselves.

"Dogs . . . " muses Reynard. He looks wan but hopeful.

They are followed by a Mexican juggler, introduced by the ringmaster as Herr Heinz of Hamburg. To help preserve the man's cover, the Calabrias take up tuba and sousaphone, and a German band is born. "*Muss I Denn*," sings the trumpet. The juggler, his dusky Latin skin showing beneath brief lederhosen, progresses from rings to pins to china plates to daggers. Gravity has been tamed. Objects shower and cascade. The band sends him off with the "Olympia Hippodrome March."

Joe appears, carried into the ring in the curl of the elephant's trunk. A rented elephant has a limited number of stock moves, but Joe exploits each one. This elephant sits on its rump, rises on its hind legs, lies down and rolls over. For a finale, it lifts Joe and swings him in its trunk. Joe exits sitting on the elephant's head, both arms raised in triumph.

"Keep back!" cautions the ringmaster. "The elephant is coming all the way around!" To "Burma Patrol," Joe and the elephant circle the dirt path at the ring's perimeter.

Then Teddy MacKay is back to work the camels. In his sheik's garb, he runs them in a circle, masses them to left and then to right, while "Caravan" screams from the band.

Joe, flushed with success, comes to sit beside us. "Wait until you see the Vietnamese!" he cries. "I was watching them warm up behind the tent."

But it is another half hour before the tumblers appear. The crowd's euphoria has waned. To hold them, we must give them our meager best. The Vietnamese, fierce with makeup and slicked hair, march sternly into the ring and cast off silver capes. Their slight bodies are taut. Even the mother is firmly muscled. Gone are the smiling children. These are warriors of the East.

Alexander's horn searches through the Mediterranean, through the Middle East, and finally locates China. An angry, harmonic minor sails through the tent, the father shouts a command, and suddenly bodies are whirling. Lime green shirts bounce and somersault, twist, and fly above the earth, separating and merging again into symmetry. The mother leaps to the teeterboard and sends a son somersaulting into the air to land on his father's shoulders. The crowd cheers.

Belle, queen mother of us all, now with a cape of feathers over her Indian dress, slips into the seat beside Joe. "Look at the baby!" she cries with delight. "Do you see? He is not afraid!"

The smallest son, the one who sat upon the pony, is coming to life.

It is as if exertion has warmed him. He is slipping into a new role. Smiles flicker on the small face. As the crowd's enthusiasm grows, his eyes light with joy. He has passed beyond himself into another existence. He is going farther. He has discovered the secret of performance. He will work this crowd himself. After each trick, as the tumblers bow, this child bows deeper, puts the faintest wiggle into the motion. The crowd loves him. He bounces between tumbles, rising two feet off the ground, arms thrown out as if to embrace his audience. The others are helpless to stop him. They hew even closer to their rigid roles, as if their discipline could pull him back to them. But it is no use. He steps to the teeterboard, grinning broadly, arms outstretched, fingers wriggling suggestively, drawing the people to him. His mother sends him sailing up to his father's shoulders as if he were completely weightless. The father catches him neatly and seems to hold him tight for a moment, as if he cannot bear to give him up. But the child is free in an instant and somersaults quickly to the ground.

From the bandstand, Alexander is watching. The trumpet calls, from Moldavia to Vietnam, and finds its answer. Across miles, across years, across language. Alexander and the child own the crowd. Time has stopped. The boy could somersault forever. But the father has begun the pyramid that will end the act. The mother leaps to the teeterboard and a brother is sent skyward, then a sister, and another sister. Then it is the boy's turn. He hesitates and, in an outrageous gesture, drops to kiss the ground. The crowd roars. Only the smallest flicker of doubt crossing the mother's face gives warning. Then she leaps to the board and the child is sent sailing, sailing. He grazes his sister's arm and sails free. For a moment, the small limbs fly out, then he gathers himself into a ball and falls almost silently to earth.

Belle, the world's expert on falls, is beside him in an instant. She requires only the briefest second of time. Then she sends Alexander a wretched glance. The trumpet explodes into the "Stars and Stripes Forever," our secret signal of distress. The clowns burst into the tent. The Vietnamese family with frozen, stricken faces, stares out at the crowd. Then, perhaps insane with fear, they bow stiffly as the child is carried out.

In another moment the ringmaster appears and the band falls

silent. "We are pleased to tell you the child is not seriously injured!" he cries. "It is only a sprain! And now, on with the show!" The crowd cheers.

But Belle's white face and slowly returning step proclaim disaster. As she reaches us, I see the pain in her eyes. "Oh, Belle!"

"Sit down, Ada!" she commands in a steely voice I have never heard before. There is an icy smile across her face. "Stay where you are. The boy is beyond help. We must think of the living. A crowd in panic now would injure many people, and it would ruin us. A horde of police descending on this place? Ada, do you think your father is the only fugitive here?"

Grim and shaken, Joe comes to her assistance. "The tumblers are professionals, new to the country but not to performing. They will leave quietly."

"And grieve in private," says Reynard, whose mind has always been quicker than mine, more canny. His eyes are bright with tears.

"But Belle—"

"Hush, Ada," she orders.

Alexander is blowing grief in a cascading wail. Then he seems to remember he is responsible for this crowd, for these clowns. The music rises as quickly as it fell. The tune is now a Yiddish *freilach.* The clowns join hands to dance, stepping lightly, then tumbling over each other. Grief and necessity ferry Alexander from Russia across the Prut River, into Rumania, the Transylvanian Alps, Bulgaria, Greece, and Turkey. They drive him through New Orleans and down Broadway. But he cannot escape. He backtracks, reworking the tunes, adjusting them. The Calabria brothers, on cornet and trombone, follow as their aging lips allow. Rick Ross drums frantically, demonically. And now the songs return transformed. They seem to remember each of the boy's movements, his incredible joy.

"And always back to the minor," says Reynard. "A music that forgets nothing."

"What did you say?"

"Ada, I suspected it from the beginning. He is a klezmer."

"A klezmer, Reynard?"

"It means itinerant musician, from Yiddish. First in Russia, then here. Everywhere, really. The everywhere is in the music. When Donald and I were young and traveling, we sometimes encountered them. They came from places with lovely musical names, Czernowitz, Smyrna, Anatolia, Salonika, Beltsy. I though they were all dead. I wonder if he is the last one."

"The last klezmer?"

"Shh, Ada. I was never able to determine exactly, but I don't think they use the word themselves. Listen, he is playing a Hebrew service for a Vietnamese child. There is always a scream when he rounds the A. I don't know if the music is crying for the past or announcing the future."

Riggers have run forward to erect nets. Only the high wire act and the flyers, our grand finalists, use nets. On the wire, the agile Mexican named Wolfgang lifts his balance pole and launches forth. Even twenty feet below, we can see tears glistening on his cheeks. He crosses and returns while Alexander, throwing caution aside, reaches out to console him with Spanish music: "In a Little Spanish Town," "Lady of Spain," "In My Adobe Hacienda." Wolfgang mounts his unicycle and shoots forward uncautiously onto the wire. Then back on his feet, hands outstretched, he reaches to pick up a handerchief with his teeth. He is unwilling to let a child die with more courage than he gives to life. He runs, he skips! The audience is enthralled, gasping now. "Cielito Lindo," plays Alexander recklessly, unwilling to be surpassed. The walker comes down to thunderous applause.

And already Luigi is swinging upside down, legs locked, hands ready to catch his wife. Cosica, in blood red, chalks her hands, catches her swing, and sails toward him. "Fascination," sings the trumpet in strictest three-four time. Cosica sails into space and is caught in Luigi's grip. The ringmaster announces a somersault, then a double. Cosica and Luigi sail flawlessly. The crowd is enraptured. Their heads move to and fro with the flyers. It is several moments before we are aware of a commotion outside; it is Reynard's instincts that come alive. "The accident has brought the police," he tells us.

But his intuition is scarcely better than that of the flyers. In an instant, Cosica has dropped to the net and somersaulted to the ground, with Luigi only seconds behind her. They streak from the ring and disappear beyond the curtain.

Then—whether by second sight or street sense, we will never know—Reynard looks over his shoulder and assesses our situation with what will prove to be complete accuracy. "There are only three officers. They are not really concerned at this point. They have heard only that there was an accident. The Vietnamese need a little longer to get away, and the flyers are illegal aliens. We must protect all of them."

The ringmaster has rushed forward to take charge. He declares our abrupt conclusion was completely planned to enhance pleasure in the drama of our performance. Then he concludes, "May all of your days be circus days!" pitting a single voice against a crowd that is growing restive.

"Look at them," says Belle. "They don't like the way the flyers left. They're putting it together, remembering the accident. We have only a minute."

Two police officers stride into the tent. "Less than a minute," says Joe.

Alexander sees it too. The band explodes into the "Washington Post March." But the crowd knows Alexander now. With the instincts of children and animals, they have seen him for the sorcerer he is, and no longer trust him.

Then some old rumble rises out of the past. How do the young ones know the mix? Is the modus operandi carried in the genes, in the dark green night of the cell? The boiler boy is at my elbow, terrified but loyal. The promise of circus savvy Joe saw in him earlier is now fully realized. His young face is alive and canny. "You gonna play that thing, Miss?"

He hurries me out of the tent. Before I am halfway up the calliope steps, he is handing me my earplugs. At the keyboard, high on the old animal wagon, I survey the world of possibility, the whole creation in an instant: a roiling crowd framed by the broad mouth of our tent, the bandstand beyond flashing brass, the proud barn rising. The opening measures of the suite whistle forth like demons released from hell. Pared down for this small keyboard, the music is a raucous, eerie plaint; but the chaos of the galloping notes inspires its opposite in the crowd. Startled and curious, they are already slipping back into docility. Below me, a police officer shouts and gestures against my noise, ordering me to stop playing. The boiler boy, with hand signs and mobile face, declares to the officer that he, too, has been driven to his limit by these queer circus folk. The officer accepts the declaration as a show of support and is mollified. The two fall into easy, mute camaraderie. I am amazed at the boy's virtuosity.

Time is the same thing in music that it is everywhere else in nature. Time is what passes while history is being made. Belle and Joe lead another officer into the seclusion of the barn where conversation will be possible, and close the door. Just inside the tent the Calabrias have taken charge of the third officer. How pleased they are he has come! They want to show him the clever construction of our bleacher seats. This is vital information that will immediately body forth all the mystery of the circus in bold relief. Has he not come on a tour of inspection? But before the man can focus on the joint of board with board, the Calabrias discover that it is, after all, the electrical wiring that requires the immediate inspection and approval of the police. They pass the silver ball of the man's attention between them.

The suite whistles on. Stripped of its auxiliary voices, it has assumed an alien life of its own. I am as curious about it as my audience. We live, after all, to know God. Beyond discovery, there is little worthy of our attention. All the seeming multiplicity of things falls into place under a single heading. On the bandstand Alexander, looking old and tired, packs instruments into cases. These performances take more out of him than he admits. He pauses to wipe finger marks from brass, to peer into the bells of horns. How much of this is meant to calm the audience, he will never tell us. He lives in our world and not in it, picking his own path through the vocabulary: con, entertainment, transcendence, oblation. Who in the crowd could be alarmed when the leader of our band looks so totally bored?

The suite, however truncated, has for the first time an audience, and by it is transmogrified. The loop of speculation it casts forth is completed now by another presence, silent but sentient. When the boiler boy turned me out of my bleacher seat, my best hope was for a novel sound to control an anxious crowd. Sometimes a question can be masked by a bigger question, a noise by a larger noise. With the bawdy instrument, the popcorn-sated crowd, the innocence of soft May sun stretching toward dusk, I did not envision a serious performance. Such is the vanity of composers. A crosshatch of response carries back to me on the gently rising wind, a cat's cradle of yeas and nays. The suite is getting mixed reviews, but it is holding together. With beginner's luck, more instinct than design, I have succeeded at the first rule of music composition: The Law of Good Continuation. My tumbling notes produce instability, and a concurrent hope for rest, a pattern laid up in our collective memory from infancy. What is holding the crowd, drawing them from the tent to the calliope, is the promise of resolution.

Reynard appears below me and raises one hand in brief salute. Trained to sound, he is not as eloquent with gesture as the boiler boy, but his meaning is clear enough. He is telling me the flyers and the Vietnamese have safely departed.

Resolution. Drawings in caves show primitive musical instruments. Who was the first man to play his ragged, abrupt grief smoothly into history? The first woman? Music, said my mother, helps us organize our lives. The suite lurches on, imagination striking a bargain with experience, giving me back what was taken from me.

Reynard conducts the closing measures of the music with speculative nods of his head, then announces, "It reads quite well, I'd say."

"There are a dozen things wrong with it, Reynard. A hundred. But I know what I have to do."

"No," he says, "you've done enough. You must move along now to the next composition."

Alexander is searching through the thinning crowd. Belle and Joe emerge from the barn, their business accomplished. Joe smooths his polished hair and shakes hands with the departing police officers. Alexander locates Belle and falls into step beside her. After a moment, he takes her hand in his own. Our opening day is over.

CARNY

Harry Crews

—Harry Crews's non-fiction piece on life with a traveling carnival originally appeared in the September 1976 issue of Playboy.

I WOKE UP SCREAMING AND kicking, catching the ride boy in the ribs with the toe of my boot (which I had not bothered to take off), and when the toe of the boot struck him just below the armpit, he screamed, too, and that caused the lot lady he was rolled in the blanket with to scream—and there the three of us were, thrashing about in my Dodge van, driven stark raving mad on a crash from Biphetamine 20's (a wonderfully deadly little capsule that, taken in sufficient quantities, will make you bigger than anybody you know for at least ninety-six hours running) and driven mad, too, by the screaming siren that woke us up to start with. It was the middle of the night—or, more accurately, the middle of the morning, about 4 A.M.—and the electronic system set to catch burglars and tire thieves had tripped, but I—addled and nine-tenths stunned from too long on the road with a gambler, chasing carnivals across half a dozen states—I didn't know it was my siren or that I was in my van or who I was with or why I was where I was.

But as soon as I opened the side door and saw the black Ferris wheel and the tents standing outlined against the sky, I calmed down enough to get the keys out of my pocket. I couldn't find the right key to turn off the alarm, though, and all the while the siren was screaming and the ride boy, who was about fifty years old, had come out of the van naked from the waist down with his lot lady, who looked like she might have been fifteen, hanging on his back.

"What the hell?" the ride boy kept shouting at me. "What the hell?"

"Alarm!" I kept shouting back. "Alarm." It was all I could get my mouth to say as I fought with the keys.

Lights were coming on in trailers all around us, and out of the corner of my eye I saw the Fat Lady from the ten-in-one show standing beside the little wheeled box that her manager used to haul her from carnival to carnival behind his old Studebaker. She was so big that her back was at least a foot deep in fat. By the time I got the key in the switch and turned the alarm off the Midget had appeared, along with several men who had apparently been gambling in the G-top. Unfortunately, the sheriff's deputy, red-faced and pissed off, had arrived, too. He pushed his flat-brimmed hat back on his head and looked at the van and then at the freaks from the ten-in-one show and then at me.

"You want to take your driver's license out of your billfold and show it to me?" he said.

"My what?"

"You want to git on back in there and put your britches on?" he said to the ride boy. The ride boy didn't move, but the lot lady, who was a local and in some danger, maybe, of being recognized by the cop, turned and got into the van.

He had a flashlight on my license now, and without looking up, he said, "You want to tell me how come you got that siren?"

"Look," I said, pointing. "There's a goddamn air jack." The sight of that jack slipped under the front end of my van made me mad enough to eat a rock.

But the deputy sheriff refused to look. He said, "Only your fire, law-enforcement, and your rescue veehicles allowed to have a siren."

The carny people had closed in around us now. The cop flashed his light once at them, but when the light fell upon the illustrated face of the Tattooed Man, he looked immediately back at the license.

"You want to—"

But I cut him off and said that two months earlier some malevolent sonofabitch had jacked up my van and taken the wheels. I'd come out of the house one morning and found it up on concrete blocks. So I had the doors and hood wired and had a mercury tilt switch rigged to the chassis. If anyone tried to jack it up, a siren went off. While I talked about the tilt switch and the rigged hood and doors, his face drew together on itself. He had never heard of such a thing, and it obviously upset him.

"You want to come on down to the station with me?" he said.

"But what for?" I was getting a little hysterical now. "What about the jack? What about the fucking jack?"

He glanced briefly at Big Bertha where she loomed enormous in the slanting light from a trailer. "You want to watch you language in front of—"

"Hello, Jackson."

We all turned, and there was Charlie Luck, sometimes called Chuck and sometimes Luck and sometimes Chuckaluck and sometimes many other things.

"This man here's got a sireen, Charlie. I think it might be illegal."

Charlie bit his lip and shook his head in disgust. "Has he still got that? I told you, boy, to git rid of that goddamn siren." He had, of course, told me no such thing.

Charlie was beautiful in a brown suit and soft brown cap and square-toed brown shoes. There was no flash to him at all. Everything he was wearing was very muted and very expensive. He came over and put his arm on the cop's shoulder. "Officer Jackson," he said in just about the most pleasant voice you've ever heard, "could I talk to you over here for a moment?"

They turned away from us, and immediately Big Bertha was struggling up the steps into her little wheeled box. The ride boy got back into the van with his lot lady, mooning us all as he went. The trouble was over. Everybody knew everything was fine, now that Charlie Luck was here. I stood watching, admiring the earnest, head-to-head talk he was having with Officer Jackson, who was nodding now, agreeing for all he was worth with whatever Charlie Luck was saying.

My feeling for Charlie Luck went far beyond admiration. I loved him. He was a hero. Some people have only one or two heroes; I have hundreds. Sometimes I meet six or seven heroes in a single day. Charlie Luck was a great man who just happened to be a gambler, in the same way that Bear Bryant is a great man who just happens to be a football coach. Bryant could have stumbled into a brokerage house when he was twenty and owned Wall Street by now. Instead, he happened into football. Same with Charlie Luck. Somebody showed him a game when he was sixteen and he never got over it. He became perfect of his kind. The perfect carny. The perfect hustler.

Charlie Luck was never registered for the draft. He's never paid any income tax. Officially, he does not exist. Or, said another way, he exists in so many different forms, with so many different faces, that there is no way to contain him. He knows a place in Mississippi where he can mail away for an automobile tag that is not registered. If somebody takes his number, it can't be traced. And even if it could be traced, it would be traced to an alias.

To my knowledge, Charlie Luck has six identities, complete with phony Social Security cards and driver's licenses, even passports. He has six, and he's contemplating more. He's very imaginative with his life. With his past. Sometimes he's from Texas. Other days, from Maine. I sometimes wonder if he knows where he's from or who he is. He's probably forgotten.

The sheriff's deputy turned and, without looking at me once, walked to his car. Charlie Luck came over to where I was. He watched me for a moment, a little half smile showing broken teeth.

"A siren?" he said. "Well, what do you know about that? I heard the thing over in the G-top. Thought it was a fire truck. Thought maybe something was burning up."

"What did you say to the cop?"

He shrugged. "One thing and another. I told him I'd shut you down, take your siren away."

"You wouldn't do that."

"Of course not." He pointed to the open door, where the ride boy was locked with the lot lady. His mouth suddenly looked as though he tasted something rotten. "I told you about letting those things use your van."

"She came up and he didn't have anyplace. I couldn't think of a way to turn him down."

"You better start finding a way or you'll queer everything." He started to walk away but then stopped. "Hang onto that jack. We'll send it into town sometime and sell it." I got back into the van and listened to the snores of the ride boy and the cotton-candy wind breakings of the lot lady. Charlie Luck was disappointed in me for letting the ride boy sleep in my van, because the workers, the guys who up-and-down the rides and operate them, are at the very bottom of a well-defined carny social structure. A lot lady is a carnival groupie. She is given to indiscriminately balling the greasy wired men and boys who spend their lives half-buried in machinery. It was definitely uncool of me to associate with them. And inasmuch as I was traveling as Charlie Luck's brother, it was even worse.

Charlie had been reluctant—very reluctant—to let me in with him to start with. But he owed me. Back in November, I had managed to persuade a cowboy down in a place near Yeehaw Junction, Florida, which is great cattle country and where they have one of the last great cowboy bars, not to clean out one of Charlie Luck's ears with the heel of his boot. Charlie had been grateful ever since. That day in Florida, he bought me a beer after the cowboy left, and we went to a back booth, where he watched me drink it and I watched him bleed.

"Name's Floyd Titler," he said. "Friends—and you definitely a friend—friends call me Short Arm."

"Harry Crews is mine." We shook hands across the table.

"Sonofabitch nearly killed me," he said, dabbing at an eye that was rapidly closing with a handkerchief he'd just soaked in draft.

"I never saw anybody do that," I said, pointing to the handkerchief.

"You just have to be careful none of the alcohol gets in your eyes. Otherwise, it's great for the swelling."

I finally got around to asking what he was doing in Florida, because nobody is *from* Florida, and he said he wintered down there and worked games in a carnival up North in the summer.

"You work hanky-panks or alibis or flats?" I said.

He stopped with the handkerchief. "You with it?" he said.

"A sort of first-of-May," I said. "I ran with a carnival a little about twenty years ago."

To a carny, you are said to be "with it" if you have been on the road with a carnival for years and run your particular hustle well enough to be successful at it. They call anyone who's been with a carnival for only a short time a first-of-May. I wanted to talk to him about his game. He didn't want to talk. Not about that. But it was easy enough to find out that he ran a flat joint, also called a flat store or sometimes a grind store or simply a flat.

"I've seen most of them," I said.

"Good," he said. "That's good." He went back to working on his eye.

The more I talked with him, the more I wanted to get back with a carnival. I thought if I did it right, I might get him to let me travel with him some the following summer. But I made the mistake of telling him I was a writer. I suppose I would have had to tell him sooner or later, anyway.

"That'd burn down my proposition," he said.

Nobody has a job in a carnival; he has a proposition.

"I've never blown anybody's cover. Never."

"It'd be dull, anyway," he said.

"No such thing as a dull subject. Only dull writers. Think about it, will you?"

"I'll think about it."

I figured I might as well remind him he owed me. That's the way I am. "You could still be over there on the floor with that cowboy walking around on your face."

It took a little doing, but he finally let me go with him for a while. I particularly wanted to see the gamblers one more time on the circuit, and I knew I had to do it soon or they would be gone forever. Twenty years ago practically every carnival had flat stores. But the flats are not welcome in very many carnivals today. Of the more than 800 carnivals that work this country, probably fewer than 50 still have flat joints. Ten years from now I don't believe there will be any at all.

They are condemned because of the heat they generate. If a flat is allowed, as the carnies say, to work strong, there will be fistfights, stabbings, and maybe even a shooting or two in a season, all direct results of the flat-store operation. Every carnival has a patch, who does just what the word says. He patches up things. He is the fixer, making right whatever beefs come down. Generally, flats keep the patch very busy.

Perhaps unique in the history of carnivals, Charlie Luck—a flattie himself—was also the patch. He was able to operate as the patch only because he usually did not actively run a joint. Rather, he had two agents who worked for him in flat stores he independently booked with the owner of the carnival. So far I'd traveled 600 miles with him and I'd seen no real violence in his flats—some very pissed-off people but no violence. And now, this was to be the last weekend before I went back to Florida. We'd just made a circus jump—tearing down and moving and setting up in less than a single day. It took me a long time to get back to sleep, because the ride boy had dropped another capsule, strapped on the lot lady, and was noisily working out at the other end of the van.

They did, however, finally rock me to sleep, and I didn't wake up until late afternoon. The carnival Charlie Luck was with worked nothing but still dates, which is to say it never joined any fairs where they have contests for the best bull or the best cooking or the biggest pumpkin. Fair dates work all day. Still dates never have much business until late afternoon and night. I changed my clothes in the van and went out onto the midway.

The music on the Ferris wheel and at the Octopus had already cranked up. The smell of popcorn and cotton candy and caramel apples was heavy on the air. A few marks from the town had showed up with their kids. Several fat, clucking mothers were herding a group of retarded children down the midway like so many ducks. I didn't know where Charlie was. He had a trailer, but he usually slept in a motel. I walked over to get a corn dog, and while I was waiting for it, I listened to two ride boys, both of them in their early twenties, talk about shooting up. They were as dirty as they could get, and as they talked, their teeth showed broken and yellow in their mouths. All the workers on carnivals have European teeth. Anybody with all his teeth is suspect. Several locals were standing about eating corn dogs, but the two ride boys went right ahead discussing needles and the downers they had melted and shot up. They were speaking Carny, a language I can speak imperfectly if I do it very slowly. When I hear it spoken rapidly, I can understand it just well enough to know what the subject of discussion is without knowing exactly what is being said.

The marks stared at the two boys babbling on in this strange language full of *z*'s and *s*'s. God knows what the marks thought they were speaking. In Carny, the word *beer* becomes bee-a-zeer and the sentence "*Beer is good*" becomes Bee-a-zeer ee-a-zay gee-a-zood. It is not too difficult as long as you are speaking in monosyllables. But when you use a polysyllabic word, each syllable becomes a kind of word in itself. The word *mention* would be spoken mee-a-zen shee-a-zun.

It is a language unique to carnivals, with no roots anywhere else, so far as I know. And it does what it is supposed to do very effectively by creating a barrier between carnies and outsiders. Above everything else, the carny world is a self-contained society with its own social order and its own taboos and morality. At the heart of that morality is the imperative against telling outsiders the secrets of the carnival. Actually, it goes beyond that. There is an imperative against telling outsiders the truth about anything. That was what made being there with Charlie Luck as risky as it was. Either one of us could have been severely spoken to if what we were doing had got out.

I ate my corn dog as I walked down past the Octopus and the Zipper and the Sky Wheel and past the House of Mirrors. I was on my way for a quick look at the ten-in-one, which I had seen every day I'd traveled with Charlie Luck. Ten-in-one is the carny name for a freak show, possibly because there are often ten attractions under one tent. This was a good one but not a great one.

I was especially fond of the Fat Lady and her friends there under the tent. I think I know why, and I know I know when I started loving freaks.

Almost twenty years ago, when I had just gotten out of the Marine Corps, I woke up one day in an Airstream trailer in Atlanta, Georgia. The trailer was owned by a man and his wife. They were freaks. I was a caller for the show. My call was not particularly good, but it was good enough to get the job and to keep it. And that was all it was to me, a job, something to do. The second week I had the job, I was able to rent a place to sleep in the Airstream from the freak man and his freak wife. I woke up that morning in Atlanta looking at both of them where they stood at the other end of the trailer in the kitchen. They stood perfectly still in the dim, yellow light, their backs to each other. I could not see their faces, but I was close enough to hear them clearly when they spoke.

"What's for supper, darling?" he said.

"Franks and beans, with a nice little salad," she said.

"I'll try to be in early," he said.

And then they turned to each other under the yellow light. The lady had a beard not quite as thick as my own but three inches long and very black. The man's face had a harelip. His face, not his mouth. His face was divided so that the top of his nose forked. His eyes were positioned almost on the sides of his head and in the middle was a third eye that was not really an eye at all but a kind of false lid over a round indentation that saw nothing. It was enough, though, to make you taste bile in your throat and cause a cold fear to start in your heart.

They kissed. Their lips brushed briefly and I heard them murmur to each other and he was gone through the door. And I, lying at the back of the trailer, was never the same again.

I have never stopped remembering that, as wondrous and special as those two people were, they were only talking about and looking forward to and needing precisely what all of the rest of us talk about and look forward to and need. He might have been any husband going to any job anywhere. He just happened to have that divided face. That is not a very startling revelation, I know, but it is one most of us resist because we have that word *normal* and we can say we are normal because a psychological, sexual, or even spiritual abnormality can—with a little luck—be safely hidden from the rest of the world. But if you are less than three feet tall, you have to deal with that fact every second of every day of your life. And everyone witnesses your effort. You go into a bar and you can't get up onto a stool. You whistle down a taxi and you can't open the door. If you're a lady with a beard, every face you meet is a mirror to give you back the disgust and horror and unreasonableness of your predicament. No matter which corner you turn on which street in which city of the world, you can expect to meet that mirror. And I suppose I have never been able to forgive myself the grotesqueries and aberrations I am able to hide with such impunity in my own life.

Inside the tent, the Fat Lady was already up on her platform, ready for the day's business. She had a pasteboard box under her chair. The box was filled with cinnamon buns that her manager bought for her. She could get through about ten pounds of cinnamon buns a day. Her manager said he'd owned her—that was his phrase, owned her—for three years and in that time he had never seen her eat any meat. She stuck, he said, pretty much to pastries.

"How is it today, Bertha?"

She nodded to me, put the last of a cinnamon bun into her mouth and reached for another one. Her little eyes deep in her face were very bright and quick as a bird's.

"You see Charlie Luck?" I said. I wasn't really looking for him. I just wanted to talk a little to Bertha.

"He was here with one-eyed Petey," she said. "You want one of these?"

"Thanks, but I just had a corn dog."

"Luck's probably back in the G-top, cutting up jackpots."

"Probably," I said.

Cutting up jackpots is what carnies call it when they get together and tell one another about their experiences, mostly lies. The Tattooed Man came in with the Midget and the Midget's mother. The Midget's mother was nearly as tall as I was and very thin. She always looked inexpressibly sad. During the show, she wandered among the marks, selling postcards with a picture of her tiny son on them for a quarter apiece. The Tattooed Man had intricate designs in his ears. Little flowers grew on his nose and disappeared right up his nostrils. He was a miracle of color.

"I surely do admire your illustrations," I said.

"How come I got'm," he said. He was from Mississippi and had a good Grit voice.

"How many dollars' worth you reckon you got?"

"Wouldn't start to know. For years all I'd do was put every nickel I could lay hand to for pictures."

He had eyelashes and an eyelid tattooed around his asshole. It looked just like a kind of bloodshot eye and he could make it wink. For $2 over and above the regular price of admission to the ten-in-one show, you could go behind a little curtain and he'd do it for you. Carnies have nothing but a deep, abiding contempt for marks and what they think of as the straight world, and nowhere is that contempt more vividly expressed than in the Tattooed Man's response when I asked him why he had the eye put in there.

"Making them bastards pay two dollars to look up my asshole gives me more real pleasure than anything else I've ever done."

Charlie Luck came in looking for me and handed me $5. "I sent the jack into town. That's your half."

"Charlie, that was a fifty-dollar jack."

"The guy took it said he got ten."

"And you believed him?"

He took another five out of his pocket and handed it to me. "What the hell, take it all. He was probably lying, and besides, it was your van. You oughtta have it all."

Charlie dearly loved a hustle, any hustle, on anybody. "Come on out here; I want to see you a minute."

As we were leaving, Bertha called around a mouthful of cinnamon bun, "That's a wonderful siren; I liked it a lot."

"Thank you, Bertha," I said. "That's sweet of you to say."

Out on the midway, Charlie Luck said, "You thought any more about what I asked you?"

"Charlie," I said, "I told you already."

"Look what I'm doing for you and you can't even do this little thing for me."

"It's not a little thing. I'm liable to get my head handed to me."

"You not working the show, you just traveling with me. You don't know anybody on this show. It'll be all right. Nobody's going to mind."

"You don't know that."

"I'm telling you I do know that. It'll be all right. You're leaving tomorrow, anyway. And I gotta know. I gotta have a firsthand, detailed report."

"Report, for Christ's sake!"

"I gotta know."

Charlie Luck's problem was this. He was nailing this lady named Rose who worked in the girlie show. Like the Tattooed Man, Rose had a specialty act that the marks could see by paying extra. Rose also had a husband. A large, mean, greasy husband who worked on the Ferris wheel. Charlie Luck wanted to know what she did in her specialty act. She wouldn't tell him. He couldn't go see for himself, because one of the strongest taboos in the carnival world is against carnies going to the girlie show. Most of the girls have carnies for husbands, and the feeling is that it is all right to show your wife to the marks but fundamentally wrong to show her to another carny, one of your own world.

"Hey, come in here and let me get my fortune told," I said. We were passing a gypsy fortune-teller, and I was reminded of the gypsies and their wagons passing through Georgia when I was a boy. But mostly I was just trying to get Charlie Luck to stop thinking about Rose and her specialty act.

"You let that raghead touch your hand and you never come on to my game again."

"I just wanted my fortune—"

"Ragheads can't tell time, much less fortunes."

Carnies are not the most liberal people in the world. A few blacks are tolerated as laborers, and maybe an occasional gypsy to run a mitt camp, or fortune-telling booth, but not too long ago, it wasn't unusual to see advertisements in *Amusement Business,* the weekly newspaper devoted in part to carnivals, that said plainly: "NO RAGHEADS."

"Look," said Charlie Luck. "You think you seen my proposition.

But you haven't seen me take any real money off anybody. Go bring this thing back for me and I'll run the game tonight. I'll run it strong."

"You don't have to run it strong," I said.

"I will, though, if you'll do this thing."

Charlie got bent bad over women. I found out later that the cowboy was on him in the bar in Yeehaw Junction over a woman, although I never found out precisely what it was about. But Charlie was, to use the kindest word, kinky when it came to ladies. Everybody I talked to said the same thing about him. I don't know why this was true, or how long it had been true of him, and I didn't try to find out. It wasn't any of my business, unless he wanted to tell me, and he didn't seem to. The girlie show had only joined us at the date preceding the circus jump. I was with Charlie Luck the first time he saw Rose in the G-top. He had known her now a total of four days, but he reminded me of the way I'd been when I fell totally and deeply in love the first time, at the age of thirteen. He'd honed for Rose from the first second he saw her and had managed to nail her two hours later in my van. He'd asked me for the van because he was afraid to take her to his trailer.

She came out of the van first and left. Then he came out—face radiant under this soft brown cap—and kept saying to me, "Did you see her? Did you?"

"I saw her, Charlie."

"Was she beautiful? God, I practically almost never seen anything like her in the world."

"Right," I said.

She looked about forty-eight years old, thick in thigh and hip, but had slender, almost skinny calves. The left calf was badly varicosed. Her face was a buttery mask of makeup. I couldn't figure what the hell she had done in there to him to string him out so bad. When I finally got into the van to drive to town, it smelled as though most of the salmon of the world had been slowly tortured to death all over my red-and-black carpeting.

"All right," I said finally, as we walked down the midway. "I'll catch Rose's bit for you, if you want me to. But I want you to remember one thing. Afterward I don't want any conversation about it. You know, they used to cut off the heads of the guys who brought bad news to the king."

"Now, what the hell's that supposed to mean?"

"Nothing," I said. "It means nothing."

"I'll catch you after the eight o'clock show," he said. "I gotta go settle a beef about a fifty-cent piece of slum. The shit I put up with."

Slum is what carnies call the cheap merchandise they give out in the little booths that line the midway. For that reason, hanky-panks and alibis are also called slum joints. Hanky-panks are simple games of skill such as throwing darts at balloons. Alibis are games in which the agent is continually making alibis about why you did not win. Also, alibis—unlike hanky-panks—are liable to be gaffed, or rigged, and they are also liable to have a stick who is said to work the gaff. A stick is a guy who pretends to be a mark and by his presence induces the townspeople to play.

I strolled down the midway and watched it all come down. A stick who was working the gaff at a game called six cat was winning tons of slum. Six cat is an alibi in which the object is to knock down two cats at once with a ball. The stick quit playing as soon as he had attracted half a dozen marks. The agent was singing his song, alibiing his ass off: "He, woweee! Look at thatl That was just a little too high! A hair! No more'n a hair an you woulda won! Too much left. Bring it down, bring it down, and win it for the lady."

I watched the mark finally get thrown a piece of plush, in this case a small, slightly soiled cloth giraffe. The poor bastard had paid only $12 for something he could have bought for two and a quarter out in the city. The six cat was gaffed and the agent had done what's called cooling the mark by rewarding him with a prize after he had taken as much money as he thought he could get away with.

Eighty-five million people or thereabouts go to carnivals every year in this country, and I do not want to leave the impression that all of them are cheated. Most of them are not. But the particular carnival Charlie Luck was running with is called a rag bag, and it means that everything is pretty run-down, greasy, and suspect. The man who books the dates and organizes the lot in such an operation will allow anything to come down he thinks the locals will stand for. Few people realize that one person or family almost never owns a carnival. One person will put together a tour—a combination of dates in specific locations—and then invite independent concessionaries to join him. If you look in the publication I mentioned earlier, *Amusement Business,* a sweet little paper you can subscribe to for $20 a year, you will find such notices as these: "Now booking Bear Pitches, Traveling Duck, can also use Gorilla Show." "Will book two nice Grind Shows. Must be flashy."

The independent concessionaries pay what is known as privilege to work these dates. The privilege is paid to the man responsible for lining up the dates, organizing and dispensing necessary graft, and arranging for a patch. It is interesting to notice that the farther south a show goes, the rougher it becomes. There may not be a single girlie show or flat in Pennsylvania, but flatties and girlies both may be playing wide open and woolly in Georgia. Whether it is true or not, it is the consensus among carnies that you can get away with a hell of a lot more in the South than you can in the North.

Carnies can conveniently be divided into front-end people and back-end people. Front-enders are carnies who work games, food, and other concessions. The back-enders are concerned with shows: freak shows, gorilla shows, walking-zombie shows, and—where I was going now—girlie shows.

The guy out front was making his call, but it wasn't a very good call. His voice was more than tired, it was dead. He rarely looked at the marks who were crowding in front of the raised platform now, and once he stopped in mid-sentence and picked his nose.

"Come on in, folks. See it all for fifty cents, one half a dollar."

Four middle-aged ladies in spangled briefs and tasseled halters—all of it a little dirty—were working to a fifties phonograph record about young love. The ladies were very active, jumping about in a sprightly fashion, their eyes glittering from Biphetamine 20's, the speeder far and away the favorite with carnies. From Thursday to Tuesday whole carny families—men, women, and children—ate them like jelly beans. Rose looked right at me but either didn't see me or didn't give a damn, for which I was grateful. I didn't want her paying any attention to me, because I kept thinking of her huge greasy husband out on the Ferris wheel right now splicing cable with his broken teeth.

I paid my half dollar, went inside feeling like a fool, and saw the same ladies doing pretty much what they had been doing out front and doing it, if you can believe it, to the same goddamn phonograph record. But before they began, the semicomatose caller pointed out that there would be a second show right after this one to which no one who was female or under eighteen would be admitted. Those who were admitted would have to pay $3 a head. That threw several good ole boys into a fit of leg slapping and howling and hot-damning. They were randy and ready and seemed to know something I did not know. Rose even permitted herself a small smile and a couple of winks to the boys who apparently knew who she was, had maybe seen her show before, and were digging hell out of the whole thing.

After the first show was over and they had made us lighter by $3, things happened quickly. Peeling the eggs took the longest. But first they added a drummer to the act. Really, a drummer. The ladies had retired behind a rat-colored curtain, and out onto the little platform came an old man dressed in an ancient blue suit with a blue cap that at first I thought belonged to the Salvation Army. And it may have. Ligaments stood in his scrawny neck like wire. He sat on a chair and put his bass drum between his legs. The caller started the record we had already heard twice, which, incidentally, was by Frankie Valli, and the old man started pounding on his drum. His false teeth bulged in his old mouth every time he struck it. Never once during the performance did he look up. I know he did not see Rose. I was fascinated that he would not look at her when she came out onto the stage. She was naked except for a halter. I swear. She had her tits clinched up, but there was her old naked beaver and strong, over-the-hill ass. She was carrying six eggs in a little bowl. She carried it just the way a whore would have carried a bowl, except she had eggs in it instead of soap and water. She squatted in front of us—taking us all the way to pink—while she peeled the eggs. When they were peeled, she placed them one by one in her mouth, slobbered on them good, and returned them to the dish. Then, still squatting, with Frankie Valli squealing for all he was worth and the old man single-mindedly beating his drum and several of the good ole boys hugging each other, she popped all of the eggs into her pussy and started dancing. She did six high kicks in her dance and each time she kicked, she fired an egg with considerable velocity out into the audience. On a bet with his buddies, a young apprentice madman caught and ate the last two.

I left the tent disappointed, though. I'd seen the act before. Once, many years ago, I knew a lady in New Orleans who could do a dozen. Not a dozen of your grade A extra-large, to be sure. They were smalls, but a dozen nonetheless,

I found Charlie Luck down in the G-top. A G-top is a tent set up at the back of the lot exclusively for carnival people to socialize with one another. Marks are not allowed there, and the carnies' socializing usually comes in the form of gambling games of one kind or another. It is not unusual for a carny to walk into the G-top at the end of the May-to-October season with $20,000 in his pocket and walk out the next morning wondering how he's going to get a dime to call his old mother for a ticket home on the Trailways. Some very heavy cheese changes hands in that tent, and I was amazed that the other carnies would sit down to a table with Charlie Luck. He had exceedingly quick hands, and more than once he showed me his short-change proposition. You could open your hand flat and he would count out ninety cents into it. You could watch him do it, but when he finished and you counted your change, you'd be a quarter short. He would press a nickel into your palm and at the same instant take out a quarter he'd just put down. He could count nine $1 bills or a five and four ones into your hand and inevitably he would take back over half of it. It's called, among other things, laying the note, and it's a scam usually run off in a department store or a supermarket.

"Down where I come from," I'd said to him once, "we don't sit down to seven card with folks who have fingers like you do."

He looked me dead in the eye and said, "These guys know I would never cheat them in the G-top. When we do a little craps or cards back there, they know that's my leisure, my pleasure. Cheating is business. The only place, and I mean the *only* place, I ever steal is when I'm working the joint right out there on the midway. I'd be ashamed of myself to do it anywhere else."

Charlie Luck saw me from across the G-top and immediately got up from the table and came to meet me. We walked back out onto the midway. It was dark now, and the lot, laid out in a U shape, was jammed with men and women and their children, laughing and eating, their arms loaded with slum. Screaming shouts of pleasure and terror floated down out of the night from the high rides, glittering and spinning there above us.

"Did you see it?" he finally said after we'd walked for a while. "Did you see her do it?"

"Yeah, I saw her do it."

"The specialty act, too?"

"I told you I'd go."

"Then lay it out for me."

I laid it out.

"Eggs? Hard-boiled fucking eggs?"

"Right."

"And she'd kick and fire?" He took out two capsules. "You want one of these?"

"You know I'm a natural wire," I said. "What I need is a drink to calm me down. Let's go by the van before we go to the game."

He swallowed both capsules and made a face, but the face was not from the dope. "Goddamn eggs and goddamn drummer. I'd need a drink, too. I may even have one."

By the time we got to the van he'd worked himself into a pretty good state over Rose and her specialty act.

"I don't put my dick where hard-boiled eggs've been," he kept saying. "Jesus, a pervert. I'm tainted."

"You ain't tainted, man," I said. "You just like you were before. I wish to God somebody could guarantee me my dick wouldn't go nowhere worse than a few boiled eggs. Besides, I don't know what you expected, taking her out of a girlie show."

"How was I to know? I never been in a girlie show once, not once," he said. "Over half my life I'm with a carnival. Never once did I go near a girlie show."

"Didn't you talk to her?" I said. "You should have asked if she ever put anything up in there."

Charlie Luck jerked his cap lower on his ears and stared straight ahead. "You don't ask a lady a thing like that," he said. He poured a little straight vodka on top of the speed, and we walked over to his proposition. The flat was near a punk ride between a glass pitch and a grab joint. The grab joint sold dogs and burgers and a fruit punch called flukum. Charlie Luck let the kid off for the rest of the night, and we got behind the counter. Charlie banged things around, positioning his marbles and his board and muttering to himself. He finally quit and stared balefully out at the passing crowd. He made no attempt to draw anybody in. Nobody so much as looked at us.

"You taking it in tomorrow?" he asked.

"I told you," I said. "I got to get back. There's only so much of this that'll do me any good, anyway."

"Maybe I'll go in, too," he said. "There's not but a little more than a week left on the season."

"I've enjoyed it," I said. "We'll cross again. Maybe we can sit down and have a beer with the cowboys."

He smiled. "Maybe." He sighed deeply. Then: "You don't gamble with cripples or ladies or children. I keep them out of my proposition. You beat one of them and you got heat, bad heat. Gamble with a fat guy who looks like he can afford it. The thing you like is if he's dressed up real good, too."

"One thing, Charlie," I said. "I been meaning to say this to you, but I didn't yet. Maybe I shouldn't now. But you don't gamble. You're not a gambler. No offense, Charlie, but you're a thief is what you are."

"Actually," he said, "I'm a gambler who doesn't lose. That's what I like to think I am. I just took the risk out of it."

"No risk, no gamble. No gamble, no gambler. You're a thief."

"Well, sort of. The word doesn't bother me. I only do what they let me do."

The thing you have to know right off is you can't win from a carny gambler unless he wants you to. And he doesn't want you to. Of course, like any other hustler, he may give you a *little* something so he can take away a *lot* of something. But that's a long way from winning.

The carny's success in flat joints depends upon having a good call and expert knowledge of just how far he can push a mark and the certainty that there is larceny in all of us. A good call simply means someone is passing on the midway and you are able to "call" him to you and get him involved with your hustle. A call itself is a hustle. The agent plays the mark off against the clothes he's wearing, or the woman he's with, or his youth, or his old age—in fact, anything that will make him rise to the challenge, which doesn't appear to be much of a challenge to start with. Many times an agent will walk out onto the midway, calling as he goes, and literally grab a mark, take hold of him, and lead him over to the proposition. I've known agents who could consistently operate like that and get away with it. Others can't. The moment I touch a guy, he swings on me. He thinks he's being attacked.

Beside me in the store, Charlie Luck had dropped another Biphetamine 20. His eyes were wet as quicksilver, and he was mumbling constantly about Rose. Finally, he said to me, "Lay it out for me again. How it was, what she did, the crowd. Six, you said, half a dozen, and none of'm mashed she fired'm out at the marks?"

I laid it out for him again, just as straightforward and with as much detail as I could, even to the smells in the tent, saving nothing.

When I finished, he seemed to think about it for a moment. "All right," he said.

"Don't you think we ought to try to take a little money now, Charlie?"

"OK. Yeah." He turned to watch a middle-aged couple approaching down the midway. He looked back at me. "One thing. Don't call me Charlie Luck anymore."

"What should I call you?"

"Tuna," he said.

"Tuna?"

"Like in fish. Tommy Tuna. A name I always liked. Brings me good things."

"I got it," I said. "OK."

"You got to be careful with names," he said. "Names can be bad for you. Or names can be good for you. You know?"

I didn't know, so I didn't say anything.

"A name can get dirty. Start to rot. Bring you nothing but trouble." He sucked his teeth and sighed. The middle-aged couple had stopped and were looking at us. The lady carried two little pieces of slum, a ceramic duck and a small cloth snake. "I don't think I'll be Charlie Luck anymore."

"You mean for a little while."

"I mean ever."

I loved him for that. He just willed himself to be someone else, submerged as Charlie Luck and came up Tommy Tuna. I know how easily I did the same thing. My fix is other people's lives. It always has been. As I stood there watching the well-dressed couple, secure in their middle age and permanent in their home, a fantasy started in me, a living thing. I felt my teeth go rotten and broken, my arms fill with badly done, homemade tattoos. I was from some remote place like Alpine, Texas, and I'd joined the carnival when I was fourteen and ever since been rootless, no home except the back of a semi carrying a disassembled Octopus, and I lived off people—marks—those two there smiling at me. I suddenly smiled back. They had no way of knowing my secret and utter contempt.

"Tuna," I said quietly, "let me take this."

"Take what?"

"These two here. Let me do it."

"Do it."

"All right, here we go," I called. "Hey! Lookahere! *Your* game. Yeah! You. Come here. Come *here.* In here and let me show you the little game. I can tell by the look on your face, big fella. This is your game! A quarter. Nothing but twenty-five cents. Win the little lady this right here. Big panda. Come here! Come on!"

They smile uncertainly at each other. The lady blushes. The guy looks away.

"*Hey,* you just married? I can see it. I can see how in love you are, how you want this right here for the little lady, right? *Come over here.*"

They've turned now and they're mine. I had thought they might walk on, and in spite of the fact that I've never been a caller who could actually grab anybody, I was ready to vault the counter and take the guy by the arm. The rule is that the mark gets deeper into your hustle with every move he makes toward you. He looks at you. He moves a little nearer. He lets you explain your game. He bets. If you can get him to do that much and don't take everything he's got, or as much of it as you want, you ought to find another business.

"See that bear? See that bear right here? You want it for the lady?" Tommy Tuna keeps his bear nice. An enormous panda under clear cellophane. The bear must be worth $20. "Look, she wants it! Look at her face! A quarter, it's yours for a quarter! OK? Can I show the game to you?"

The lady is blushing and squeezing the guy's arm and pressing into him. And he's already got his quarter out.

"Look, I got marbles and I got a board." I whip the board out and show it to him. The board has little indentations on it. On the bottom of each indentation is a number: a one or a two or a three on up through nine. There's a little chute that leads down to the board. "You need a hundred points to win this game. Right? One hundred points to win that bear. Cost you a quarter. You roll the marbles down the chute, we add up the total. Each total gives a number toward the hundred points you need. Right?"

He's still got his quarter in his hand. Both of them are leaning over the board. He wants to give me the quarter so bad it's hurting him and he's not even heard the game. He just knows he's risking only twenty-five cents.

"Right? Each total gives a number toward the hundred points you need." I look him in the eye and smile. I take him by the wrist and pull him a little closer. "Here's the kicker. You keep rolling till you get the hundred points you need to win. *Without paying another penny*." I pause again. He's smiling. She's smiling. I'm smiling. Tommy Tuna's smiling. "Unless . . . unless the total you roll is thirty. If you roll a thirty, the cost of the game doubles, but you *keep* the points you've earned toward the hundred and roll again."

The lady says, "Do it, honey. Oh, do it."

And here is where much of the carnies' contempt for the mark starts. The guy walks up to *my* game. He doesn't know the game, has never seen it. He sure as hell doesn't know me. He doesn't see or doesn't care that on the board there are not an equal number of ones, twos, threes, and so on. If he cared to check the board or think about it, he'd see the odds are overwhelming that he'll roll the losing number nearly every time. And each time you roll a 30, though you keep the points you already have, you don't get to count the 30.

He rolls the marbles. As soon as they stop in the slots, I'm taking them out again as fast as I can, palm partially obscuring the board, adding aloud in a stunned, unbelieving voice, "Two and nine, eleven, and six is seventeen and, wow, oh golly! Nine and nine and nine . . . twenty-seven to the seventeen and . . . that's forty-four *big* points, almost half of what you need to win that bear for the little lady. This must be your lucky night!"

He had, of course, rolled a 30. He takes the marbles again, and I quick-count him to 52. "Hey, this bear's gone tonight. It looks like your night." He's flushed. You'd think he had $5000 on the line. He whips down the marbles, and guess what? He rolled that 30. But he's got fifty cents out almost before I can count the losing number for him. We go again and I take him up to 65. He rolls and loses. The bet's $1. Before he knows what's happened, he's looking at an $8 bet and he needs only 22 points to win.

I was just about to give him the marbles and made the mistake of looking at the lady. You'd have thought the guy was losing the mortgage on the house. She was nearly in tears. I hand him the marbles. He rolls a 30, but I count him into 105. Pandemonium squeals. Hurrahs. Down comes the bear and off they go. Tommy Tuna took me by the arm and led me to the back of the booth.

"You sonofabitch," he said.

"Yeah, I guess. But don't come down on me too hard. I'll pay you for the bear."

"Not the point. You had the gaff so deep into that fucker, you coulda made him bet his wife."

"It was the lady. Hadn't been for the lady, I could've done it."

"It's all right. You done good, anyway." He smiled toward the front of the booth, where four marks—all men, well fed, well dressed and apparently at the carnival together—were yelling to come on and play the game. They had been drawn to the booth by my loud counting, and they'd stayed to see the man easily win the bear.

Tommy Tuna went over to the four marks. He shrugged, looked sadly at his board. "Maybe I'm crazy," he said, "but I feel like a little action." He leaned closer to the marks. "Fuck the bears. Let's bet some money." He went into his pocket and came out with the biggest roll of bills I've ever seen. He showed the roll to the marks. I saw nothing but hundreds. "I'll play you no limit. Just like with the fucking bear, it takes a hundred points to win. The first bet'll cost you a buck. The bets double after that. I'll pay ten to one. Did you get that? Ten to one I'm paying. If you're betting a hundred dollars when you reach the hundred points to win, I'll pay you a thousand."

He said it quickly, in a flat, unemotional voice. They were into it immediately, and Tuna quick-counted them to 37 points. There seemed to be no way to lose. All four guys were pooling their money with the intention of splitting the take. But by the time they had accumulated 82 points, they'd lost $255. The next bet was gonna cost them $256. The whole thing had taken about five minutes, but Tuna pointed out they needed only 18 more points to win, and after all, he *was* giving ten-to-one odds.

"Sumpin might goddamn funny goin on here," said the biggest and meanest-looking of the four.

"Gee," said Tommy Tuna in a quiet, sad voice. "You fellas do seem to be having a real bad run of luck. I can hardly believe it myself."

They withdrew a few steps to consult and then came back and went for the bet. They rolled a 30. Tommy Tuna scooped up the money. All four of them howled simultaneously as if they'd been stung by wasps. They'd been cleaned out. The big, mean one moved to come over the counter when, as if by magic, Officer Jackson appeared on the midway, only a few feet away.

He came over and said, "You want to tell me why you hollering like this?"

The big one said, "This bastard's running a crooked game, that's why."

"You want to tell me what kind of game?"

He told Officer Jackson what kind of game. He also told him they'd been taken for over $500 in less than ten minutes.

"Gambling?" Officer Jackson could hardly believe it. "That's against the law. It's against the law for everybody here. If it's true, I'll have to lock you up. *All* of you." Then he turned to the four guys and actually said: "And if I do, and if it's true, he's got your money to bail hisself out with." He paused and looked at each of the four in turn. "You want to tell me what you want to do?" After the four guys had left, Officer Jackson and Tommy Tuna went over to the corner and had a short, earnest conversation, which I did not hear. Then Officer Jackson left.

Tommy watched the cop disappear down the midway and said in a wondering voice, "You know, I once took twelve thousand dollars off a oilman in Oklahoma. He never said a word about it. A real fine sport."

I said, "Some days chicken salad. Some days chickenshit."

FROM THE ADVENTURES OF HUCKLEBERRY FINN

Mark Twain

—Huckleberry Finn *is one of the most celebrated literary works in the American canon. In this chapter Mark Twain (1835–1910) takes dead aim on mob mentality, and offers some shrewd, albeit disturbing insights on the nature of spectacle.*

THEY SWARMED UP TOWARDS Sherburn's house, a-whooping and raging like Injuns, and everything had to clear the way or get run over and tromped to mush, and it was awful to see. Children was heeling it ahead of the mob, screaming and trying to get out of the way; and every window along the road was full of women's heads, and there was nigger boys in every tree, and bucks and wenches looking over every fence; and as soon as the mob would get nearly to them they would break and skaddle back out of reach. Lots of the women and girls was crying and taking on, scared most to death.

They swarmed up in front of Sherburn's palings as thick as they could jam together, and you couldn't hear yourself think for the noise. It was a little twenty-foot yard. Some sung out "Tear down the fence! tear down the fence!" Then there was a racket of ripping and tearing and smashing, and down she goes, and the front wall of the crowd begins to roll in like a wave.

Just then Sherburn steps out on to the roof of his little front porch, with a double-barrel gun in his hand, and takes his stand, perfectly ca'm and deliberate, not saying a word. The racket stopped, and the wave sucked back.

Sherburn never said a word—just stood there, looking down. The stillness was awful creepy and uncomfortable. Sherburn run his eye slow along the crowd; and wherever it struck the people tried a little to out-gaze him, but they couldn't; they dropped their eyes and looked sneaky. Then pretty soon Sherburn sort of laughed; not the pleasant kind, but the kind that makes you feel like when you are eating bread that's got sand in it.

Then he says, slow and scornful:

"The idea of YOU lynching anybody! It's amusing. The idea of you thinking you had pluck enough to lynch a MAN! Because you're brave enough to tar and feather poor friendless cast-out women that come along here, did that make you think you had grit enough to lay your hands on a MAN? Why, a MAN's safe in the hands of ten thousand of your kind—as long as it's daytime and you're not behind him.

"Do I know you? I know you clear through was born and raised in the South, and I've lived in the North; so I know the average all around. The average man's a coward. In the North he lets anybody walk over him that wants to, and goes home and prays for a humble spirit to bear it. In the South one man all by himself, has stopped a stage full of men in the daytime, and robbed the lot. Your newspapers call you a brave people so much that you think you are braver than any other people—whereas you're just AS brave, and no braver. Why don't your juries hang murderers? Because they're afraid the man's friends will shoot them in the back, in the dark—and it's just what they WOULD do.

"So they always acquit; and then a MAN goes in the night, with a hundred masked cowards at his back and lynches the rascal. Your mistake is, that you didn't bring a man with you; that's one mistake, and the other is that you didn't come in the dark and fetch your masks. You brought PART of a man—Buck Harkness, there—and if you hadn't had him to start you, you'd a taken it out in blowing.

"You didn't want to come. The average man don't like trouble and danger. YOU don't like trouble and danger. But if only HALF a man—like

Buck Harkness, there—shouts 'Lynch him! lynch him!' you're afraid to back down—afraid you'll be found out to be what you are—COWARDS—and so you raise a yell, and hang yourselves on to that half-a-man's coat-tail, and come raging up here, swearing what big things you're going to do. The pitifulest thing out is a mob; that's what an army is—a mob; they don't fight with courage that's born in them, but with courage that's borrowed from their mass, and from their officers. But a mob without any MAN at the head of it is BENEATH pitifulness. Now the thing for YOU to do is to droop your tails and go home and crawl in a hole. If any real lynching's going to be done it will be done in the dark, Southern fashion; and when they come they'll bring their masks, and fetch a MAN along. Now LEAVE—and take your half-a-man with you"—tossing his gun up across his left arm and cocking it when he says this.

The crowd washed back sudden, and then broke all apart, and went tearing off every which way, and Buck Harkness he heeled it after them, looking tolerable cheap. I could a stayed if I wanted to, but I didn't want to.

I went to the circus and loafed around the back side till the watchman went by, and then dived in under the tent. I had my twenty-dollar gold piece and some other money, but I reckoned I better save it, because there ain't no telling how soon you are going to need it, away from home and amongst strangers that way. You can't be too careful. I ain't opposed to spending money on circuses when there ain't no other way, but there ain't no use in WASTING it on them.

It was a real bully circus. It was the splendidest sight that ever was when they all come riding in, two and two, a gentleman and lady, side by side, the men just in their drawers and undershirts, and no shoes nor stirrups, and resting their hands on their thighs easy and comfortable—there must a been twenty of them—and every lady with a lovely complexion, and perfectly beautiful, and looking just like a gang of real sure-enough queens, and dressed in clothes that cost millions of dollars, and just littered with diamonds. It was a powerful fine sight; I never see anything so lovely. And then one by one they got up and stood, and went a-weaving around the ring so gentle and wavy and graceful, the men looking ever so tall and airy and straight, with their heads bobbing and skimming along, away up there under the tent-roof, and every lady's rose-leafy dress flapping soft and silky around her hips, and she looking like the most loveliest parasol.

And then faster and faster they went, all of them dancing, first one foot out in the air and then the other, the horses leaning more and more, and the ringmaster going round and round the center-pole, cracking his whip and shouting "Hi!—hi!" and the clown cracking jokes behind him; and by and by all hands dropped the reins, and every lady put her knuckles on her hips and every gentleman folded his arms, and then how the horses did lean over and hump themselves! And so one after the other they all skipped off into the ring, and made the sweetest bow I ever see, and then scampered out, and everybody clapped their hands and went just about wild.

Well, all through the circus they done the most astonishing things; and all the time that clown carried on so it most killed the people. The ringmaster couldn't ever say a word to him but he was back at him quick as a wink with the funniest things a body ever said; and how he ever COULD think of so many of them, and so sudden and so pat, was what I couldn't noway understand. Why, I couldn't a thought of them in a year. And by and by a drunk man tried to get into the ring—said he wanted to ride; said he could ride as well as anybody that ever was. They argued and tried to keep him out, but he wouldn't listen, and the whole show come to a standstill. Then the people begun to holler at him and make fun of him, and that made him mad, and he begun to rip and tear; so that stirred up the people, and a lot of men begun to pile down off of the benches and swarm towards the ring, saying, "Knock him down! throw him out!" and one or two women begun to scream. So, then, the ringmaster he made a little speech, and said he hoped there wouldn't be no disturbance, and if the man would promise he wouldn't make no more trouble he would let him ride if he thought he could stay on the horse. So everybody laughed and said all right, and the man got on. The minute he was on, the horse begun to rip and tear and jump and cavort around, with two circus men hanging on to his bridle trying to hold him, and the drunk man hanging on to his neck, and his heels flying in the air every jump, and the whole crowd of people standing up shouting and laughing till tears rolled down. And at last, sure enough, all the circus men could do, the horse broke loose, and away he went like the very nation, round and round the ring, with that sot laying down on him and hanging to his neck, with first one leg hanging most to the ground on one side, and then t'other one on t'other side, and the people just crazy. It warn't funny to me, though; I was all of a tremble to see his danger. But pretty soon he struggled up astraddle and grabbed the bridle, a-reeling this way and that; and the next minute he sprung up and dropped the bridle and stood! and the horse a-going like a house afire too. He just stood up there, a-sailing around as easy and comfortable as if he warn't ever drunk in his life—and then he begun to pull off his clothes and sling them. He shed them so thick they kind of clogged up the air, and altogether he shed seventeen suits. And, then, there he was, slim and handsome, and dressed the gaudiest and prettiest you ever saw, and he lit into that horse with his whip and made him fairly hum—and finally skipped off, and made his bow and danced off to the dressing-room, and everybody just a-howling with pleasure and astonishment.

Then the ringmaster he see how he had been fooled, and he WAS the sickest ringmaster you ever see, I reckon. Why, it was one of his own men! He had got up that joke all out of his own head, and never let on to nobody. Well, I felt sheepish enough to be took in so, but I wouldn't a been in that ringmaster's place, not for a thousand dollars. I don't know; there may be bullier circuses than what that one was, but I never struck them yet. Anyways, it was plenty good enough for ME; and wherever I run across it, it can have all of MY custom every time.

Well, that night we had OUR show; but there warn't only about twelve people there—just enough to pay expenses. And they laughed all the time, and that made the duke mad; and everybody left, anyway, before the show was over, but one boy which was asleep. So the duke said these Arkansaw lunkheads couldn't come up to Shakespeare; what they wanted was low comedy—and maybe something ruther worse than low comedy, he reckoned. He said he could size their style. So next morning he got some big sheets of wrapping paper and some black paint, and drawed off some handbills, and stuck them up all over the village. The bills said:

AT THE COURT HOUSE! FOR 3 NIGHTS ONLY! The World-Renowned Tragedians DAVID GARRICK THE YOUNGER! AND EDMUND KEAN THE ELDER! Of the London and Continental Theatres, In their Thrilling Tragedy of THE KING'S CAMELEOPARD, OR THE ROYAL NONESUCH! ! ! Admission 50 cents.

Then at the bottom was the biggest line of all, which said:

LADIES AND CHILDREN NOT ADMITTED.

"There," says he, "if that line don't fetch them, I don't know Arkansaw!"

THE FROG PRINCE

Johnny Meah

—Writer and carnival sign painter Johnny Meah recounts the true story of the most fascinating person he ever met, sideshow fixture Otis Jordan, the Frog Prince. The piece originally appeared in volume five of Shocked and Amazed!, *published in 1998.*

I'M WRITING THIS ARTICLE with the assumption that most readers of a journal as specific as this already know something of sideshows. I feel it would make for a pretty tedious reading to have to explain the socio-economic background of either the shows or those who presented themselves in them. There are books on the market that attempt this sort of explanation, providing you're sufficiently stoked-up with coffee to combat drowsiness while reading them.

Sideshows are not for the placard-carrying-social-awareness-crowd. Most of them seem to lack the ability or determination to cope with their own problems and find some weird solace in joining groups which espouse public outrage concerning issues that are generally so abstract that they defy definition much less solution: "Yes, I'm a fat slob, no, I don't know where my teenage daughter slept last night or why she smokes crack but, by God, I do know that they shouldn't put monkeys in cages."

I so love these brainless ditto-heads. The next time one of them uses one of those, "What kind of message are we sending here?"

phrases on me I think I'll barf all over them so they can take my message down to the corner dry cleaners.

So much for the pre-story ranting; now on to Otis Jordan.

Nineteen sixty-eight was a year of changes, an evolutionary year for me in which I discarded—in the order of their importance to me at the time—two vehicles, an occupation, and a marriage. I was at that wonderful age when I regarded all temporary setbacks as "learning experiences." That year, after the divorce and the donation of a truck and trailer to resolve same, I realized that I was learning myself into instant poverty. Also, as part of this cavalcade of revelations, I discovered that I was sick of extracting money from the patrons of carnival games. This, I had decided, was not show business.

Fortunately for me and my sagging economic situation, show business—or at least a reasonable facsimile—was only a few steps away at the back end of the midway.

The "back end" of this particular carnival offered four girl shows and a sideshow. It was early afternoon and the banners on the ten-in-one were down and rolled up. I remember thinking that, no matter what acts were advertised, they'd have an awfully hard time grabbing attention away from the four prurient pleasure palaces.

I cautiously ducked under the teaser curtain, half expecting to encounter a snarling dog or an ill-tempered roughie who'd encourage me to leave. Finding neither, I stood and surveyed the tent's interior. It was a pretty average-looking sideshow. A long main stage with the usual props: an electric chair, a sword ladder, a nail board and so on. A small platform with a bladebox sat at one end of the tent and a blow off curtain sectioned off the opposite end. I had worked a lot of shows that looked just like this one. I guess it would add a touch of romanticism to say that the sight evoked some sort of Thomas Wolfe moment for me but it didn't. I was, in fact, on my way out of the tent, mentally resigning myself to a lifetime of petty larceny on the front end when a voice stopped me.

"Johnny?"

I couldn't quite imagine who'd know me here, nor could I quite determine where the voice was coming from.

"Johnny," the voice came again, this time with a hint of urgency.

I made my way to the end of the main stage since the voice seemed to be coming from somewhere behind it.

"Yeah, I'm coming," I ventured, now even more puzzled as there was nobody in the area behind the stage.

"Oh, sorry—you're not Johnny," the voice said from under the stage.

"Well, I was a few minutes ago," I replied, now bending down to see the challenger of my identity.

"You're not black," the voice that had now grown a body—or sort of a body—retorted.

Peering into the dim light beneath the stage, I found myself staring at a rather bemused looking black man with twisted arms who was, for some reason, propped up in a washtub.

"This is true," I said. We observed each other for a second or two and then burst out laughing.

The man in the washtub was Otis Jordan, "The Frog Boy" as he was titled in the sideshow business.

The urgency that I'd detected in his voice was very legitimate. He needed to use the toilet and the man he'd been calling to was not around, so I carried him to the public restroom. In doing so, I discovered that his legs were in the same condition as his arms—about the size of a four-year-old child's and paralyzed.

For the next three years, I carried Otis in and out of restrooms, restaurants and motels. I helped him dress and undress (a pretty complicated maneuver, sort of like dressing a corkscrew). I bathed him, processed his hair and became, for all practical purposes, his arms and legs. Best of all, I became his friend.

I eventually bought my own sideshow and the last year we were together, Otis worked for me.

At this point I've given you a sketchy rundown of what Otis looked like. Although Otis and I would have never met had he not been a sideshow attraction, I feel that his deformity was very secondary to his personality, a fact that anyone who knew him would readily attest to. I will, however, quickly describe him physically because a large segment of the *Shocked and Amazed!* readers probably never saw him.

The stock "lecture" on Otis referred to his condition as "arrested development." Although this term probably leaves a lot to be desired from a clinical standpoint, I'll let it stand. Actually, Otis's physical dilemma was the result of several things but, unless you own a dictionary of medical jargon (and understand it), "arrested development" will do just fine. The only part of Otis's body that would pass as normal was his head. The rest of him was, as previously mentioned, about like a four-year-old child in size. A paralyzed four-year-old with the exception of the thumb and index finger of his right hand. Everything above the shoulders worked and his internal organs functioned properly. He had developed the ability to propel his body in whatever direction he desired by using his neck muscles, thereby throwing his shoulders and the frozen anatomy below them from side to side. This took a great deal of effort but he would wobble himself around pretty well in this manner.

So there you have Otis Jordan, the Anatomical Jigsaw Puzzle—an unusual sight to be sure. But then there was that face. A noble, scholarly face that instantly drew your attention away from the cruel prank that Mother Nature had played on the rest of him. Without uttering a word Otis's face would convey—"All that down there? That's The Frog Boy you paid to see. Up here? This is the part I analyze *you* with."

As you travel Interstate 75 in Georgia, you'll see an exit marked "Barnesville" somewhere between Macon and Atlanta. Otis Jordan was born there—long before the Interstate was thought of, long before the Civil Rights Movement and long before even the brightest and whitest medical practitioners could offer much more than sympathy to parents of such an unfortunate child.

The Jordan home sat at the end of a dusty dirt road in an area dotted with similarly sparse little dwellings that housed the black population of the town. At that point in time, dealing with social oppression was a fact of life for anyone in Otis's circumstances; however, there seemed to be an unending supply of jokers in the deck at the Jordan household. Besides being poor, black and deformed, Otis next became aware that his brothers and sisters were ashamed of his appearance. This manifested itself in the form of their refusal to take him to school with them. It was at this point that Otis discovered that inner force called determination.

Even as a youngster, Otis had the enviable ability to not only absorb knowledge but to equate it to his own needs and implement it. Here, for example, we had a forlorn child left to his own devices in a yard containing, among other things, a rusty toy wagon and several goats. He and the goats had established a rapport due, perhaps, to the fact that they were about the same height.

Over a period of a month, Otis fashioned a crude harness from old ropes and a broken broomstick. Convincing the goats that they were to be the power department was a far more frustrating task. For weeks, they'd either balk at his coaxing to pull the wagon or run off, wagon in tow. But determination won out at the end, and one day Otis's father returned from the fields to find his son, the teamster, proudly circling the house in his goat-drawn chariot.

"My Daddy laughed and laughed—and then he cried and hugged me," Otis told me. "Next day he fixed up a real little harness and board with an old pillow that I could sit on."

One evening, seated on the front steps and observing Otis's progress with his transportation, his older brother hollered, "Where you think they're gonna take you, Macon?"

"Maybe," Otis grinned. "First they're taking me to school." And for the next twelve years, they did just that.

Otis's first title before an imaginative showman dubbed him "The Frog Boy" was "The Goat Boy." "The Goat Boy of Barnesville, Georgia" was a familiar sight to the townspeople as he made his way to and from school each day. Otis eventually captured the attention of the local newspaper and they did an article about him, his goats and his quest for an education. Several out-of-town papers ran articles and photo coverage as well.

The black VFW, in an effort to call attention to the plight of young, southern blacks wishing to enroll in college, decided that Otis was the perfect individual to pinpoint the issue. Otis would, according to their plan, make his way via goat express, from Barnesville to Washington, D.C., garnering both media coverage and donations for his college tuition. Otis considered it and decided against it. Why? "Well, it would've been pretty hard on the goats," Otis told me with a wry grin. And we both laughed, much the same way we laughed when we first met and for pretty much the same reason.

Otis remained in Barnesville for the next fifteen years, taking mail order courses on a variety of subjects and selling newspapers in the town square. He helped his father repair neighborhood cars and pickup trucks, his contribution being instructional. Through his correspondence school training and armed with a repair manual for the vehicle being worked on, he'd be hoisted up in sight of the problem area, then orally guide his father or brother through the actual repair operation.

He also learned to repair small electric appliances and motors. This he'd do mostly by himself using his mouth and two functioning digits.

Otis bought a car, a DeSoto I seem to recall, and orchestrated the outfitting of it so he could drive it. He got his driver's license, amazing a rather skeptical Department of Motor Vehicles examiner with his driving abilities. He had come full circle from the question regarding his destination with the goat wagon. Yes, he could get to Macon, but then what? Could he make even a semblance of a living anywhere other than Barnesville, Georgia? Could he make enough money to help ease the financial burden at home?

It was September and the County Fair opened its annual run in Barnesville. Most fairs in the South were now integrated; however, Otis had only been to the "colored fair" a few years before. It had been fun for Otis. A friend had pulled him around in his wagon. Even with the promise of his friend holding him, the ride operators wouldn't allow him to board the whirling amusement devices. Still, he enjoyed the fair from his own vantage point.

His neighbors would shout and wave to him. His friend bought him cotton candy and someone boosted him up on a game counter to throw (or, in Otis' case, blow) darts at balloons. Otis was very proficient at darts. He could place one in his mouth sideways and blow it very accurately at any given target. That day he won the game's limit of three stuffed toys.

Of course, the "colored fair" was played by a lesser carnival company than the "white fair," usually a week apart, the first (naturally) being the white version.

But now the fair was integrated and slowly regaining its attendance, which dropped to less than half when they "started leaving them niggers in."

Otis could hold his own in the face of bigotry but, like most sensible people, tried to avoid unnecessary confrontations. He had mixed emotions when asked by a group of his friends if he'd like to go to the fair. After much nagging, he did, however, agree to go.

There was no way he could have known that the canvas-colored version of Macon was out there waiting for him.

Since arriving earlier in the evening, Otis had decided that this fair wasn't going to be much fun. Small groups of blacks clustered together and moved apprehensively through the mostly white attendees. One of Otis's friends confided that a group of white high school toughs were circulating through the fairgrounds trying to provoke a fight with any blacks they encountered. No, this wasn't going to be much fun at all.

They had stopped to buy sodas when Otis jerked his head toward an area of the midway beyond them and asked, "What's down there?"

"Don't think we should go down there," one of his friends commented with a frown.

"Why's that?" Otis inquired.

"That's where those hootchie-cootchie shows are."

"Yeah?" Otis beamed.

"They don't like us looking at them white ladies."

"Oh," Otis said dejectedly, then regaining enthusiasm, "maybe we could just kinda peek."

Otis persuaded his cohorts to at least venture a short way down the forbidden path, and they were passing an array of huge canvas paintings in front of one of the shows. Suddenly a man standing on a platform in front of the paintings began beating on a bass drum and hollering over a microphone.

"This where the hootchie-cootchie ladies are?" Otis grinned.

"No," his friend said uneasily. "We should go back," and began to turn Otis's wagon around.

"Wait. Wait," Otis said irritably. "I want to see. What is this place?"

As Otis related the story to me, he recalled his friend looking down at him with a strangely sad look, and mumbling a reply. He asked his friend to repeat what he said.

"It's—freak people."

At this point in the story I think it would be improper to speculate on Otis's reaction to his friends' obvious discomfort. I know that Otis was always very insightful concerning people's inner emotions—as he would be at this moment regarding my efforts in trying to relate this portion of the story to you.

They remained well in the back of the small tip that was gathering near the platform where the man was shouting and beating on the drum.

"Gonna bring 'em all out now—those strange, odd and unusual people," the drum beater said. A few pretty average-looking people in costumes were now joining him on the platform.

Otis looked up at the paintings that were flapping in the night breeze. There was a picture of a man swallowing a sword, another of a person who was supposed to be half man, half woman. At home Otis had a book called *Medical Anomalies* that showed a picture of a person with breasts and a penis and he wondered if this could be the same person. In the same book was a photo of a white man whose body looked something like his own. He'd bought the book at a musty smelling little store called Trash and Treasures and had it hidden away in his room. From time to time he'd feel an inexplicable urge to dig it out and look through it. Now he seemed to be confronted with a tent full of curious people from the book which, like the book itself, made him feel "creepy."

The talker, actually the owner of the sideshow, ceased his drum thumping and advanced to the front of the bally platform to begin the third opening of the night. This was the last fair of the season for him.

The year had not been good, and he was relieved that this was the season's closing engagement.

Throughout the "opening" his eyes kept returning to a small group of blacks hovering toward the rear of the "tip." In their midst was a studious looking black man seated, or so it appeared, in a wagon. The man's face was so serenely expressionless that at first he thought that they were hauling a bust of George Washington Carver around. This all changed when a young black girl holding a snake joined him on the platform. The statue now broke into an ear-to-ear grin.

When he finished the opening, turning a disappointingly small group of customers into the tent, his interest in the man in the wagon greatly intensified. Now, unblocked by the crowd that had stood in front of him, it became clear that the man's head was supported by something that looked like the body of a poorly crafted ventriloquist's dummy.

He climbed down from the platform and made his way toward the man in the wagon and his entourage, them eyeing him more gravely with each step.

That was the night Otis met Dick Burnett or "Commodore Dick" as he was referred to in sideshow circles. The beginning of a profitable, if sometimes rocky, three years' association that would forever change the life of the young black man from Barnesville, Georgia.

Burnett, an affable actor-turned-midway-showman, enjoyed a reputation of being the premier promoter of freaks in the industry. He possessed the uncanny ability to approach even the most unlikely candidates and somehow convince them that sitting on a sideshow platform was second only to a career in Hollywood. If you or I ever attempted what he seemed to accomplish with ease, we'd have nursed many a black eye. ("Hi there. Hate to interrupt your dinner, but I just wanted to offer your wife a job as a sideshow fat lady!" As I said, many a black eye.)

To his credit, Dick did not ply his promotional talents on the mentally handicapped. His star attractions were usually people that were socially and/or economically disadvantaged and looking for any ray of sunshine they could find. As a result, at a time where most sideshow operators were lucky to have one bona fide "feature freak," Commodore Dick usually had three or four.

Strangely enough, Burnett never had a good route, despite a show literally bulging at the seams with acts and oddities. When other operators were playing major fairs and cranking out big grosses with less of a show, Burnett would be playing spots like, well—Barnesville. As a result, his equipment usually looked a little scruffy and paydays were sometimes missed. Despite Commodore Dick's shortcomings, most of his help remained loyal to him, even upon discovering that the other operators paid appreciably more.

Otis joined Burnett's show the following spring. Although it was yet another mediocre tour for the show, he faired far better than he had in Barnesville and returned home at the end of the season with money in his pocket and a new outlook on life.

In a career that spanned over twenty-five years, Otis appeared with a host of sideshows owned by such operators as Elsie Sutton, Jeff Murray, Dean Potter, Ward Hall and myself. Each one of them has their own "Otis" stories to tell, some funny, some poignant but all with reverence for the fact that their lives had been touched by a very unique human being.

I, of course, have a favorite story regarding Mr. Jordan.

In his earlier sideshow days, Otis was always "lectured on." The inside lecturer (*emcee* for the sideshow-vernacular-impaired), would introduce Otis, tell you why he was called "The Frog Boy" (in case your imagination wasn't up to making the quantum leap to make this observation for yourself), and then do a quasi-medical explanation of his condition. Some of these "lectures" were pretty brutal, particularly when the lecturer mangled medical terms or, worse yet, invented new ones. When I first knew Otis, the magician was also the lecturer. To be as charitable as possible, he was a good magician. Each day I endured his Walter Brennan-style delivery of, "Little Otis was born in a small town in Georgia of normal parents." I often wondered how many people went home and tried to locate Normal Parents in their *Rand McNally*.

At any rate, the lecture would wind up with a brief question and answer period.

"How old are you, Otis?"

"Thirty-two."

"How tall are you?"

"Twenty-seven inches."

After this exhilarating exchange the lecturer would pitch Otis's miniature bibles for fifty cents, the proceeds of which, ostensibly, did everything from staving off off-season hunger pangs to building a national research center to cure frogboyitis.

There were human oddities on the circuit that did their own lecture, doubtless inspired into doing so to salvage whatever dignity they could after being subjected to the forgoing repartee.

Otis was terribly "mike shy." When I began doing his lecture I tried to expand on the little "man-on-the-street" segment by tossing in questions that required more than a monosyllabic answer. I'd either get a terrified look or an inaudible grunt in return. It appeared that the audio portion of the Otis Jordan show was always going to remain at "thirty-two" and "twenty-seven inches."

Then came that sweltering hot night in New Britain, Connecticut. It was Otis's first year of employment with me and I'd managed to buy him a nice little trailer that had everything except an air conditioner. We closed the show at around midnight and it was still about 85 degrees. I'd just finished dropping the banners and walked back into the tent, preparing to carry Otis to his trailer.

"Gonna be awful hot in there tonight," Otis said. "Think maybe I'd rather sleep out here," adding, "Got my gun, I'll be all right."

It was a rubble-strewn urban lot and we'd already had problems with neighborhood gangs. I knew Otis could handle his *Pirates of Penzance*-looking gun pretty well, but I was still uneasy about leaving him alone in the tent. He was, however, not about to give up the idea of "camping out." Reluctantly, I trudged off to my own humid trailer.

My wife and I had almost fallen asleep when she nudged me awake with a hushed, "Did you hear that?"

Whatever "that" was, I didn't hear it.

"Shhh—" she whispered, "listen."

It was a kind of electronic buzzy sound interspersed with a faint voice.

"Somebody's TV," I said.

"Light plant's off," she countered.

"Somebody's battery TV."

"Get up and check," she said, ignoring my comedic efforts.

I opened the trailer door and listened. The sound was coming from inside the tent. Drawing myself up to my not particularly imposing five foot eight inches, I lifted the sidewall, expecting to find Otis holding a group of thugs at bay with his comic opera pistol.

"—chickens," an unexpectedly melodious baritone voice was singing. "Ain't nobody here but us chickens."

Oblivious to my sidewall entrance, Otis continued to croon into the mike. "Ain't nobody here but us chickens."

"A star is born!" I announced from the shadows.

"Didn't think you could hear me," said Mr. Jordan with a kid-with-his-hand-in-the-cookie-jar grin.

The next day Otis began lecturing on himself.

Otis's final years of sideshow performing were spent in Coney Island in the employ of John Bradshaw and Dick Zigun.

Here Otis appeared as the "Human Cigarette Factory" rather than "The Frog Boy." The age of political correctness was now upon us. Other than the new title, nothing changed in his presentation.

Many physically handicapped sideshow acts performed some feat or another to illustrate how they'd overcome their particular disability. Armless people would, for example, draw, typewrite, or knit using their feet. In Otis's case, he'd roll and light a cigarette and then puff smoke rings and make it disappear and appear—"sleight of mouth," as I referred to it. Hence the new "Human Cigarette Factory" title.

Ironically, if Otis was still alive today he'd be out of business with *that* title, as cigarette smoking has now been added to freak gawking by the tongue-clucking set.

A new title for Otis? Well, I'd probably lock horns with the legal folks at *Reader's Digest,* but my vote would have to go to, "The Most Unforgettable Person I've Ever Met." It'd be the most factual title I ever painted on a banner!

LADY OLGA

Joseph Mitchell

—Joseph Mitchell (1908–1996) is one of the foremost chroniclers of New York City's splendid underbelly. Bearded lady Jane Barnell is one of the many colorful characters Mitchell encountered when frequenting his favorite watering hole—which provided the title for his collection McSorley's Wonderful Saloon *(1943).*

JANE BARNELL OCCASIONALLY CONSIDERS herself an outcast and feels that there is something vaguely shameful about the way she makes a living. When she is in this mood, she takes no pride in the fact that she has had a longer career as a sideshow performer than any other American woman and wishes she had never left the drudgery of her grandmother's cotton farm in North Carolina. Miss Barnell is a bearded lady. Her thick, curly beard measures thirteen and a half inches, which is the longest it has ever been. When she was young and more entranced by life under canvas, she wore it differently every year; in those days there was a variety of styles in beards—she remembers the Icicle, the Indian Fighter, the Whisk Broom, and the Billy Goat—and at the beginning of a season she would ask the circus barber to trim hers in the style most popular at the moment. Since it became gray, she has worn it in the untrimmed, House of David fashion.

The business of exhibiting her beard has taken her into every state in the Union. In fact, she has undoubtedly travelled as widely in the United States as any other person, but she has always been too bored to take much notice of her surroundings and probably would not do well with a grammar-school geography quiz. "I been all over everywhere, up, down, and sideways," she says. "I've hit thousands of towns, but I don't remember much about any of them. Half the time I didn't even know what state I was in. Didn't know or care." Miss Barnell is sixty-nine years old and was first put on exhibition shortly after her fourth birthday; she claims she has been bearded since infancy. As Princess Olga, Madame Olga, or Lady Olga, she has worked in the sideshows of at least twenty-five circuses and carnivals for wages ranging between twenty and a hundred dollars a week. She has forgotten the names of some of these outfits; one circus she remembers only as "that ten-car mess on the West Coast where I and my third husband had to knock the sideshow manager on the noggin with a tent stake to get my pay." She started out with a tramp circus, or "mud show," whose rickety, louse-infested wagons were pulled by oxen, and worked her way up to Ringling Brothers and Barnum & Bailey.

She spent six years in the Ringling circus. She was with it last in 1938, when its season was cut short by a strike in Scranton, an occurrence which made her hysterical. Ringling's sideshow, the Congress of Strange People, is as highly esteemed by freaks as the Palace used to be by vaudeville actors, but she would not sign a contract for the 1939 season. It pained her to make this decision; for six consecutive seasons she had occupied the same berth in Old Ninety-six, the Ringling sleeping car for sideshow people, and had grown attached to it. "Once I heard about a man in the penitentiary who broke down and cried when he finished his term and had to leave his cell for the last time," she says. "It had got to be a home to him. That's how I felt about my berth." She turned down the 1939 contract because she had become obsessed with a notion that out on the road she would somehow be forced to join the circus union. Unions frighten her. Although she has never voted, she is a violently opinionated Republican. Also, she is a veteran reader of Hearst newspapers and believes everything she reads in them. She thinks the average union organizer carries a gun and will shoot to kill. When she sees pickets, she immediately crosses to the other side of the street. "Just as sure as I go back to Ringling's, that union will get me," she told a circus official who tried for hours to reason with her, and added, "To tell you the truth, I think that old union is a corporation, like everything else these days." She also has a fear of corporations; to her, they are as sinister as unions. Since she left, Ringling's has been without a bearded lady. Fred Smythe, manager of the Congress, offers her a contract every spring, but she always tells him that she will never again work for the Big Show. This never surprises Smythe. "Short of blasting," he says, "there's no way of getting a fool notion out of the head of a freak. I'd sure like to get her back. She's the only real, old-fashioned bearded lady left in the country. Most bearded ladies are men. Even when they're women, they look like men. Lady Olga is a woman, and she looks like a woman." Smythe says that bearded ladies are not particularly sensational but they are traditional in sideshows, like clowns in the circus itself. "People don't laugh at clowns anymore but they want to see them around," he says. "Likewise, if there isn't a bearded lady in a sideshow, people feel there's something lacking."

Miss Barnell has not been on the road since leaving the Big Show but has stuck pretty close to New York City, which, as much as any other place, she considers home. In the winter she works intermittently in the basement sideshow of Hubert's Museum on West Forty-second Street. She has shown her beard in practically every dime museum in the country and likes Hubert's best of all; she has come to look upon it as her winter headquarters. Professor Le Roy Heckler, who operates the Flea Circus concession in Hubert's, is an old friend of hers. They once lived in the same farming community in Mecklenburg County, North Carolina, and she worked in circuses long ago with his father, the late Professor William Heckler, who was a sideshow strong man before he developed a method of educating fleas and established the family business. She has great respect for Le Roy; she calls him "the young Professor" and says she has known him since he was "diaper size." In the summer she divides her time between Hubert's and Professor Sam Wagner's World Circus Side Show, also a dime museum, in Coney Island. She likes Coney because she feels that salt air is good for her asthma; also, she has a high regard for the buttered roasting-ear corn that is sold in stands down there.

On the dime museum circuit she does not work steadily; she works two or three weeks in a row and then lays off for a week. "I don't want to go nuts," she says. In museums, her hours are from 11 A.M. to 11 P.M. There is an average of two shows an hour and during a show she is on the platform from five to ten minutes. Between appearances, she is free. At Hubert's she kills most of this time dozing in a rocking chair in her dressing room. Sometimes she visits with other performers, usually with Albert-Alberta, the half-man-half-woman. Twice a week she goes into Professor Heckler's booth and watches him feed his fleas. This spectacle always amazes her, although she has seen it scores of times. The Professor rolls up one sleeve, picks the fleas out of their mother-of-pearl boxes with tweezers, and drops them, one by one, on a forearm, where they browse for fifteen minutes. While the fleas are feeding, the Professor reads a newspaper and she smokes a cigarette. They seldom say anything to each other. Taciturn herself, Miss Barnell does not care for talkative people. At least once an afternoon she wraps a scarf around her beard and goes out for coffee or a mug of root beer. She usually goes to the lunchroom in the American Bus Depot, a few doors west of Hubert's. She finds the atmosphere of a bus terminal soothing to her nerves. When showing in Coney Island, she takes brisk turns on the boardwalk between appearances.

In the past, while filling engagements in and around the city, Miss Barnell always lived in small Broadway hotels. A year or so ago she gave up hotel life. One Saturday night, after working late in Hubert's, she walked into a hotel off Times Square in which she had been living since the Ringling strike and a drunk in the lobby saw her and said, "By God, it's the bearded lady!" He followed her to the elevator, shouting, "Beaver! Beaver!" Next day she moved out and took a furnished apartment in a theatrical rooming house on Eighth Avenue, not far from the Garden. The house was recommended by a colleague, a man who eats electric-light bulbs. Among the other tenants are a magician, an old burlesque comedian, a tattooed woman, and a retired circus cook. Surrounded by such people, she feels at ease; when she meets them on the stairs they simply take her for granted and do not look startled. "If an old baboon was to walk down the hall tooting on a cornet, nobody in my house would give him a second look," she says.

Miss Barnell would like to spend the rest of her life in the city, but she knows that sooner or later she will become a stale attraction in the dime museums and will have to run an "At Liberty" notice in *Billboard* and get a job with a circus or carnival again. She wants to put this off as long as possible because she has grown to like apartment life; it has given her a chance, she says, really to get acquainted with Thomas O'Boyle, her fourth husband, and with Edelweiss, her cat. O'Boyle is a veteran Joey, or clown, but recently he has been employed as a talker—the sideshow term for barker—on the box at the gate at Hubert's. He is nineteen years younger than Miss Barnell and, unlike her, is enthralled by sideshow life. He wears dark-blue shirts, lemon-yellow neckties, and Broadway suits. He believes Miss Barnell is one of the great women of all time and treats her accordingly. When she comes into a room he leaps to his feet, and when she takes out a cigarette he hurriedly strikes a match for her. They were married after working together during the season of 1931 in the Johnny J. Jones Exposition, a carnival. Both are short-wave-radio fans, and O'Boyle says that this mutual interest is what brought them together. "Since our marriage, I and Mr. O'Boyle have travelled with the same outfits," Miss Barnell said recently, "but I never felt like I really knew him until we settled in an apartment. In a sleeping car you just don't feel married. To get to know a husband, you have to cook and wash for him." Next to O'Boyle, Edelweiss is her chief concern. Edelweiss is a sullen, overfed, snow-white Persian, for which she paid twenty-five dollars when it was a kitten and which now weighs sixteen pounds. She has nicknamed it Edie, and when she speaks to it she uses baby talk. She owns a comfortable old canvas chair—it came out of a circus dressing tent—and she likes to loll in this chair, hold the cat in her lap, and sing to it. Interminably, one after the other, she sings "Eadie Was a Lady" and "Root, Hog, or Die," an old circus song. Cats and dogs are not permitted in the sleeping cars of most circuses, so when she is on the road she usually has to board Edie in a pet store. "Sometimes out in the sticks," she says, "I get so lonesome for Edie I feel like I just can't bear it." She thinks Hubert's is much nicer than other museums because the manager there understands how she feels about the cat and lets her bring it with her to work. While she is on the platform, Edie sits beside her, purring. After cats, Miss Barnell likes horses best. She is one of those women who cannot pass a horse standing at a curb without trying to stroke its head; she keeps a handful of wrapped cube sugar in her bag for horses. Once a month, no matter how lean the season, she sends a contribution to the ASPCA. "To an animal, if you're bearded, it don't make no difference," she says.

Miss Barnell has not only a beard but side whiskers and a droopy mustache. In a white, loose-fitting house dress, she looks like an Old Testament prophet. Her appearance is more worldly when she dresses for a party; on such occasion she uses lipstick and rouge. Monty Woolley saw her once when she was dressed for the evening and said she looked like Elsa Maxwell in a property beard. Someone repeated Woolley's remark to her and she snorted with indignation. "Mr. Woolley must not have good eyesight," she said. She is not as plump as Miss Maxwell. She is five feet five and weighs a hundred and eighty-three pounds. She does not look her age; she has few wrinkles and she walks with a firm step. Her face is round and gloomy. Her bobbed gray hair is brushed pompadour style, and on the platform she wears a Spanish comb and two side combs. Once a year she gets a permanent wave. Before going on the street, she always covers her face with a veil and wraps a Paisley scarf around her neck, hiding her beard. To keep it curly, she sleeps with her beard in a pigtail plait; on days off she does not unplait it. She wears a thick gold wedding ring. Her voice is low and feminine.

Years of listening to barkers has had an effect on her speech; she makes long words longer. To her, a monstrosity is a "monsterosity." She uses some circus slang. The men who haunt the pinball machines on the first floor of Hubert's and never spend a dime to visit the sideshow in the basement are "lot lice" to her; in circuses, this term is applied to townspeople who do not buy tickets but stand around the lot, gaping at everything and getting in the way. She uses the word "old" to express contempt. She once said, "If that old Mayor they have here can't think up anything better than that old sales tax, he ought to lay down and quit." She consistently says "taken" for "took." This is a sample of her conversation: "When I was a young'un I taken the name Princess Olga. After I first got married I changed to Madame, but when every confounded swami-woman and mitt-reader in the nation taken to calling herself Madame So-and-So, I decided Lady was more ree-fined." She has a dim but unmistakable Southern accent, and many of her habits of speech are North Carolinian. She heavily accents the first syllable in words like "hotel" and "police." She uses "one" as a contraction for "one or the other." She says, "I'm going to the movie pitchers this afternoon, or down to Coney Island, one." When she gets ready to do her kitchen shopping, she doesn't say, "I'm going up the street"; she says, "I'm going up street," or, "I'm going down street." Another heritage from her years in rural North Carolina is a liking for snuff. She and O'Boyle own an automobile, and occasionally they get it out of storage and take a long trip. While riding along with the windows lowered, they both dip snuff. "Out in the country, snuff is better than cigarettes," she says. "Of course, I'd never think of using it indoors." She smokes a pack and a half of cigarettes a day. The use of tobacco is her only bad habit. As a rule, sideshow performers are fond of the bottle, but she is a teetotaler and a believer in prohibition.

On a sideshow platform or stage, Miss Barnell is rather austere. To discourage people from getting familiar, she never smiles. She dresses conservatively, usually wearing a plain black evening gown. "I like nice clothes, but there's no use wasting money," she says. "People don't notice anything but my old beard." She despises pity and avoids looking into the eyes of the people in her audiences; like most freaks, she has cultivated a blank, unseeing stare. When people look as if they feel sorry for her, especially women, it makes her want to throw something. She does not sell photographs of herself as many sideshow performers do and does not welcome questions from spectators. She will answer specific questions about her beard as graciously as possible, but when someone becomes inquisitive about her private life—"You ever been married?" is the most frequent query—she gives the questioner an icy look or says quietly, "None of your business." Audiences seem to think that this is admirable. Now and then, after she has told off a persistent or insulting questioner, people will applaud. Miss Barnell's temper has been a blessing; it has kept her from succumbing to utter apathy, which is the occupational disease of freaks. "I don't take no back talk from nobody," she says. She guards her dignity jealously. Once she slapped an apology out of a carnival owner who had suggested that she dye her beard so he could bill her as "Olga, the Lady Bluebeard." Wisecracking professors, or talkers, annoy her; she prefers to be introduced by one who is deadly serious and able to use long medical words. Except for midgets, the majority of freaks in American sideshows are natives, but talkers hate to admit this. Consequently, at one time or another, Miss Barnell has been introduced as having been born in Budapest, Paris, Moscow, Shanghai, and Potsdam. In one carnival she was "the daughter of a Hungarian general," and in another "the half sister of a French duke." She does not have a high opinion of foreigners and is sorely vexed by such introductions. She was grateful to the late Clyde Ingalls, who was once married to Lillian Leitzel and preceded Smythe as manager of Ringling's Congress, because he never seemed to resent the fact that she was born in North Carolina. Ingalls would bow to her, turn to the audience, click his heels, and say, "It gives me the greatest pleasure at this time to introduce a little woman who comes to us from an aristocratic plantation in the Old South and who is recognized by our finest doctors, physicians, and medical men as the foremost, unquestioned, and authentic fee-male bearded lady in medical history. Ladies and gentlemen, Lay-dee Oolgah!"

Among freaks it is axiomatic that Coney Island audiences are the most inhuman, but Miss Barnell has found that a Surf Avenue dime museum on a Saturday night is peaceful compared with a moving-picture studio at any time. She talks bitterly about her experiences in Hollywood, where she has been used in a number of horror and circus pictures. Her most important role was in "Freaks," a Metro-Goldwyn-Mayer study of sideshow life filmed in 1932. It was probably the most frightening picture ever made. In it, among other things, a beautiful trapeze girl of a European circus permits a dwarf to fall in love with her in order to obtain some money he has inherited. At their wedding feast, with a fantastic group of sideshow people around the table, she gets drunk and lets slip the fact that she despises the dwarf. A few nights later, during a terrible storm when the troupe is on the road, the freaks climb into her private wagon and mutilate her, turning *her* into a freak. Miss Barnell thinks this picture was an insult to all freaks everywhere and is sorry she acted in it. When it was finished, she swore she would never again work in Hollywood.

Her self-esteem suffers least of all when she is working in circuses, where sideshow class distinctions are rigidly observed. She herself divides freaks into three classes: born freaks, made freaks, and two-timers. Born freaks are the aristocrats of the sideshow world. She, of course, is a member of this class. So are Siamese twins, pinheads, fat girls, dwarfs, midgets, giants, living skeletons, and men with skulls on which rocks can be broken. Made freaks include tattooed people, sword-swallowers, snake charmers, and glass-eaters. Normal people who obtain sideshow engagements because of past glory or notoriety are two-timers to her. Examples are reformed criminals, old movie stars, and retired athletes like Jack Johnson, the old prizefighter, and Grover Cleveland Alexander, the old ballplayer, both of whom starred for a while on the dime museum circuit. Because Johnson wears a beret and because she has heard that he sips beer through a straw, she particularly dislikes him. "To the general public, old Jack Johnson may be a freak," she says, "but to a freak, he ain't a freak." Paradoxically, she bears no animosity toward fake bearded ladies. They amuse her. She was greatly amused when Frances Murphy, the Gorilla Lady in the "Strange As It Seems" sideshow at the New York World's Fair in 1940, got into an altercation with a truck-driver and was exposed as a male. "If any man is fool enough to be a bearded lady," she says, "it's all right with me."

Some of Miss Barnell's genuine but less gifted colleagues are inclined to think that she is haughty, but she feels that a woman with a beard more than a foot long has a right to be haughty. She undoubtedly does have the most flamboyant female beard in American sideshow history. The beard of Joséphine Boisdechêne, a native of Switzerland and one of P. T. Barnum's most lucrative freaks, was only eight inches long, and she had no mustache. She did, however, have a bearded son—Albert, billed as "Esau, the Hairy Boy"—who helped make up for this shortcoming. Grace Gilbert, who came from Kalkaska, Michigan, and spent most of her professional life in Barnum & Bailey's Circus, had a lush beard, but it was only six inches long. Miss Gilbert used peroxide and was billed as "Princess Gracie, the Girl with the Golden Whiskers." Records of non-professional female beards are scarce. Margaret of Parma, Regent of the Netherlands from 1559 to 1567, had a "coarse, bushy beard." She was proud of it, believing it gave her a regal appearance, and she required court physicians to mix tonics for it. Charles XII of Sweden had a bearded female grenadier in his army, a reputedly beautiful amazon, who was captured by the Russians in the battle of Poltava in 1709 and subsequently taken to St. Petersburg and presented to the Czar, at whose court she was popular for several years. There was a Spanish nun called St. Paula the Bearded, who grew a miraculous beard, according to sacred history. She was being pursued one night by a man with evil intent when hair suddenly sprouted from her chin. She turned and confronted the man and he fled. No reliable statistics on the length of these beards have come down to us.

Most freaks are miserable in the company of non-freaks, but unless she is sunk in one of the morose spells she suffers from occasionally, Miss Barnell welcomes the opportunity to go out among ordinary people. One morning in the winter of 1940 Cole Porter went to her dressing room at Hubert's and asked her to go with him to a cocktail party Monty Woolley was giving at the Ritz-Carlton. Porter told her that Woolley was a student of beards, that he was known as The Beard by his friends, and that he had always wanted to meet a bearded lady. "I'll have to ask my old man," Miss Barnell said. O'Boyle told her to go ahead and enjoy herself. Porter offered to pay for the time she would lose at the museum. "Well, I tell you," she said, "I and you and Mr. Woolley are all in show business, and if this party is for members of the profession, I won't charge a cent." Porter said non-professionals would be present, so she set a fee of eight dollars. Late that afternoon he picked her up at her house. She had changed into a rhinestone-spangled gown. In the Ritz-Carlton elevator she took off the scarf she was wearing around her beard, astonishing the other passengers. There were more than a hundred stage and society people at the party, and Porter introduced her to most of them. Woolley, who got quite interested in her, asked her to have a drink. She hesitated and then accepted a glass of sherry, remarking that it was her first drink in nine years. "I like to see people enjoying theirselves," she said after finishing the sherry. "There's too confounded much misery in this world." She was at the party an hour and a half and said she wished she could stay longer but she had to go home and cook a duck dinner for her husband. Next day, at Hubert's, she told a colleague she had never had a nicer time. "Some of the better class of the Four Hundred were there," she said, "and when I was introduced around I recognized their names. I guess I was a curiosity to them. Some of them sure were a curiosity to me. I been around peculiar people most of my life, but I never saw no women like them before." She was able to recognize the names of the society people because she is a devoted reader of the Cholly Knickerbocker column in the *Journal & American.* She is, in fact, a student of society scandals. "The Four Hundred sure is one cutting-up set of people," she says.

Several endocrinologists have tried vainly to argue Miss Barnell into letting them examine her. She is afraid of physicians. When sick, she depends on patent medicines. "When they get their hands on a monsterosity the medical profession don't know when to stop," she says. "There's nobody so indecent and snoopy as an old doctor." Her hirsuteness is undoubtedly the result of distorted glandular activity. The abnormal functioning of one of the endocrine, or ductless, glands is most often responsible for excessive facial hair in females. Hypertrichosis and hirsutism are the medical terms for the condition. Miss Barnell once read a book called *The Human Body* and is familiar with the glandular explanation, but does not take much stock in it. She says that her parentage was Jewish, Irish, and American Indian, and she believes vaguely that this mixture of bloods is in some way to blame, although she had three beardless sisters.

Miss Barnell has to be persuaded to talk about her early life. "What's the use?" she tells people. "You won't believe me." She says that her father, George Barnell, an itinerant buggy- and wagon-maker, was a Russian Jew who had Anglicized his name. Around 1868, while wandering through the South, he visited a settlement of Catawba Indians on the Catawba River in York County, South Carolina, and fell in love with and was married to a girl who had a Catawba mother and an Irish father. They settled in Wilmington, the principal port of North Carolina, where Barnell established himself in the business of repairing drays on the docks. Miss Barnell was their second child; she was born in 1871 and named Jane, after her Indian grandmother. At birth her chin and cheeks were covered with down. Before she was two years old she had a beard. Her father was kind to her, but her mother, who was superstitious, believed she was bewitched and took her to a succession of Negro granny-women and conjure doctors. Around her fourth birthday, her father inherited some money from a relative and went up to Baltimore to see about starting a business there. While he was away a dismal little six-wagon circus came to Wilmington. It was called the Great Orient Family Circus and Menagerie, and was operated by a family of small, dark foreigners; Miss Barnell calls them "the Mohammedans." The family was composed of a mother, who was a snake charmer; two daughters, who danced; and three sons, who were jugglers and wire-walkers. The wagons were pulled by oxen, and the show stock consisted of three old lions, a few sluggish snakes, some monkeys, a cage of parrots, an educated goat, and a dancing bear. There were many tramp circuses of this type in the country at that time. On the last day of the Great Orient's stay, Mrs. Barnell sold or gave Jane to the Mohammedan mother. "I never been able to find out if Mamma got any money for me or just gave me away to get rid of me," Miss Barnell says bitterly. "She hated me, I know that. Daddy told me years later that he gave her a good beating when he got home from Baltimore and found out what had happened. He had been in Baltimore two months, and by the time he got home I and the Mohammedans were long gone. He and the sheriff of New Hanover County searched all over the better part of three states for us, but they didn't find hide or hair."

She does not remember much about her life with the Great Orient. "My entire childhood was a bad dream," she says. The Mohammedans exhibited her in a small tent separate from their circus, and people had to pay extra to see her. On the road she slept with the Mohammedan mother in the same wagon in which the snakes were kept. Her pallet on the floor was filthy. She was homesick and cried a lot. The Mohammedans were not intentionally cruel to her. "They did the best they could, I guess," she says. "They were half starved themselves. I didn't understand their talk and their rations made me sick. They put curry in everything. After a while the old Mohammedan mother taken to feeding me on eggs and fruits." The circus wandered through the South for some months, eventually reaching a big city, which she thinks was New Orleans. There the Mohammedans sold their stock and wagons to another small circus and got passage on a boat to Europe, taking her along. In Europe, they joined a German circus. In Berlin, in the summer of 1876, after Jane had been exhibited by the German circus for four or five months, she got sick. She thinks she had typhoid fever. She was placed in a charity hospital. "I was nothing but skin and bones," she says. "The day they put me in the hospital was the last I ever saw of the Mohammedans. They thought I was due to die." She does not remember how long she was in the hospital. After she recovered she was transferred to an institution which she thinks was an orphanage. One morning her father appeared and took her away. "I disremember how Daddy located me," she says, "but I think he said the old Mohammedan mother went to the chief of police in Berlin and told who I was. I guess he somehow got in touch with the chief of police in Wilmington. That must have been the way it happened."

Barnell brought Jane back to North Carolina but did not take her home; she did not want to see her mother. Instead, he put her in the care of her Indian grandmother, who, with other Catawbas, had moved up from the settlement in South Carolina to a farming community in Mecklenburg County, near Charlotte. Jane worked on her grandmother's farm, chopping cotton, milking cows, and tending pigs. She never went to school but was taught to read and write by a Presbyterian woman who did missionary work among the Catawbas. Jane remembers stories this woman told her about Florence Nightingale; they made her long to become a nurse. In her teens she taught herself to shave with an old razor that had belonged to her grandfather. When she was around seventeen she went to Wilmington to visit her father, and a doctor he knew got her a place as a student nurse in the old City Hospital. She worked in the hospital for perhaps a year, and she still thinks of this as the happiest period of her life. Eventually, however, something unpleasant happened which caused her to leave; what it was, she will not tell. "I just figured I could never have a normal life," she says, "so I went back to Grandma's and settled down to be a farmhand the rest of my days." Three or four years later she became acquainted with the senior Professor Heckler, who owned a farm near her grandmother's; he worked in circuses in the summer and lived on the farm in the winter. Heckler convinced her she would be happier in a sideshow than on a farm and helped her get a job with the John Robinson Circus. As well as she can remember, she got this job in the spring of 1892, when she was twenty-one. "Since that time," she says, "my beard has been my meal ticket." Until the death of her grandmother, around 1899, Miss Barnell went back to North Carolina every winter. She had three sisters and two brothers in Wilmington, and she visited them occasionally. "They all thought I was a disgrace and seeing them never gave me much enjoyment," she says. "Every family of a freak I ever heard of was the same. I've known families that lived off a freak's earnings but wouldn't be seen with him. My parents passed on long ago, and I reckon my brothers and sisters are all dead by now. I haven't seen any of them for twenty-two years. I had one sister I liked. I used to send her a present every Christmas, and sometimes she'd drop me a card. She was a nurse. She went to China twenty-some-odd years ago to work in a hospital for blind Chinese children, and that's the last I ever heard of her. I guess she's dead."

Miss Barnell was with the Robinson Circus for fourteen years. While with it, she was married to a German musician in the circus band. By him she had two children, both of whom died in infancy. Soon after the death of her second child, her husband died. "After that," she says, "I never got any more pleasure out of circus life. I had to make a living, so I kept on. It's been root, hog, or die. When I got sick of one outfit, I moved on to another. Circuses are all the same—dull as ditch water." She left Robinson's to go with the Forepaugh–Sells Brothers' Circus and Menagerie, leaving it to marry a balloon ascensionist. He was killed about a year after they were married; how, she will not say. "He was just killed," she says, shrugging her shoulders. Her third marriage also ended unhappily. "That one treated me shamefully," she says. "If he was in a bottle, I wouldn't pull out the stopper to give him air. I taken out a divorce from him the year before I and Mr. O'Boyle got married."

Miss Barnell is disposed to blame circuses for much of the unhappiness in her life. Consequently she does not share her present husband's enthusiasm for them. O'Boyle was an orphan who ran away to work with a circus, and has never become disenchanted. Every week he reads *Billboard* from cover to cover, and he keeps a great stack of back copies of the magazine in their apartment; she rarely reads it. Like most old circus men, he is garrulous about the past. He often tries to get his wife to talk about her circus experiences, but she gives him little satisfaction. O'Boyle is proud of her career. Once he begged her to give him a list of the circuses and carnivals she has worked for; he wanted to send the list to the letters-to-the-editor department of *Billboard.* She mentioned Ringling, Barnum & Bailey, Forepaugh-Sells, Hagenbeck-Wallace, the World of Mirth Carnival, the Royal American Shows, the Rubin & Cherry Exposition, and the Beckmann & Gerety Shows, and then yawned and said, "Mr. O'Boyle, please go turn on the radio." He has never been able to get the full list.

In the last year or so Miss Barnell has become a passionate housekeeper and begrudges every moment spent away from her apartment. About once a week she rearranges the furniture in her two small rooms. On a window sill she keeps two geranium plants in little red pots. On sunny afternoons during her days off she places a pillow on the sill, rests her elbows on it, and stares for hours into Eighth Avenue. People who see her in the window undoubtedly think she is a gray-bearded old man. She spends a lot of time in the kitchen, trying out recipes clipped from newspapers. O'Boyle has gained eleven pounds since they moved into the apartment. Before starting work in the kitchen, she turns on four electric fans in various corners of the apartment and opens all the windows; she does not trust gas and believes that stirring up the air is good for her asthma. While the fans are on, she keeps Edie, the cat, who is susceptible to colds, shut up in a closet. She has developed a phobia about New York City tap water; she is sure there is a strange, lethal acid in it, and boils drinking water for fifteen minutes. She even boils the water in which she gives Edie a bath. In her opinion, the consumption of unboiled water is responsible for most of the sickness in the city. On her bureau she keeps two radios, one of them a short-wave set. On her days off she turns on the short-wave radio right after she gets up and leaves it on until she goes to bed. While in the kitchen, she listens to police calls. The whirring of the fans and the clamor of the radio do not bother her in the least. The walls are thin, however, and once the burlesque comedian who lives in the next apartment rapped on the door and said, "Pardon me, Madam, but it sounds like you're murdering a mule in there, or bringing in an oil well."

Miss Barnell's attitude toward her work is by no means consistent. In an expansive mood, she will brag that she has the longest female beard in history and will give the impression that she feels superior to less spectacular women. Every so often, however, hurt by a snicker or a brutal remark made by someone in an audience, she undergoes a period of depression which may last a few hours or a week. "When I get the blues, I feel like an outcast from society," she once said. "I used to think when I got old my feelings wouldn't get hurt, but I was wrong. I got a tougher hide than I once had, but it ain't tough enough." On the road she has to keep on working, no matter how miserable she gets, but in a museum she simply knocks off and goes home. Until she feels better, she does not go out of her apartment, but passes the time listening to the police calls, playing with Edie, reading *the Journal & American,* and studying an old International Correspondence Schools course in stenography which she bought in a secondhand-bookstore in Chicago years ago. Practicing shorthand takes her mind off herself. She is aware that such a thing is hardly possible, but she daydreams about becoming a stenographer the way some women daydream about Hollywood. She says that long ago she learned there is no place in the world outside of a sideshow for a bearded lady. When she was younger she often thought of joining the Catholic Church and going into a nunnery; she had heard of sideshow women who became nuns, although she had never actually known one. A lack of religious conviction deterred her. Religion has been of little solace to her. "I used to belong to the Presbyterians, but I never did feel at home in church," she says. "Everybody eyed me, including the preacher. I rather get my sermons over the radio."

Most of Miss Barnell's colleagues are touchy about the word "freak," preferring to be called artistes or performers. Years ago, because of this, Ringling had to change the name of its sideshow from the Congress of Freaks to the Congress of Strange People. Miss Barnell would like to be considered hardboiled and claims she does not care what she is called. "No matter how nice a name was put on me," she says, "I would still have a beard." Also, she has a certain professional pride. Sometimes, sitting around with other performers in a dressing room, she will say, with a slight air of defiance, that a freak is just as good as any actor, from the Barrymores on down. "If the truth was known, we're all freaks together," she says.

THE PASSING OF PHILOMENA MARKER

James Taylor

—James Taylor is the publisher of the carnival sideshow journal Shocked and Amazed!, *and the co-founder of the American Dime Museum in Baltimore, Md. This story is a work of fiction.*

OTTO "OTTS" NOON—"DOC SIDESHOW" AS HE WAS KNOWN TO THOSE WHO WERE "WITH IT"—TOLD MANY STORIES IN HIS TIME, SOME OF WHICH WERE EVEN TRUE. OFTEN, HE TALKED OF PHILOMENA MARKER.

PHILOMENA MARKER WASN'T YOUNG or beautiful or half the bearded lady she claimed she was, but by the time she got to the big lot in the sky, she got what she wanted. I should know. She asked for me to come, and the roughies come to get me. But I'm ahead of myself again. That's my problem.

I first met Philly down to winterquarters on a day when nothing should've happened. Dexter, wise work that he was, came out the trailer laughing and scratching. "Hey, punk," he called to me, "got somethin to learn ya about. Come here." I dropped what I was doing, of course. I wasn't stupid, just a kid next to Dexter, and he was the boss besides. "I just got a 'portant call," he put his arm around my shoulders, not a good sign if you'd asked me, "from a freak worked for me couple seasons back. One of the best. I doubt she'll show, mind ya." Dexter wrinkled his lips. "I just couldn't carry her fare down here from Eugene. It'll be a hell of a haul for the old broad, but she might make it 'fore the first of May." He walked me out past the lumber I'd been painting for the sideshow's banner line, all white and blue stripes, like wacky barber poles. "So I was sayin, I need you to make sure she feels comfortable and gets settled in OK. OK?" He asked me the question, but he knew that I knew it wasn't a question at all. "And while you're at it, let Skippy finish that paint job." Dex let go my shoulders with a slightly less than gentle shove. "I need you to change the juice in Benny. Just dump what's there now. And fill him back up slow so he don't kick up too much a stink." He laughed when he said it. "I ain't shittin ya on that. Cloudy's one thing, but if the suckers can't see shit in the blow I'll get a lot of beefs."

I didn't care for doing anything with Benny Benjamin, our pickled punk, least of all change the formaldehyde on him. In his gallon jar he floated, a botched twin, two heads, an arm coming out of his neck, eyes like slits, lips pushed into a kiss kiss. Dex wouldn't carry bouncers, the rubber freak babies so called, though I never saw any of them bounce anywhere. I suppose you could get them to rock and shimmy some if you twirled the jar. Old Man Dex said it was gypping the public to give them bouncers instead of genuine punks. Of course it never hurt him none to talk up any old trash about Benny, depending on what he thought the tip wanted to hear, anything to get the rubes to fork over an extra dime. He'd pitch Benny as the horrors of drug abuse, the nightmare of brother-sister marriage, or an out-and-out "facts of life" show—which always meant sex to the crowd debating whether to pay extra for the blow-off, which is where Dex always had Benny set up. But then, if you don't promise people something strong, something so damn godawful peculiar you can't even pitch it on the front, then you'll never get them to fork over.

It was only a couple days before Philly showed up. Damn good time for coming a couple thousand miles, especially the way she got there. This big blue sedan pulls up, pretty damn dirty for so new a set of wheels, and behind that sedan a tiny-ass trailer. All bolted and riveted up to beat the band. A lot more hard miles on her than that sleek blue baby towing her would put in in maybe ten years. The traveler who dragged his stiff self out of the driver's seat was smooth too. Slick as a seal. Too damn well oiled for his own good. Salesman written all over him. Brushes maybe. Nah. Shoes looked too good for door to door. Shit on it. The gypsies in the mitt camp are better at this sort of thing anyway. Gypsy there'll tell you your weight, age, occupation and the next time you're likely to get a piece.

It didn't take no damn witch doctor, though, to tell that that salesman hadn't gotten much of what he'd expected from Philomena Marker. From the passenger side, she unfolded herself until she stood a full head taller than that fella that brought her to winterquarters. It was pretty clear what he saw in her, she looking every inch what the old timers would've called a tall glass of water. From the tip of her satin turban, to the half-opened blouse under which as fine a set as you'd want to set eyes on swung free as you'd please, down past a skirt you just know she had to be greased into, and all of this set atop snake skin cowgirl boots, well, none of it matched the picture of dejection and bafflement on that poor bastard's face who drove her to us. Maybe it was Philly's two foot of auburn beard put him off. He drove slow and confused off the winterquarters lot after she'd given him an affectionate peck on the cheek. Philly gathered me up then in a smile wide as a highway as she told me she'd hitchhiked all 2700 miles from Eugene. Trailer and all. And the sucker in the blue sedan wasn't even her first lift.

You couldn't be around Philly and not drink. A lot. "As though," she'd say, "there was any other way, my dear." We'd left the lot in some town or another, some burg where Philly felt safer dressing down into an outfit that was harder to call as either male or female. "Whiskey," Philly called to the bartender, a raw beef-faced character with mitts the size of my head. "Neat, of course." Philly and the barkeep both looked at me then. "And you're having?" I swallowed. A big lump. For the first time since I'd met her, Philly looked damn good. All twenty-odd years my senior, beard, mannish clothes and all. What else could I say but, "The same?"

I wasn't so much the drinker then, and I didn't have a damn to eat that morning, so I learned quick where whiskey can take you. Of course Philly already knew and was looking forward to the trip. As best I could, I took it like the man I didn't feel much like at the time, and thought I did damn good keeping the tears in my eyes from rolling down my cheeks as the cheap booze scoured its burning trail to the place where my breakfast should've been. The barman just looked at me and grunted. Damn virgin. Philly arched her back and cocked her head to the left, slow. Then she reached up and cupped her hand around mine holding the glass on the bar. "Now that," she said softly, "wasn't so hard."

A bunch more drinks came and went that morning and early afternoon. And Philomena sang songs about her years and years with the shows, doing the bearded lady, the half-and-half, whatever else the show needed. Well she might not have sang, but it all sounded like music to me, hardly out and away myself from home, still unsure whether I was with it. The light in the bar, as they say, grew amber like the whiskey in the jar. Philly realized it first, that it was drawing on to show time, about the middle of her story of the St. Louiee Exposition, where you could step into the x-ray show and your friends could see right through you. She called the barkeep over for our last round.

She gave me a break, seeing as how I still had two shots keeping me company, but told the bartender she'd need a double. Through the blurred and doubled vision of too much drink, I could still see the beef-faced son of a bitch lift the bottle, catch sight of something, hesitate, then pour anyway. " 'At there's a little stiff, sweety, but the balance's on me. Here's how." He tossed the bottle into what sounded like a steel can under the bar, empty except for another empty or two in the bottom. The glint in Philly's eyes, bright and fluttering, nearly distracted me from what I saw in her glass, what I thought I'd seen in the wall of the bottle as the bartender faltered in his pour: the wasp-waisted hour glass on the satin stomach of the black thing, its eight short legs made long and sleek by the curve of the whiskey.

"Miss Philly," I touched her arm, soft, like she'd held my hand earlier, "don't. Look."

She didn't bother. "Not to worry, child. It's just another trick of the glass." She downed the double in a gulp, spider and all. "Besides, it's not the beasties kills ya, child. The water of life'll do that all on its own."

We'd done a lot of filming that day. Sid and I were worried sick about the camera we actually went out and rented, of all things, to film the performers for the planned blow-off movie, a first. Actually, the idea was more Sid's than mine. He was always full of himself, which made him full of ideas I guess. More ideas than money, money we always seemed to be making hand over fist at the next spot, never at the spot we'd just played. That movie seemed as good a shot as any I suppose. It was different anyway. But Sid handled the money in those days. I was the half of the show handled the reality. And the half that worried.

We'd filmed lots of old junk in the morning, photos of famous freaks, mule women and seal boys, half girls and human torsos, which we had none of on the show, which didn't matter since the marks were going to be pretty put off anyway by the fact of paying extra to watch a grainy movie. They'd've been pissed even if you'd showed them *The Ten Commandments*. That would be some of them anyway, the rest would be standing in the annex so spooked at what they were seeing, or thought they were seeing, you better not so much as brush against them or they'd turn in a panic and slug you. Of course, we had some stuff that was legit. An alligator boy and a elephant-skin girl. And then there's Philly. I'd not seen her in years, and it showed all around. The cheek bones were still as lofty as ever, and the drink had only been as tough on her as it had to be. Of course, I guess it hadn't done much good by me neither. Philly had kept her hair hennaed as she'd gone more and more to gray, at least I suspected that was the reason. Christ knows, maybe she thought it brought out the color in her. She still had a body that, for a broad her age, was pretty knock out, at least it seemed to be under her outfit.

"Philly," Sid called over to her, "any time you get your act together." Sid and I were inseparable since we partnered up. Grafted at the hip as one of the other showman once told me. Still, Sid's tone with her, when he knew I was in ear shot, was too sweet. Unnatural. I liked him better straight up: nasty as a hot snake when he needed to be, kind to the punks when he knew their parents were around. I knew he didn't like Philly much. Said she was on the bottle too much, even though she never missed a performance and her half-and-half, as strong as anything in the damn show, made the nut for us nine spots out of ten.

"I'll get this squared away, Sid." Sid knew I saw through the horse shit, all that sweetness and light. "Philly, why don't I get some shots of you just stroking your beard, maybe one with you on the platform lecturing on yourself." Something was wrong. Philly got up slow, I knew partly from her age but partly from something else, something that looked like reluctance. Sid would've said obstinateness. She tossed her reddened, straw hair and raised her chin, then pulled her fingers through her beard like a comb. Then she raised her hand to me in a gesture to have me take it like I would the hand of some great lady. And she winked. "How do you want me?"

Sid pretty much disappeared while I filmed Philly stroking her beard, prettying her hair in front of a vanity mirror. I shot that bit over her shoulder, getting her and her reflection both. It was pretty arty too, if you ask me. I had a couple of the boys stand in front of the platform so I could shoot up through their heads at Philly lecturing on herself. Through the view finder, it looked just like she was doing her show for the marks, and that's the way she handled it. Don't ever let anybody tell you over thirty years in the business isn't good for something.

When it came time to shoot her doing the half-and-half, Philly lifted her long, dark gypsy skirt, revealing the most mysterious of the mysteries of life as she'd say. But I knew we were in trouble, because what showed wasn't just her act. That she did like few others. What Philly showed was all the years, coursing in lines that ran the length of her legs, even her inner thighs, like she was some mummified animal pumped back to life, only half full of the spirit and damn little of the flash. "Is this going to do the trick?" Philly turned away, appeared to diddle herself, then turned back as a man, showing her other half. "Sure, Philly," I lied. "You bet." On film, no sucker would even know what they were looking at. On the screen in the blow-off, it would all flicker and flutter like a bad dream anyway.

Not even my girl show, just one of my "Noon's No. One Shows," was drawing a tip and it was the last spot of a season that was mostly blanks. Rain and mud. Too damn hot when it wasn't wet. Everything wrong. I guess I should've expected the worst to cap it off, so when one of the boys from my ten-in-one came running up all flustered, I wasn't hardly surprised. "Mr. Otts," he mumbled under his harelip. "You better hurry up over to the show. Miss Philly's asking for you."

I'd seen it coming. I always seen it coming. Got to the point where I should've been doing my own damn mentalist act, except all I'd have been able to see is bad news for the future, and you don't win a lot of repeat customers with that kind of fortune. Philly, though, any blind guy could've seen coming. Years of abuse, 99 percent self-inflicted. I took her back after years of her being who knows where. I guess I was just always a soft touch for the old girl.

They told me they'd dragged her out of the blow-off where she'd been doing the half-and-half when she'd gone wacky and started ranting. The rubes laughed it off at first, but Philly started talking in tongues or something and then the whole mob scattered. By the time I got to the back of the show all my boys had gotten her over to her place and stretched her out in bed. Nice as you please is what I was going to say, but there wasn't much nice about the way Philly was going.

The last bits of spit and foam were still in her beard, and her outfit, that sequined gown, was all twisted around. I couldn't tell whether it was the boys manhandling her into the trailer or what she'd done on her own when she went into that fit they told me about.

The way her hair and beard were tossed around, she looked more ready for my wild man show than anything else. With her eyes closed like they were, I thought she might already be gone. But that would've been too lucky for me at the time.

"Freddie?" Philly half opened her eyes and lulled her head my way. "I wanted you to come, Freddie."

"No. No. It's me, Philly. Otts."

"Thank the Lord you've come, Freddie." I didn't bother to correct Philly again. I didn't know who Freddie was, but it did make me wonder who in hell my boys thought I was. She squeezed her eyes together hard, like she had some kind of pain, but she made no motion otherwise. "It's an old footstool, Freddie, an old footstool of a world. And life," she looked into me, her eyes red and runny,

"Freddie, life's a broken straw." Now when Philly moved, it was pain. But I couldn't for the life of me tell where. And when she shifted in that sequined gown, it sounded like wind blowing slow through tall grass. Philly's eyes got all bedroom-like, in spite of herself I suppose. I couldn't tell whether it was her act or the moment or what. "It's time, Freddie. Time to get folded double, folded in the wings of the great anonymity." Philly paused for a second, then tried to reach for my hand which, even though I sat on the bed, she couldn't quite reach. "Have you got anything to drink, Freddie?" And then her eyes glazed over and she was gone.

I ran into trouble in twos, as they say, after Philly died. That spot alone, because we had her billed all over the county as the Great Bearded Philomena, greatest bearded lady of the freak shows, fell in around us once they found out the gaff of her other act, the half-and-half. Of course almost every half-and-half ever displayed themselves was a gaff, but not any of them I knew ever did a bearded woman show too. At least, none except Philly. And when the hick town coroner got a good look at her, no amount of fixing on my end did a damn. As far as the medical examiner was concerned, male organs meant a man behind them. Philomena, being a bit shy on the female reproductive end, since she didn't have any parts there that was female at all, well, that spelled publicity that closed my ten-in-one for the remainder of that date and damn near got my ticket seller killed just after the news broke. We limped back to winterquarters. If it hadn't been for my girl show, I'd have died there on the lot too.

That wasn't the final hurrah to all this though. Philly's wish, told to me over and over over the years, was to be buried on the lot where she died. A damn hairy wish if you ask me, one no normal man would promise to keep. Too many years of too much drink, though, made me make that promise. Worse was that I found I wanted to see it through. Philly and I, you see, had gotten a bit distant over the years. As I rose in the ranks of the shows to finally own my own, Philly rose to the occasion, but we'd both grown apart the further I'd gotten from having to wait on her, hand and foot. I suppose guilt and being with her at death side carried more weight than I expected it would.

It took two seasons for me to get that spot back, and I didn't have the freak show by then either. My girl show was still roaring though, and the carny I was with was running wide open that year. Every game a grift, every show a hootchie cootchie. And we all made out like robbers. The rubes didn't remember me from Philly, the bearded lady who wasn't, and I sure didn't want to remember any of them, though I did secretly hope I'd see that coroner again, especially after he'd told me to my face he'd think over keeping Philly's secret, then ratted us out to the papers.

So halfway through the week, just as we were opening for the evening, just before sunset, another show pulls onto the lot. Trailer mount. And he and his crew start setting up, and as it goes up, in the midst of all that hot flesh and fast money, I see that the last empty spot on the lot hadn't gone to another posing show. It hadn't gone to another firecracker-hot "review." The last spot had gone to this guy's wax museum. And not just any wax show either. This was the Lord's Last Supper.

Well I couldn't stand it. I thought I was gonna laugh till I wet myself. The whole live long night, all of us doing land office business, I watched the poor bastard probably take in no more than a handful of hard money. He'd have had a better time competing with a hundred different Visit to the Holy Land or devil baby shows. What, you're going to go into three, four shows chock full of broads, lose two months rent in a flat store, then want to stare at a wax Jesus? Worse yet, *pay* to stare at a wax Jesus. Of course, you had to admire the guy's guts, even to pull onto the lot.

"Hey, Gab!" I'd ambled over to his ticket box. "Your show?"

He was sour looking, obviously pissed he was drawing a blank for the spot.

"Yeah. So what? You from the office?"

"Hell no. But how's it goin' tonight?"

He eyed me up. I probably shouldn't have asked him, but I wanted to see whether he'd lie in front of Jesus. His eyes went hard and glassy. "I'm makin' the nut."

"Yeah," I lied back, "guess so. Still, I'd've expected you'd try to get some mileage out of the disaster they had here a couple years back."

He perked up. "Can't say I know anything about it. What they have? Some kinda blow-down or somethin'?"

"No no no." Time for the reel-in. "Ten-in-one caught a lot of beefs over this bearded lady half-and-half," I winked and poked him one in the ribs, "you know the drill. Philomena Marker she called herself. Old bird up and died. Right here on," I paused and did a theatrical scan of the midway, "right here on your territory in fact." I could tell from the look on his face he couldn't put two and two together, but with the midway packed like it was, and not a one of them going into his show, he couldn't afford to blow me off. "I, ahhh, I don't see how that's gonna do anything for my show."

I turned astounded and did half a double take. " 'Don't see how . . . ' Jesus H. Lordee there, pilgrim. You should be tellin' them newspaper boys you're here to redeem that falsehood. You're here to present the 3-D, hard as wax plea of forgiveness for that show's cruel trick on this righteous community. The Lord's Last Supper itself, in all its animated glory, to wash clean the stain of the dead, bearded morphodite." I patted him on the ribs, then ran my hand up his side to his arm pit. "All for just half a dollar. Five thin dimes for the kiddies." I pulled my hand back and reached down to rearrange my privates. "Watcha think there?"

Well, he thought plenty, once I told him what to think about. The next morning's papers carried a fair-sized spread on his show. And the marks did just what I, and he, knew they'd do. Start coming to the carny for another reason. The pious and self righteous now had their excuse to lose the farm: Now it was sanctioned. None of this bothered the rest of us at all. The wax show owner took his best holt, which meant he finished the week off the nut, and it was all after the rubes had already spent the rest on the broads and the hanky panks.

I suppose about now you're wondering, What in hell happened to the promise to Philly? I carried it out you know. You see, I'd had Philly cremated. Burned her up and put in a can. And that can I lugged till I made it back to that spot, like she wanted. And the afternoon after the Lord's Last Supper hit the papers, when nobody was on the front, I made good on my word. At the foot of the entrance stairs to the show, I spread Philly's ashes, the crumbled bones, the fine dust. And all that night and for the next three, till the show closed, the rubes in that two-bit town got Philly all over them, worked her into the soil on the lot, and tracked her into the show with them when they went to stare at Jesus and his merry men.

You know, a hundred years ago, people used to hang on last words. Last words from their friends and family, the famous. I suppose those few utterances were meant to redeem the whole damn life, make it make some sense. I'd like to say that about Philly's last words to me, but I'd be talking out both sides of my mouth. Hell, the last thing she asked me, or I should say "Freddie," heaven knows who that was, the last thing Philly asked me for was a drink. Come to think of it, that was just about the first thing she ever asked me for. Which has a kind of circular ring to it, if I do say so myself.

THE PEN PAL FROM GEEK LOVE

Katherine Dunn

—Katherine Dunn's novel, originally published in 1983, about the Binewskis, a dysfunctional carnival clan, is now a cult classic. In this chapter, entitled "Pen Pal," Arturo The Amazing Aqua Boy puts his questionable theories on beauty to the test on a loyal fan.

IT WAS EARLVILLE, ON the Gulf of Mexico. One hundred windless, muggy degrees. Mosquitoes drowned in your neck creases. The only industry in town was the federal penitentiary. The midway was jammed and the show tents bulged with sweating, stinking, bad-tempered drawls. It got dark but it didn't cool off.

The fat woman surfaced at Arty's last, hottest show for the day. She was young but her colorless hair was scraggled up into tight separate curls with so much scalp between them that she looked old and balding. She was crying as she stood up on the fifth tier of the bleachers and pushed her clasped hands out toward the tank where Arty was deep in his pitch.

"You, darling," said Arty, and the feel of "darling" rose up through her puffy ankles and through every buttock in the bleachers. The crowd sighed. The fat woman sobbed.

"You feel ugly, don't you, sweetheart?" and "ugly" and "sweetheart" thrummed the crowd, and they all gasped and she wasn't the only one nodding.

"You've tried everything, haven't you?" said the bright floating spirit in the tank. "Everything," murmured the bones of the people.

"Pills, shots, hypnosis, diets, exercise. Everything. Because you want to be beautiful?"

Arty was building it up now, winding them tight.

"Because you think if you were beautiful, you would be happy?" He had the timing pat. Arty was a master of tone and timing. I leaned on the last steel strut of the bleachers in the aisle and smiled, though I'd seen him do it all my life.

"Because people would love you if you were beautiful? And if people loved you, you would be happy? Is it people loving you that makes you happy?"

Now the pitch drops a full octave into the groin groan. I can feel it even in the support poles. The asses on the seat boards must be halfway to orgasm.

"Or is it people not loving you that makes you unhappy? If they don't love you it's because there's something *wrong* with you. If they love you then it must mean you're all right. You poor baby. Poor, poor baby."

The place was full of poor babies. They all sighed with tender sympathy for themselves. The fat woman's nose ran. She opened her mouth and cried, "Hoooh! Hoooh! Hoooh!"

Now Arty was gentle and low as a train a mile off in the night.

"You just want to know that you're all right. You just want to feel all right."

And now he dives into the sneer. Arty's sneer could flay a rhino.

"That's all you need other people's *love* for!"

The crowd is shocked into stillness. Arty grabs their throats while they're down and starts pumping the tempo.

"So, let's get the truth here! You don't want to stop eating! You love to eat! You don't want to be thin! You don't want to be beautiful! You don't want people to love you! All you really want is to know that you're *all right!* That's what can give you peace!

"If I had arms and legs and hair like everybody else, do you think I'd be happy? NO! I would not! Because then I'd worry did somebody love me! I'd have to look outside myself to find out what to think of myself!

"And you! You aren't ever going to look like a fashion queen! Does that mean you have to be miserable all your life? Does it?

"Can you be happy with the movies and the ads and the clothes in the stores and the doctors and the eyes as you walk down the street all telling you there is something *wrong* with you? No. You can't. You cannot be happy. Because, you poor darling baby, you *believe* them. . . . Now, girl, I want you to look at me and tell me, what do you want?"

Arty expected her to stay tongue-tied and blubbering so he could say the next line. That's the way it always worked. But this fat woman was so used to blubbering that it didn't slow her down. She opened her mouth wide and, though I've never really stopped hating her for it, I have to admit she was just saying what all the rest of the damp, wheezing crowd was thinking. She screamed, "I want to be like *you* are!"

Arty stopped dead still. His flippers froze and he began to sink slowly with his face pressed into the speaking mask and his eyes close to the glass staring out. There was sobbing in the crowd. Soft voices murmured, "Yes, yes." Arty was silent for far too long. Had he had a stroke? Was it a cramp? I started forward, ready to run around behind the tank and up the ladder. Then his voice came.

"Yes," he said. "Yes, that's what you want." And I could hear his breath go in, Arty's breath. Arty could control a mike and he never breathed so you could hear it.

"And that's what I want for you."

He didn't go on with his usual talk. He said that he'd have to think how to give this gift to her. He said they should all come back the next day—though he knew few of them would—because he would have something to say to them.

McGurk didn't know what to do with the lights. He was flickering a rainbow that made Arty almost invisible in the water. Finally Arty himself hit the switch that blacked out the tank.

The crowd started to trickle away as I ran to the back of the tank. Arty was already out on his platform and rolling in his towel.

"Arty, what's wrong?" I whispered as I scrambled up the ladder.

"Not a thing," he said. His face popped out of the towel and he grinned hugely, excited.

"Let's get over to the shower quick. I want to see Doc P. right away."

The woman who wanted to be like Arty came back the next day. The crew had just finished sweeping down the bleachers in Arty's tent and were raking the sawdust. The first show had gone as usual and it was an hour until the last show began.

I was next door in the ticket booth of the twins' tent snagging the take out of the till drawer into a bag, and punching in totals. A finger tapped the SOLD OUT sign in the barrel window in front of me.

"All sold out!" I hollered, and locked the cash bag.

"There's a dame in Arty's tent!" It was the crew foreman, shrugging at me. I took the cash bag and went with him.

She was sitting up on the fifth tier, where she'd sat before, but now she was the only one. The heat in the tent was heavy and dead. She had a shopping bag beside her and she looked ready to collapse. Her face was dark red. Her eyes were blood-spatter over yellow. She had a little face set into a big pillow of a head, and her arms and legs stuck out of a dress that would have been loose on a linebacker but looked like cheap upholstery on her. She was just sitting, staring at the unlit tank, listening to the gurgle of the pump that aerated and filtered the water.

I climbed up toward her. She looked at me, got a ripple of fear on her face, and grabbed at her shopping bag.

"Hi," I said. She clutched her bag and nodded, warily. She expected to be chased. I expected to chase her. "I work with this show, can I help you?" I stood still at the end of the tier and didn't go any closer. She flapped her jaws and then came out with a tiny shrill voice.

"I'm just waiting for the Aqua Man. I'm going to pay but there wasn't anybody to sell tickets. I'll pay when the ticket booth opens."

Her eyes ran over me cautiously. I was wearing one of the blue sailor dresses that Lil made for me. The blue matched the lenses of my sunglasses. I wasn't wearing a cap so the woman's eyes spent a lot of time on my bare skull.

"I'll sell you a ticket right now so you won't have to worry about it," I offered, helpfully. I had a roll of tickets in my pocket, and I needed to make sure she wasn't going to pull an automatic out of her shopping bag and perforate Arty. She fumbled out money.

"You were here yesterday, weren't you?" I asked.

"He spoke to me," she said, counting out coins. "He said to come back. He would help me."

I sat down next to her and watched the heat rash on the insides of her elbows and the backs of her knees and in the folds of her chins as she talked. She had got herself into a terrible jam, she said, and it had made her realize . . . She was from Warren, Ohio, and her mother was a schoolteacher but had died last year. She took a photo album out of the shopping bag and showed me a picture of a fat old woman.

"What kind of a jam are you in?" I pushed. If she had strangled her old mother I was going to have her escorted to the gate, heat rash and all. "It's a man," she said coyly. I couldn't help looking at her with suspicion. She bubbled into tears right away. I looked at the photo album in her lap. She had drawn pink daisies on the cover. I figured she was the type who would doodle LOVE in big, loopy letters and dot her *i*'s with hearts. Her name was Alma Witherspoon. She was twenty-two riding hard on fifty-five. It seems she was a pen pal. She'd always been a pen pal. Seems she'd got the address of a twenty-to-life bank blaster a year or so before. He was up the road in the Earlville Federal Pen. She'd sent him a photo of one of the cheerleaders in her high school. After her mother died she moved down here so she could send him fresh cakes and cookies.

"We're in love," she said. It sounded like L[heart]VE. "He wants to marry me!" she moaned. "And the warden has agreed! But I thought we'd do it by telephone and now the warden says I have to go out there and do it in his office and Gregory will see how I really *look!*" So she needed to see the Aqua Man. She didn't know anybody in this town. She had no relatives left to turn to. Her heat rash looked contagious. I gave her a show ticket and got away from her. "You just wait here for the show. Nobody will bother you."

I took the cash bag to the safe and went over to help Arty get ready. I told him about Alma Witherspoon while I greased him. He lay on the massage bench and nodded. His eyes were eager. He had a funny half smile the whole time.

"She's probably been spinning whoppers to her pen pals for years about being beautiful and popular."

"No relatives? No friends?" he asked.

"So she says."

"Good," grinned Arty. He stretched and rolled his back under my kneading fingers.

I was doing my talk in front of the twins' tent, "Siamese beauties linked in harmonious perpetuity . . ." I always had a great time with "perpetuity"—it was a word you could play like a flute, rolling it up a full octave and whistling "Dixie" on that last syllable. The crowd was pretty good and most of them were already inside; the last twenty were shuffling in line for tickets.

That's when I saw Alma Witherspoon go by with two of the redheads who helped out in Arty's tent. The tall women beside her made Alma look even wider. She rolled along with her shopping bags and her purse and her photo album all folded sweatily into different rash-angry creases of her dreary body.

Alma couldn't have made a penny as a pro. She didn't weigh as much as a single leg of "Eleven Hundred Pound Jocko!" or "Pedrita the Plump!" but she wasn't healthy. Jocko and Pedrita were the proudest people who'd ever worked for the show, according to Papa. Alma Witherspoon had the pride of a squashed possum.

". . . Twin musicians! Twin miracles!" I rolled on, watching the redheads gently guide the wobbly Alma up the ramp to the shower van parked behind the Games of Chance. She put her foot on the top and heaved lopsidedly upward as the door opened. I could see the startled jerk of Alma's wispy head as she saw the staunch white-clad figure in the doorway. Dr. Phyllis nodded, her white mask flashing glare into her thick glasses. Her white glove lifted, beckoning. Alma Witherspoon stepped into the shower.

"There is no shock. There is no danger of infection. Young Fortunato's techniques eliminate that entirely."

Dr. Phyllis watched Arty as she talked; her eyes swiveled behind her pool-deep lenses, probing for an argument that would change his mind.

Arty was looking through the glass window at the sterile infirmary where Alma Witherspoon lay sleeping, with Chick perched beside her on a three-legged stool. Chick was wrapped in one of Dr. P.'s white coats with the sleeves rolled up. His glowing face was bent toward the pillow. His eyes grazed lovingly over the sodden grey folds of Alma's cheeks and chins.

"Did you look at that chart I gave you? The healing rate on that spiral fracture was triple the normal expectancy for a patient that age. Arturo? Are you able to comprehend what I am conveying?" Dr. P.'s thin, perfect diction entered the ear in a surgical manner. Arty, who had been absorbed in his view of the lumpy sheets and the doughy mound on the pillow, turned to her calmly.

"Doc, I know you can cut her down all at once. I know it would be more efficient. But I want her to have a lot of chances to change her mind." He turned back to look through the window again. He relaxed against the back of the wheelchair. His face was easy as he looked at the creature asleep in the next room. His mouth looked soft. There was a sleepy pleasure about him, almost peaceful, almost warm. There was, oddly, a look of Chick on Arty's face. Arty was happy. He was deeply happy and it was, in some way I didn't grasp, all because of moldy Alma Witherspoon having had all her toes cut off and then, when she'd recovered from that, having begged for the privilege of having her feet and legs nipped away as well.

Dr. P. and Chick kept Alma in the infirmary. Arty went frequently to park his chair in the observation room at one end and sit staring through the glass at her bandaged body lying on the second bed from the end.

Once a week, on Sunday mornings, Arty would flick on the

intercom and watch Alma's face through the glass as his voice pumped at her from the speakers. She was always overjoyed to hear him. She called him "Aqua Man" and said she was fine and when could she have more of herself taken away? "I can't tell you what it means to me each time they clean a little more away, even a little toe. Once it's gone I feel what a weight of rot it was for me. Oh, Aqua Man, you are so kind to me. I thank the stars in heaven for leading me to you . . ." and so on like that. She'd blubber away, a pen pal to the core. Her message was always How soon would they take her feet off? When would they take her hands? Could she, by a special dispensation from His Wateriness, skip the feet and have Doc P. just take off her whole legs one at a time? They were such a burden to her and she was in such a hurry to be like HIM.

Arty didn't talk about it but I could see it meant a lot to him. The whole thing had me fuddled. Why should this Alma make him happy? He'd never been that way about any of his visiting night girls—at least not by the time I brought in his breakfast the next morning. He was working harder than ever, reading more, vomiting nervously before each show—"To clear my head," he claimed. He schemed and planned with McGurk for hours every morning, playing with lights and sound. But I'd never seen him smile the smiles he smiled in those days, great soft openings of his face with no biting edges at the eyes.

We were up in Michigan when Alma started testifying. She was down to her nubs by then. Her legs were gone from the hip and her arms ended at the elbow. She looked better. Her front still flopped but she'd been eating Dr. P.'s Vegetarian Nutri-Prescription for months. Her skin had some tone and she'd dropped a few chins along with her limbs. More of her face was visible and her wispy hair seemed to have less expanse to drift away from. She was chipper, and she proved that "feeling good" about herself, as she called it, didn't make her any less irritating than being pathetic. There was a difference, though. Where she had been wetly repellent she was now obnoxious.

"I should say she might feel good about herself, the great lazy lump," said Lil. "Lying up there being fed and waited on. When does my

Chick get to play? A child his age needs frolic and silliness, not mooning about spooning green gruel into that blob and worrying over her every minute for fear she might feel a twinge of pain! All my other children had time to play even though they worked every day."

I had nothing to do with Alma. To my recollection I never spoke to her directly after the first time in Arty's tent. But I watched her. To give them both credit, Alma was terrified of Doc P. and said nothing but yes'm and no'm whenever the good doc was around. And Alma worshiped Chick. But Chick was her painkiller so I figured her love for him had the same virtuous weight as an addict's for his drug.

Alma's testimony started in the Michigan factory towns. The redheads would wheel her out onto the stage beside the tank before Arty made his appearance. Alma's twittering bat voice fed down through a button mike on her white robe and McGurk bled a little timbre in before he shot it out through the speakers.

"My name is Alma Witherspoon," she'd begin, "and I just want to take one minute to tell you all about a wonderful thing that happened to me. . . ."

The rodent squeak chittered in her chest and her stump arms waved in the white spotlight and the bright green tank gurgled, huge, beside her on the dark stage. The funny thing was that it worked. By the time Arty exploded in a rush of bubbles from the floor of the tank, the folks in the stands were ready for him, dry-mouthed and open. And those certain few in the bleachers, those stone-eyed kettles boiling with secret pain, received her message. Those who had been waiting finally found a place to go.

That's the way it began. It was Alma "Pen Pal" Witherspoon who actually founded what came to be known as "Arturism" or the "Arturan Cult."

There were just a few converts at first, but Alma took over the process of organizing with a smug zest that made me want to kick her.

She was all humility and worship to Arty—a kind of "Kiss the Ground on Which Your Blessed Brown Balls Drag" smarminess. But with the converts she reigned as a high priestess, prophet, and megabitch. She originated the concept of "Artier than Thou." She ordered, organized, and patronized. The redheads, who had to wait on her and wheel her around in a replica of Arty's chair, hated her. Soon there were enough of the "Admitted" to give Alma a full-time staff. The redheads went thankfully back to balloon games, popcorn, and ticket sales.

Not that Arty was ever less than In Charge. Though he appeared only in his tank and did no trivial fraternizing, he knew everything. Most likely the whole thing in all its details was Arty's invention. He gave orders to Alma by intercom.

She sat in her commandeered trailer office chirping earnestly into the box on her desk and listening reverently to replies. Her method of passing orders on to the lesser members was as snooty as that of any conveyor from on high. She set Arturism up like a traveling fat farm for nuns. Though she herself had lucked onto Arty while flat broke, all who came after paid what she called a "dowry." Arty said, in private, that the scumbags were required to fork over everything they had in the world, and, if it wasn't enough, they could go home and get their ears pierced or their peckers circumcised and see what that did for them.

The thing grew. Arty's fans—or the "Admitted," as Alma insisted on calling them—began to trail after the show in cars and vans and trailers of their own. From a half-dozen simple characters wandering the midway with white bandages where fingers or toes had been, there grew a ragtag horde camped next to the show every place we stopped. Within three years the caravan would string out for a hundred miles behind us when we moved.

Papa hired more guards and had the Binewski vans wired for security. After a month of phoning and looking and asking, Papa bought the biggest tent any of us had ever seen and set it up around Arty's stage-truck.

Dr. P. got a big new surgery truck with a self-contained generator. Two of the big trailers were converted to post-operative recovery wards. Chick was with Dr. Phyllis from early morning until supper every day. He was getting thinner and he fell asleep at the table leaning on Mama night after night.

"When does he play?" she would ask, her eyes blinking at the air directly in front of her.

Papa talked to Arty and Arty passed the word to Doc P. Dr. Phyllis didn't like it, but two hours each day, one after breakfast and another before supper, Chick was ordered to play where Mama could see him. She started reading fairy tales to him during the morning hour. In the afternoon he dutifully pushed toy cars around the floor of the family van, making motor noises, so Mama could hear him as she made supper.

Having established the chain of command, having petrified two dozen finger-and-toe novices into doing all the paperwork, Alma shed her left arm to the shoulder. She spent hours crooning to herself on her infirmary bed with the screen drawn around her for privacy. Her voice grew frail and she stopped testifying.

She was replaced immediately. Dozens clamored for a chance to testify at Arty's shows. There were thousands waiting, willing to pay, for the right to see and listen.

I was walking by when Dr. P. walked out of her big new surgery truck and heaved the plastic bag containing Alma's last flabby upper arm into an ice chest for Horst to dispose of. She dusted her white gloves against each other and nodded to me. "Well, that's finished," she announced through her mask. "It took a year and a half. I could have done the whole job in three hours."

After a while, Alma wasn't around anymore. Arty laughed when I asked about her. "She's retired," he said. "She's gone to the old Arturans' home to rest in peace." I thought he meant she was dead.

FROM LOBSTER BOY

Fred Rosen

—True crime author Fred Rosen has covered some of the most bizarre and heinous events in recent American crime. But none of them reach the shocking proportions of the story of Lobster Boy. This selection traces the story of Grady Stiles Jr. from his birth up to and including his 1978 trial for the murder of his daughter's fiancé.

N 1937, EDNA AND Grady Stiles already had two children. On a carny's salary, it was hard to make ends meet.

Grady Stiles worked in the carnival, where he exhibited himself as one of life's human oddities. Grady was born with a birth deformity that gave him fused hands in the shape of lobster claws.

"Hurry, hurry, hurry, and see the Lobster Man," the bally man would shout to the throng assembled on the midway. "Hurry, hurry, hurry."

They would pay their nickel and step inside a tent. On a raised platform sat Grady Stiles.

"Ladies and gentlemen, I am Grady Stiles, the Lobster Man," he said, holding his claws up proudly. "I am a product of a genetic condition, which has run in the Stiles family since 1840. In scientific circles it is known as ectrodactyly.

"Ectrodactyly is a genetic condition. Affecting one in ninety thousand at birth, a baby is born with the absence of the third digit and the fusing together of the remaining fingers and toes into claws. Sometimes it affects all four limbs, sometimes two. In my case, as you can see, I have normal legs.

"Once the gene has latched onto a family, every child born has a fifty-fifty chance of getting the condition, which is also known as 'lobster claw syndrome.' "

He never bothered to add that the only way to get rid of the offending gene was not to have children, a choice the Stiles family had rejected.

Since Zachary Taylor was president, the Stileses bore children. Their attitude was "Hell, if a child was born a freak, it was the child's problem, the child's and God's. Besides, fifty-fifty weren't bad odds."

Grady and Edna Stiles had had three children. Big sister Margaret was born normal, but her life came to a tragic end. One day while selling tickets at the carnival, she keeled over and died of a cerebral brain hemorrhage, only weeks before she was to be married.

Their middle child Sarah was born with the "lobster claw syndrome," in her case, with a lobster claw for one hand, and one stunted foot with lobster claw for toes. She later had the foot amputated and an artificial leg made. A marriage to an alcoholic ended in divorce, but the products of the union, one boy and two girls, grew up to marry and have normal lives.

Then came Edna's third pregnancy. Grady, Jr., who came into the world on July 18, 1937, was born with ectrodactyly. The condition was so bad that not only did he have claws for appendages, he had legs whose growth was stunted and ended at the knees.

On the north side of the Ohio River, which cuts the city of Pittsburgh in two, is a series of slums. It is the place where those without money and those without hope settle. Every city has a place like that and in Pittsburgh it's called, not coincidentally, the North Side.

Edna and Grady, Sr., rented an apartment on the North Side. As a toddler, Grady, Jr., crawled on his back and on his stomach on the apartment's bare, wooden floors. Without legs, he could not stand; without hands, he would gradually have to learn a special type of manual dexterity.

In the eyes of the residents of the tough North Side, he was a freak, constantly pointed at whenever he appeared on the street, constantly made fun of and demeaned by children and adults alike. Grady, Sr., was always on the road with the carnival, traveling throughout the forty-eight states, so Grady, Jr., had no father to teach him what it meant to be a man, to teach him how to weather life's adversities, of which there were many for a child who was called "freak" to his face.

Parents held their children tight and pointed with mixed awe and revulsion at the freak with lobster claws. Silent prayers of "There but for the grace of God go I," superstitious women spitting to ward off the evil eye, and taunts from schoolmates of "Hey, freak" accompanied him wherever he went. The world did not accept him. And then, fate gave young Grady a reprieve.

The Stileses had already discovered the Gibsonton area. It was the place to winter when the carnival shut down for the cold weather. Real estate was cheap in Florida in those days and from his carnival wages, Grady, Sr., was able to buy a house on Marconi Street in the Palmetto Beach area, across the bay from Gibsonton proper. In 1944, Grady, Sr., settled his family for good in their new Florida home. But young Grady, then seven years old, had little time to enjoy his new locale.

The Stiles family was still struggling along from day to day. Everyone had to do their share, including Grady, Jr. It was time for the child to go out and make a living like everyone else. His father decided he would join the family business. Young Grady would become a carny.

Grady, Sr., forced his son to quit school and join the carnival. From small town to small town, across the northern plains and the southern panhandle, into the cool New England forests and the muggy northeastern states in the summers, young Grady climbed up onto the platform with his father.

"Hurry, hurry, hurry," the bally man shouted. "Step right up, pay your money and see 'The Lobster Family!' "

People would pay money, get a ticket, and enter a small, canvas tent. Upon entering, they would see a raised, wooden platform, on which Grady Stiles, Sr., and his son sat in chairs. As they gazed at this exotic form of human oddity, Grady, Sr., began his routine. As he had throughout his carnival life, Grady would entertain the folks by relating the story of his family's disability, pointing to his smiling son, Lobster Boy, as the next generation who had to grin and bear it.

In those days, the carnival was indeed a family. There were none of the "forty-milers" you have now, those that join the carnival briefly and move on. In those days, people joined up for the duration; they stayed with the same carnival through thick and thin, through mud and rain or locusts or whatever. They were there for each other, The Fat Man, The Bearded Lady, the roustabouts, the strippers, the workers in the "grab trucks," who sold the equivalent of junk food.

The living conditions in the back of drafty trailers and tents were abysmal, but young Grady, Jr., enjoyed being a showman, exhibiting himself on the platform, earning a salary like his father.

The Stileses signed on with the Lorow Brothers and were put in a "ten-in-one" show that featured ten "freak" acts under one tent for the same price. The Lobster Family became the star attraction.

During the winter months, Grady traveled with his father back to Gibsonton and lived there with his mother and sisters. Unlike his experience in Pittsburgh, he was not ridiculed for his appearance. After all, the odd was usual in Gibsonton. It was a show town, filled with carnival and circus oddities.

Young Grady fit in with the local kids. He could play baseball like they did and he loved to wrestle. It was fun getting his strong arms around his opponent and squeezing until they had no choice but to submit and cry uncle or be further crushed in Grady's python-like arms. As for locomotion, he was as fast on his hands as most people were on their feet. Even faster.

Yet despite his adaptation to his handicap and the acceptance he received in Gibsonton, Grady grew up bitter at the world at large for not accepting him. Determined to prove to the world he was just as good as they were, he got stronger than anyone else.

All Grady had was his arms. Years of crawling around on them, of supporting his entire body weight on those appendages, made them strong. His claws had bone and muscle and sinew in them, too. He gradually learned how to use his claws, to do nearly everything anyone else could, from simple tasks like washing to more complex ones like writing, and later, much later, firing a revolver . . . accurately. And they became powerful enough to crush anything he grasped with them, powerful enough to inflict pain. His strength allowed him to indulge a sadistic side that had built up in him over the years. He enjoyed inflicting pain, especially when he was drunk.

If anyone bothered him, Grady's claw shot out and slapped the malefactor alongside the head. Those who were hit by his claw said it felt like being hit with a board. Before his victim could stand, Grady would scuttle over and head butt him in the stomach. An explosion of air and his opponent went down again. Then Grady would place his powerful arms around the target's throat and began squeezing.

As for his parents, not much is known about Grady's relationship with them. In later years, he talked rarely to his wife, Teresa, about his childhood and adolescence. If his parents abused him in any way, he did not tell. He did, however, acquire a taste for liquor, and drank with Grady, Sr., and Edna as he grew older. Grady favored Seagram's 7.

Years later, all that bitterness he'd stored up as a child and adolescent would come raging out of control when he drank too much, which was, his family would say, every night. God forbid if you were a family member who got in Grady's path when he got drunk.

Mary Teresa Herzog was born April 23, 1938, in a small town in Vermont, where a cold winter's day could find the temperature plunging to ten below zero. What she remembered most from her childhood was the cold, mostly the frost in her home.

Her mother, Jean, and father, Harvey, did not get along and when she was six, they divorced. Her mother married Frank Tyler. Until Grady, he was the most important man in her life.

In those days, incest was not talked about. It was even more taboo than now. And so, having no choice, having no power, young Teresa submitted to her stepfather's frequent sexual abuse for years. However, one of the things that made her life bearable was the circuit carnival that stopped at her town several times a year.

"The carnival fascinated me. I guess it fascinated most young people. I thought the lights and the excitement were just great," Teresa recalls.

Teresa wanted to get closer to the carny, so whenever the carnival came to town, she helped sell tickets—until one day in 1956. When she was eighteen years old, she shook off that small-town New England routine for good and joined the carnival.

On a warm May day in Trenton, New Jersey, in 1959, the charming Lobster Boy and the incest victim from New England met and fell in love.

Grady had already seen her selling tickets and secretly admired her. But within the hierarchy of the carnival, he was on the top as a performer and she was on the bottom as a worker. Grady and his father, while still a team, were now billed as "The Lobster Family—4th and 5th Generation" of freaks. They worked for Stan Wright and Jimmy Steinmetz in the World of Mirth carnival that toured the forty-eight states.

Fate intervened when the bosses, sensing her potential, offered her a job as a bally girl working the sideshow. Grady knew that if she were closer to the show, he would be able to date her more easily.

For Teresa, it meant more money and a chance to escape the monotony of the ticket booth. Teresa readily accepted. She became a full-fledged carny. Soon, she had graduated from bally girl into part of an act, as "The Blade Box Girl." Her role was to enter a box and seemingly be stabbed by swords thrust into it from every angle.

Teresa became a carnival jack-of-all-trades. She was so good as The Blade Box Girl, she also became "The Electrified Girl."

Teresa would sit in a throne-like chair similar to one used to execute prisoners. When her assistant threw the switch, an electrical glow formed around her, and lightning bolts leaped from hand to hand. She seemed in a semistupor, yet she remained unharmed. When the current was finally turned off, she stood and gazed down at her adoring crowd, as they applauded the illusion.

To Grady, it made no difference whether she was in an electric chair or a blade box. It was all just making a living, and who cared what you did? What he really cared about was that once he set eyes on her, he wanted to have her.

Grady courted her with attention and presents. Never had Teresa been so loved and so wanted by anybody as she was by Grady Stiles. He wined and dined her, made her feel like part of his family.

"Grady was such a charming man," Teresa recalls, her voice filled with love and nostalgia. "Everyone enjoyed being in his company."

Here was a man, a real man, despite his deformity, who wanted to take care of her. Finally, they began living together.

They made a decent living in the carnival. During the off-season, Teresa took a job in a shrimp factory in Tampa to help make ends meet. She and Grady lived together for nine years before he officially married her.

Grady was a good provider. However, when he was drinking, Grady started beating Teresa early in their relationship, taking care to keep his blows to the body. It wouldn't do for her to be seen on the midway with a battered face.

The first child born to Grady and Teresa was named Margaret. Margaret died after twenty-six days. Teresa says the cause of death was pneumonia.

The second child born to Grady and Teresa was named David. David died after twenty-eight days. Once again, Teresa says the cause of death was pneumonia. Apparently, the constant travel and the drafty living conditions on the road caused both infant deaths.

The family problems continued.

"Grady's father became ill and couldn't really do the work," Teresa recalls. By 1961, in failing health, Grady Stiles, Sr., quit show business for good.

"His father wasn't making it here in Florida, and the cost of living was too much for him, so he moved back to Pittsburgh. Grady was still living in Florida [with me] and he'd go to Pittsburgh when his father got ill. He got an apartment to be close by. We almost lost him a couple of times."

While Grady was in Pittsburgh, Teresa recalls that he "drank with his parents. They drank a lot. They drank beer while Grady drank whiskey."

To make ends meet, Grady and Teresa went into Tampa and opened up a single low—carnival slang for a show just featuring one act which, of course, was Grady on the platform. And during the season, they would travel.

In 1963, their third child, Donna Marie, was born. This time, the Stileses were blessed. Not only was Donna a healthy child, she was born without her father's deformity.

She would not have to go through life a freak. It was something he should have been thankful for. Instead, it embittered Grady even more.

Right after Donna's birth, Grady started drinking heavily. He would stay out late at night drinking liquor and playing cards with his carnival buddies. Sometimes, he'd go on drinking binges and be away from home for days at a time. When he did come home, he would generally make it to the living room and pass out on the floor. Sometimes, he'd throw up first and then sleep in his own vomit.

In the morning, Debra and Donna would get up, get washed, and change into their school clothes. They would have to step over Grady to get out of the trailer.

None of this was lost on Grady. He might not have had formal schooling, but he was still a smart man. Part of him warred with himself to become more of a father, someone his kids could look up to, at least figuratively. He made a strong effort to change. He stopped drinking as much and started to come home more often.

During this brief period of semisobriety, when Teresa heard him come home, she would make the children go to their room.

"I want you to be very quiet," she told them, "and not disturb your father."

What she did not tell them was that it was in their own best interests because when he was drunk, Grady liked to beat his kids. There is no indication that Teresa ever tried to stop him. Perhaps she was too busy protecting herself. Sometimes, Teresa says, the beatings she suffered were so severe that she could barely get out of bed in the morning.

Their fourth child, Catherine, who would become known as Cathy, was born in 1969. She was born with the same deformity as her father.

She would have to grow up with lobster claws and stunted legs that ended just below the knees.

Strolling by the trailer in Gibsonton, the Stiles place looked like any other, slightly run-down, but not seedy. Just hard-working carny people trying to make a go of it.

Inside, Donna Stiles, a sad-eyed, towheaded child, would see the same thing every day. And it seemed normal, just like other families. When you're five or seven, everything seems normal, just like other families.

Donna was born April 29, 1963, in Syosset, a middle-class suburb in Long Island, New York. Grady and Teresa had been on the road playing Long Island when her water broke. Teresa was rushed to the hospital. The child she gave birth to was completely normal.

Donna was raised in Gibsonton, and most of her early childhood years remain a blur. Her earliest memories come from about the age of seven. "There was nothing really good I can recall," she says now. "He [her father] always drank. Continually drank. I really started noticing it at about seven because he would yell at us if he was drinking at home."

Day after day, Grady would get drunk. He'd scream at the kids. Then he would give them beatings or spankings. Sometimes, it would happen if one of his kids talked back to him.

"Who the fuck you think you're talking to like that?" Grady would shout, and the claw would shoot out like lightning and smack his child across the mouth.

Sometimes, he'd beat his kids without provocation, just to keep them in line.

Donna remembers one night in particular during the latter part of 1972. They were home in the trailer in Gibsontown. "He was arguing, he was really drunk, real bad. And he was fighting, arguing with Mom."

While World War III raged in the living room, all the kids went to bed. They were in a separate part of the trailer. Lying in bed in the dark, staring up at the ceiling, they could hear their parents arguing and fighting.

"Then I heard a big bang," Donna says, "a very *loud* bang."

They got up and came running out of the bedroom, into the living-room light.

"He had my mom in the middle of the living-room floor, and he was punching her in the sides, and the legs, and in the arms and face."

"Stop it, stop it," Debbie screamed in tears.

"Daddy, please, stop . . . ," Donna sobbed.

Teresa collapsed in Grady's arms. Her eyes rolled back in her head. Her breathing became shallow.

Debbie raced across the room and put her thin arms around his neck, pulling him back. Trying to help, Donna took hold of his arm, too.

Looking down at the limp rag of a woman in his arms, Grady's rage subsided. He let her go and she collapsed to the floor in a heap.

"I ought to finish you," he snarled. "I ought to finish you off right here. I don't need you. You're nothing but a dirty bitch!"

He turned and looked at Donna.

"You're too much like your mother," he muttered coldly, staring at the petrified child. "Too much."

Taking in deep gulps of air with every breath, Grady put his claws down on the floor and scooted across the room to his armchair. He turned on the TV and finished drinking his Seagram's 7 and Coke like nothing had happened.

As the television's light flickered across the room, the children knelt down around their mom and tried to wake her up. Struggling mightily, they half carried and half dragged her out. Eventually, Teresa regained consciousness.

"Mom, I'll call the cops," Debbie said.

"No, no," Teresa answered anxiously. "Don't worry about it. He's just drunk."

The night her parents separated remains indelibly etched in Donna's mind.

"I don't remember where it was, or the exact month, or the town, but we were on the road, and he was drinking all day. He drank all the time when he was working."

Many times, when the marks would come into the tent to see Grady on top of the platform, reciting his speech about how long the "lobster claw syndrome" had been in his family, his words would be slurred from all the booze he'd been drinking.

"That night, after closing, he called Mom out in the show. They were arguing. She came back into the trailer, crying. And then he came back to the trailer, pulled the door open, let it slam real hard, and he took twenty dollars and he threw it at her."

"Take your fucking kids and get out of my face," Grady screamed.

"She did," Donna continues. "She told all five of us to go get packed. She was scared and crying real hard. She packed a couple of suitcases herself and she took us with her across the street to a motel. There was no way she'd leave us alone with him when he was drinking."

After Teresa and the kids checked in, she called Midget Man to come to her rescue.

Harry Glenn Newman, a.k.a. Midget Man, was actually a welder by trade. Unlike normal-sized welders, at a little over three feet, Glenn was lower down to the material he was working on and consequently inhaled some of the fine metal filings he shaved with his blow torch. Respiratory problems followed. Rather than keep risking his health, he joined the carnival.

As Midget Man or The World's Smallest Man, he toured the carnival circuit, eventually hooking up with Grady Stiles, who became one of his friends, and later, his employer. To see Lobster Boy and Midget Man together was indeed a strange sight for the casual bystander.

Over the years of their friendship, Glenn came to know and admire Teresa Stiles. A truly compassionate person, he had a friendly shoulder she could lean on. Glenn was always there to help out.

"When my mom called Glenn the night she was thrown out, Glenn quit work. He had a little camper. He came over to the motel and tried to calm Mom down. He says, 'Don't worry, if he throws you out, I'll help you get straightened around.' "

• • •

The entire family traveled to Ohio and moved in with Glenn's mother.

Things were quiet then. Glenn would come around every day. Frequently, he played with Cathy. One day, he brought her a puppy as a present. For the first time in their lives, the Stiles family, minus Grady, lived a normal life. There was no fighting. Teresa was more relaxed.

"When we got up for breakfast every morning, it was quiet. Glenn would come over for dinner, and it was nice. He would joke around. We were able to go shopping," Donna recalled.

With Glenn footing some of the bills, the Stiles family was able to make a go of it. Then, one day, four months into the honeymoon, "Mom took us someplace to this courthouse. I think it was in Pennsylvania. I remember the day because Cathy had just lost her first front tooth that day.

"We were sitting in a room, and Dad and Mom was in another room. I don't know what happened. We went downstairs to a cafeteria, and then she took us off to the side and said we had to go with him, had to go with my dad. Cathy was crying, and I ran to Glenn's pickup and locked myself in it. I think it was Mom that eventually talked me out of there."

Without Teresa's knowledge, Grady had filed for divorce. Since Teresa never knew about the proceedings and didn't participate in any of them, the court awarded Grady an uncontested divorce and custody of the kids.

"We left the courthouse, but I don't know where he was living at the time. But we ended up in Florida, back on Trenton Street in Tampa. He still had the house."

Not for long, though. They were only there long enough for Grady to sell the house and all the furniture in it. "He gave all of Mom's whatnots, lamps and all of her stuff to his sister. He would not let her come back to the house to get her clothes, which included a fur coat and some evening dresses. He gave away all of her clothes. Jewelry, and everything else, he gave to Barbara."

By that time, Grady was living with Barbara Browning Lucille. With his divorce final, they married.

"Barbara had a sunken face and stringy, light brown hair. She was very, very skinny. She wanted to put herself in my mom's place. She wanted to be our mother. She tried to force herself onto us."

Donna hated her. But the idea wasn't to be a nurturer, the way Teresa was. It was "a role [she was playing] to try to get closer to my dad, and to try to get us away from my mom. I think she had a drinking problem like my dad did, because they would go out drinking together a lot," unlike Teresa, who so hated drinking she would only do it if Grady forced her.

Barbara had one child from a previous marriage, a daughter named Susan. Along with Susan, who everyone called Susie, the reconstituted Stiles family consisted of Grady, Cathy, Donna, and Barbara. Debra, who was older, went out on her own.

Being the oldest, Donna was forced to adopt adult-sized responsibility. Though she wasn't close to her stepsister Susie growing up, she helped raise her.

"My dad had me take care of [all] the kids," Donna continued. Sometimes, the responsibility overwhelmed her and she cut school. When Grady found out, he beat her with his belt. "I'm gonna send you to juvenile," he threatened, as the belt bit into her skin.

Grady beat his new wife, too, but unlike Teresa, whom he preferred to beat around the body so the bruises did not show, he wasn't as careful with Barbara; when she appeared in public, it was not uncommon to see her face bruised, her eyes blackened, her lips puffy.

Donna still had her own survival to consider.

By 1974, Grady had relocated the family again, this time back to his hometown of Pittsburgh. He was hoping to organize a sideshow with him as the star attraction. They settled in his old stomping grounds on the city's North Side, in a tenement, which had a fine view of other tenements. Then, in 1976, Barbara became pregnant.

"My dad knocked Barbara down and continued to punch her in the stomach when she was pregnant with [Little] Grady," Donna recalls.

Grady Stiles III was born on July 26, 1976. He had the family trait of lobster claws and truncated legs.

Teresa continued to live with Harry Glenn Newman. He was a good husband and made a living from a tire business he had established.

On June 8, 1974, Teresa gave birth to Harry Glenn Newman, Jr. He would become known as Glennie to the family.

The joy of having her sixth child, a healthy baby boy, should have lasted, but Teresa's heart ached. She missed her kids terribly. "He [Grady] wouldn't allow me to have contact with the kids," she remembers.

By 1976, Grady still had custody, and Christmas was approaching.

Against Glenn's best advice, Teresa called Grady anyway.

"Grady, I was wondering if I could see the children so I can take them home with me to Vermont to see my mother for Christmas."

"That would be okay," said Grady.

"Okay, so I'll come by your place—"

"No, why don't we meet at Harry's Bar? You remember where that is, right?"

"Yeah, but—"

"Okay, so we'll meet at Harry's, have a couple of drinks, and then go back to my house to pick up the kids."

"I don't trust him," Glenn warned, after Teresa hung up. "You never know what Grady might do."

"Look, Glenn, I miss those kids. I really want to be with them."

Midget Man knew better than to argue with his wife when she had her mind set on something, especially seeing the kids. He knew how much they meant to her. Still, he felt uneasy about the trip. But they went anyway, along with baby Glennie.

They met at Harry's, where Grady tossed back double shots of Seagram's and 7-UP on the rocks.

"The girls are at my apartment," Grady said, slugging the drinks down. "You gotta go in to take them."

Glenn didn't want to. He smelled something wrong, and told her that. But Teresa was heartsick. She needed her babies.

After he finished his fifth double shot, Grady took them all to his apartment. The kids were nowhere to be found.

"Go fix yourself a cup of coffee," Grady said casually.

Teresa didn't know what was happening. She decided to play

along. When she came out of the kitchen, Grady leaned back on the couch. Deftly, he reached underneath the cushions and pulled out a revolver. He pointed it at his guests, who stood paralyzed in fear.

"Ever see a gun like this?" he asked menacingly.

"Yes, I've seen a few," Teresa replied.

Grady put his free claw in his mouth and whistled.

The back door opened. They heard a lumbering sound getting closer and closer. He plodded into the living room, all six hundred pounds of him.

His name was Paul Fishbaugh, a carnival "Fat Man" whom Grady employed. To Teresa and Glenn, he was distinguished not so much by his impressive bulk but by the even more impressive shotgun cradled in his fleshy arms.

Fishbaugh sat down on a chair by the kitchen door. It was surprising the chair would support his weight.

"Cover them, Paul," Grady said.

Fishbaugh pointed the shotgun at Teresa, Midget Man, and their baby boy. It is doubtful that Midget Man could have taken The Fat Man under any circumstances. Still, Lobster Boy was taking no chances.

"Come over here to the couch, Teresa," said Grady.

Teresa did as she was told.

He hit her with the claw that was hard as a board.

The baby screamed.

"For God's sake, Grady, let them leave! I'll stay," Teresa shouted.

Grady ignored her pleas and continued to beat her. Teresa's mind drifted. It seemed like forever.

When he finally finished, Grady told Teresa, "Don't bother me anymore or next time, I'm going to kill you, Glenn, *and* your son."

Then he let them go.

On April 29, 1978, Donna turned fifteen. Escape from Grady was paramount in her mind. But what kind of escape could a fifteen-year-old hope for?

Her hope for freedom resided with Jack E. Layne, Jr. A strapping eighteen-year-old, six feet three inches, and a solid 210 pounds, he had black hair and a handsome face.

They were introduced by Donna's cousin, who had previously gone out with him. Jack and Donna, who was then attending Allegheny Junior High School, hit it off almost immediately.

In early September of that same year, Donna ran away from home. She met Jack in a public park, which was about four blocks from the apartment she shared with her family. Jack took her to his sister Jenny Layne's house, in the Brighton Heights section of Pittsburgh. A few days later, Donna called Grady.

"Where the fuck are you?"

"Dad, listen—"

"No, you listen," he screamed into the receiver. "You get right back here now, or else!"

Donna said no.

"All right, all right," Grady acquiesced. "I'll let you go with your mom. You come home, I'll call your mom, and you can go with your mom."

"You're lying." Donna spit the words out. "You won't even let us talk to her and you expect me to believe you'd let me go and live with her?"

"Listen, you fucking—"

And Donna hung up the phone. Three or four days later, she called again.

"I got detectives looking for you," Grady said menacingly. "They'll find you and when I find that boy that's with you, I'm going to kill him and—"

Donna hung up.

Pit Loan was a pawnshop on the North Side. Philip Archer was behind the counter on September 11 when he saw a strange sight: a legless man in a wheelchair with lobster claws for hands. He wheeled himself up to the counter.

"I want to buy a gun," he said.

Archer filled out the state-mandated "Application for Purchase of Firearms," and noted the following information:

APPLICATION FOR PURCHASE OF A FIREARM
Name: Grady F. Stiles, Jr.
Date of application: 9-11-78
Date and place of Naturalization: 7-18-37
Male, 41 years of age, white, 4 feet 3
inches, 185 pounds, black hair, blue
eyes.
Make: H&R
Model: 732 .32 caliber
Length of Barrel: 2.5 inches

In a scratchy script, Grady signed the document. As the seller, Archer countersigned.

Another few days passed. Donna made another phone call.

"The cops are looking for you this time," Grady said evenly. "With my detectives. I'm gonna send you to juvenile," he added.

This time, Donna was scared. Something about this threat made her sit up and take notice.

She hung up. She needed to do something before the door burst in and they came to get her and sent her back.

She picked up the phone and dialed.

"Dad."

"Yeah, Donna."

"Dad, listen. Jack and I want to get married. I—I'm pregnant."

Nothing could have been further from the truth. Donna was playing on Grady's paranoia. In fact, not only wasn't she pregnant, she was still a virgin. The most they'd ever done was neck a little bit.

Grady got very quiet on the phone. He didn't say anything for a while. Finally, he said, "Since you've already been with him, I'll sign the papers."

September 28 was set as the wedding date. During the week, Grady made one last effort to dissuade her. When Donna remained true to her dream of escape, Grady relented and told her that he would keep his promise and let them get married.

As promised, Grady signed a form agreeing to the marriage.

Letter in hand, Donna and Jack went to the county clerk's office where, on September 20, they applied for a marriage license.

September 27, 1978, dawned with a chill in the air, but by midmorning, the temperature was climbing into the sixties and the sun came out.

Donna walked through the sunshine, and got to Jack's house at approximately eleven A.M. Together, they went to Dr. Rob Slotkin's office, where blood was drawn from both of them, as required by the state for couples marrying. Then they walked over to the barber's school on East Ohio Street, where Jack got a haircut. Jack then walked Donna to her father's house where she was to clean the house, getting ready for the planned wedding reception. When they got there, Grady was already gone.

A few blocks away at Harry's Bar, Grady was perched on a barroom stool, doing what Harry loved: being one of his best customers.

By seven o'clock, Grady had consumed twelve whiskey doubles. It was a wonder he could still crawl without tipping over, let alone talk. Because of his years of alcohol abuse, his alcohol tolerance was so high that to the average bystander, he appeared barely inebriated.

Grady left the bar in his wheelchair and headed home. He got there just as Jack, Donna, Barbara, and Grady III were leaving to buy food for the wedding reception.

They were planning on buying a lot of potato chips to feed the guests. While the others left, Donna stayed behind at Grady's behest.

"Look, I really don't think you should marry him."

"Daddy, we've been over this—"

"You know, I love you so much I paid an investigator one hundred dollars up front to find you?"

"Daddy—"

"And then I owed him another two hundred dollars, so I went over to Dover [Ohio] and worked in the sideshow to pay the guy off."

"Look, Daddy, I'm going to marry Jack!"

"He's not good enough for you!"

Grady reached for his jug of whiskey. Grady usually had a gallon jug of whiskey around. He would drink almost a whole one of those by the time he went to bed.

By 7:30, the group was back with the chips. Donna has a vivid recollection of what happened next.

"We went out, Jack, Barbara, me, and Little Grady, and I think Susie was with us. Cathy was behind the house in the alley, playing with one of her friends.

"We went to the mall. My father gave me some money. I was supposed to pick out a dress to get married in. We selected a dress at Zayre's Department Store and put it on layaway to be picked up tomorrow morning. We had an appointment with the judge to be married on the morning of the twenty-eighth.

"A few hours later, we came back. Susie ran out back to play."

The first thing they noticed when they got back was that Grady's wheelchair was missing. Usually, Grady's wheelchair was kept right outside the house for easy access. Donna, Barbara, Jack, and Little Grady went inside.

"What happened to the wheelchair?" Barbara asked.

"It was sitting here," Grady replied. He sat calmly in his briefs. "Pittsburgh, in the streets, people steal things."

"Okay, we'll go out and look for it," said Donna, and she, Barbara, and Jack trooped to the door.

"No, you, why don't you stay, Jack? Close the door and sit down."

Jack stayed.

"So, Barbara and I went around into the metered parking lot out back, looking for the wheelchair," Donna continued. "Still not finding it, we searched in the bushes.

"We were just about halfway around, and I heard a bang. And I looked at Barbara and said, 'What do you think that was?' "

"Don't worry about it, it's not your father," Barbara replied.

"Then I heard a bang again immediately after and I said, 'Yes, it is something,' and I ran back toward the house. When I got there, Jack comes stumbling out of the house. He was holding his chest in the middle."

"He shot me." Jack coughed out the words, and fell straight down to the ground in front of Donna.

"It didn't seem real. It seemed like a joke. And I shook Jack. He didn't move. And he was coughing. There was blood coming out of his mouth. And I looked up, and Dad was standing on his knees looking out the window, smiling at me. It really surprised me that he was doing that. I said, 'Why did you do this?' "

"Because I told you I would," Grady smirked.

"You'll die for this, you son of a bitch!"

"Don't give me that shit!" Grady shouted back.

"I'll see you in your grave!"

From off in the distance, Donna could hear sirens. And then she heard the crying and screaming from inside the house. Little Grady.

Panicking, her heart beating wildly in her chest, she ran to her grandmother's house twelve blocks away.

The public safety building in downtown Pittsburgh was the home of the Pittsburgh Department of Public Safety. At 11:23 P.M., Condemi and Stottlemyre removed Grady from the bull pen holding cells on the second floor and took him to the homicide office, and sat him down on a chair in the interrogation room. Condemi read from a prepared form.

"At this time, it is my duty to inform you of the rights that you possess while in custody. Under law, you cannot be compelled to answer and you have the right to refuse to answer any questions. While you are in custody, if you do answer such questions, the answers given by you will be used against you in a trial in a court of law at some later date. Do you understand?"

"I understand," Grady replied soberly.

"The answers are to be recorded in the suspect's own words. You are also entitled to talk to a lawyer and have him present before you decide whether or not to answer questions or while you are answering questions. If you do not have the money to hire a lawyer, you are entitled to have a lawyer present before you decide whether or not you will answer questions and while you are answering questions. Do you understand?"

"I understand."

"You can decide at any time before or during to exercise these rights by not answering any further questions or making any further statements. Do you understand?"

"I understand."

"Knowing these rights, are you willing to answer questions without the presence of a lawyer?"

"Some of them," Grady replied.

The detectives signed the form as witnesses and Grady gave his statement.

"I suffer from emphysema, cirrhosis, and various other ailments," he complained. "Two of my five children have the 'lobster [claw] syndrome' and my income at the present time is derived from Social Security.

"I use the wheelchair when I'm out of the house, otherwise I have to crawl around. I have the equivalent of an eighth grade education. I'm so concerned about my kids. What's going to happen to them?"

The detectives noted in their subsequent report Grady's ". . . sincere concern for the welfare of his children. He appears to be sober at this time."

"Mr. Stiles, why don't you tell us how all this happened?"

"Well, about three weeks ago, Donna, she's fifteen, she ran away from home with Jack Layne. I went to the city police and the state police to do something about Layne running away with my underage daughter, but I received no help. No help."

"What did you do next?"

"Well, I-I contacted a private investigator to help me find her."

"You know the PI's name?"

"No, I don't recall. I do remember that his fee was like eighty to a hundred dollars a day plus expenses. I gave him one hundred dollars to start with. Then a little while later, I got a call from Donna. Donna told me that she did not want to come home."

"Did she say why?"

"Yes, she said she was in love with Jack and wanted to marry him."

"How did that make you feel?"

"Oh, I was so upset. This is hard to talk about."

"Take your time, Mr. Stiles."

"Well, Donna, she, uh, she was a virgin and a good girl until Jack Layne came along."

"What did you do?"

"What could I do? I finally gave in and told her I'd sign the necessary papers for her to marry him. She came home the next day. By that time, she'd been gone six days, and I owed the investigator two hundred dollars."

Neither detective bothered to tell him that his math didn't add up. They just let him keep talking.

"So, last week," Grady continued evenly, "I went to Dover, Ohio, and worked in the sideshow for the Dine Amusement Company. I worked from Wednesday to Friday, earning a little over three hundred dollars. And then I paid off the investigator.

"When I got back, I heard some street talk that Jack Layne was bragging about Donna living with him. This really upset me but I didn't say anything to Layne or Donna, but I did try to talk Donna out of the marriage. With no success, I might add."

And then he related what happened that day.

"I woke up about ten-thirty and went down the street to Harry's Bar. I was there until seven P.M., when I came back home to watch the news."

"How much booze did you drink?"

"About twelve doubleheaders of whiskey."

"That's a lot."

"I'm good at holding my booze."

"Go on."

"Well, Donna and Barbara, she's my wife, and my son, Grady, and Layne, they went to Allegheny Center to buy a wedding dress. They came back about nine and that's when I called Layne into the living room."

"The others went outside?"

"Right. To look for my wheelchair."

"What'd you say to Jack?"

"He was sitting on the sofa. I told him, 'You have her. Don't laugh and make a mockery of this.' "

"What did Jack do?"

"He smirked, and said, 'I told you I'd get her.' "

"And that's when you shot him?"

"I pulled my gun from the side of the cushion of the chair I was sitting in and shot two times at Layne. Layne got up from the sofa and walked outside. I had taken all I could at the time. The guy gave me no choice."

"How about the gun?"

"What about it?"

"When and where did you buy it?"

"I bought it about three weeks ago from a loan company down on East Ohio Street."

"Know how to use a gun?" Condemi asked, looking dubiously at Grady's claws.

"I've owned several in my time."

"Well, why'd you buy this one?"

"In the evening, when I'm alone downstairs, I watch TV. I like to keep the gun with me to ward off any intruders, who may be thinking about breaking into my home."

"Have you ever been robbed or broken into?" Stottlemyre asked.

"No."

"Where do you keep the gun?"

"In a drawer in my upstairs bedroom."

"So, since you haven't been robbed or broken into, you really wouldn't have any reason to bring the weapon downstairs?"

"Right."

"Then why'd you bring the gun downstairs today?"

Grady thought for a second.

"Now that's a good question," Grady smiled. He wouldn't answer any more questions. The interview ended.

At approximately 11:55 P.M., the detectives notified the coroner's office that they had the accused in custody and they wanted him arraigned as soon as possible. Could a deputy coroner come to their office for the arraignment because the accused was in a wheelchair?

At approximately 1:10 A.M. on September 28, 1978, Deputy Coroner Phillips came to the homicide office and began the arraignment at 1:18 A.M. Grady Stiles, Jr., was officially charged with the murder of Jack Layne. Phillips then set a hearing for October 6 at eleven A.M., and Grady was taken back to a cell to wait for justice to unfold.

On October 6, a hearing was held before Coroner's Solicitor Stanley Stein. A special van with a hydraulic lift transported Grady to the hearing. It made for a heartrending photograph in the *Pittsburgh Post-Gazette* to see the crippled man when he was lowered to the ground.

Donna testified that Grady had not been happy about her impending nuptials to Jack.

"He [Grady] said Jack could come for supper but for him not to smile or snicker at me," Donna testified.

Donna then said that she was with Grady when he purchased the murder weapon. "He told me the gun was for Jack and me," Donna said.

Dressed in a shabby pair of blue trousers, white shirt, and white sweater, Grady could only shake his head in astonishment at Donna's testimony. He still had no conception of the tragedy he'd caused.

She then recounted her shopping trips on the day of the shooting, and what happened when they returned to Foreland Street.

Stottlemyre then took the stand and told Stein how he had taken Grady's statement after he was taken into custody, and the content of it.

It didn't take long for Stein to remand Grady to the County Jail without bail pending trial.

All alone in his jail cell, Grady had time to think. Despite what the police had told him, he was smart enough to know he was in hot water. They had charged him with first degree murder.

In the state of Pennsylvania, first degree murder is punishable by death in the electric chair. Grady knew that unless he found a good attorney, he would be convicted.

The taxicab left Grady and Barbara off on Grant Street, in downtown Pittsburgh. They paid for the cab with the little funds they had left. The state had moderated their initial demands and had let Grady out on $10,000 bond.

Barbara helped Grady into his chair, then wheeled him up the sidewalk and into the Grant Building.

When they got off the elevator, they found themselves in a reception area, off which were the offices of five different criminal defense lawyers.

"Can I help you?" the receptionist asked.

"We're here to see Anthony DeCello. We have an appointment," Barbara answered.

They were ushered into DeCello's office. It was very plush and expensive-looking. There was a big, dark mahogany desk, arranged neatly with a phone/intercom, a dictating machine, yellow foolscap pad, pen and pencil set in holders, pictures of DeCello's family, and a statue of St. Anthony. The saint of lost things, St. Anthony was DeCello's patron saint.

In front of the desk were chairs made out of a lighter colored wood than the desk, upholstered in a soft, cushiony fabric. To complete the look of elegance, all the walls were paneled in dark wood.

"The first time Grady came into my office with Barbara, he was in a wheelchair," DeCello recalled. "She did everything for him as far as pushing it. He wanted me to know immediately about his physical condition, which was quite obvious."

During introductions, Grady shook DeCello's hand. The attorney would later find out that this was Grady's favorite thing to do when meeting someone for the first time. He always wanted a formal introduction. That's when he could establish his strength by literally crushing the other person's outstretched hand in his iron grip.

Throughout the morning, Grady had been drinking. DeCello smelled the booze on his breath. When he tried to tell DeCello what had happened and why he was there to seek his help, the words came out in a drunken slur.

DeCello knew how difficult it was defending any defendant accused of murder, but one who was a drunk, whose behavior was unpredictable, was just too problematic. He told Grady to go home and the next time he showed up for an appointment, he'd better be sober. Otherwise, he would have nothing else to do with his case.

Few people talked to Grady like that and got away with it, but Grady was fresh out of options and staring the electric chair in the face. When he and Barbara showed up for his next appointment a few days later, he was sober.

Barbara, still thin to the point of emaciation, was dressed in ill-kept jeans and a raggedy shirt. "She looked like she fought Sonny Liston and lost. She was bad. She always was bruised. Every time I saw her she had bruises. She was ugly and she was very stupid," DeCello recalls. "And she smelled."

As for Grady, despite the fact that he was in a place of business, he, too, was dressed shabbily. His pants, cut off at the knee, and button-down shirt were wrinkled and faded.

But if Grady was not flashy in appearance, he was still a showman.

He had Barbara position his wheelchair next to one of the overstuffed armchairs in front of DeCello's desk. As DeCello watched openmouthed, Grady used his claws to flip himself from one chair to the other in a single, neat motion. It showed the dexterity he had with his claws, all right, but DeCello wondered why he was trying to impress him so. Coupled with his antagonistic way of shaking hands, DeCello figured he was trying to show off his immense physical strength.

DeCello asked Grady to tell him the truth in his own words of exactly what had taken place because he didn't want to be surprised in court.

Instead, Grady began to discuss the fact of his physical disability. His tone was sarcastic, and DeCello soon realized that the disability was his armor plate against everything, that because he was physically disabled, everyone should take pity on him.

Finally, after Grady finished trying to garner the lawyer's sympathy, DeCello was able to turn the conversation around to the crime Stiles had been charged with.

"Jack had taunted me and made fun of me and ridiculed me," Grady said in his whiskey-soaked voice. "He told me that he'd had sex with Donna and there was nothin' I could do about it. And then he made fun of me. He said, 'I'm gonna dump you out of the wheelchair anytime I feel like it.' "

To DeCello, though, Grady's fears did not seem real. He could tell from talking to Grady and from the man's physicality that he was not the defenseless cripple he tried to make himself out to be. He was a very strong man who was able to do almost everything a normal man could, including firing a gun.

Despite the fact that Grady was hardly defenseless, he insisted that Jack Layne continued to taunt him with all kinds of names until finally, he just couldn't take the verbal abuse anymore. He thought that in the best interests of Donna, and for his own sake, he had to do something about Jack.

"Donna, she deserved better than this bum," Grady said.

After that second meeting, Anthony DeCello remembers feeling sorry for Grady Stiles. "Hell, any normal person would have feelings of remorse that someone would have to live a life with those claws. He was poor, he was downtrodden and his own family, he claimed, made fun of him," said DeCello.

Regardless of what Stiles had done, he deserved help. And DeCello was going to give it to him. He would plead "not guilty" by reason of self-defense. Whether he believed Grady or not was not relevant. The man was entitled to the best defense possible. He would do what the law allowed—present his defense as the facts allowed.

In court, DeCello would try to minimize the seemingly cold-blooded nature of the crime with the mitigating factors of Jack's alleged threats, Grady's fear, and, of course, his client's pitiable physical condition.

While Anthony DeCello was trying to figure out a way to rescue Grady from the electric chair, Robert Vincler was doing the exact opposite. As sure as the sun would come up in the morning, Vincler was certain that Grady Stiles had committed first degree murder. As assistant district attorney, and supervisor of general trials for the district attorney's office of Allegheny County, Vincler's job was to make sure that Grady Stiles, Jr., was convicted.

Yet despite the facts of the case, Vincler was struck by the tragedy of the whole thing. Here was the sad case of a young girl who had gone out to buy a wedding dress and returned to her home, only to have her future husband shot by her father and die in her arms. It was also astonishing to Vincler that Grady had so much dexterity with his claw, he was able to pull the trigger on the gun.

Donna was going to be the prosecution's star witness; she was going to testify against Grady. Over the course of the next five months, Vincler spoke frequently with Donna over the phone. She was still pretty broken up about the crime.

After Jack had been killed, his sister and his family blamed Donna for his death. For a time, she hid out at her girlfriend's house. Cathy had been living with Barbara at the Salvation Army. Then, one day, Donna's grandmother, Edna Stiles, called her up on the phone.

"Donna, your mom's been in touch with me. Your mom's sending an airplane ticket to get you and Cathy," Edna continued.

"My . . . mom was only going to take me, because she didn't know if she was allowed to have Cathy. And Grandma says [to Teresa], 'You better take Cathy with you. You take both of these girls and get them out of here.' "

Teresa sent her the plane tickets. Donna and Cathy left Barbara with her children, Little Grady and Tammy.

"We left Pittsburgh and met her and Glenn [Sr.] in Dallas. They were helping a friend with a show. They were sort of taking a vacation and working at the same time."

Glenn was working the bally stage for Ward Hall, a famous carnival entrepreneur. Eventually, they moved back to Ohio.

Donna stayed with her mother and Glenn in the Buckeye State, where Glenn supported the family from a tire business he had established. Because Teresa rarely spoke to Vincler, the task of explaining the family circumstances fell to Glenn, Sr. Vincler found himself liking the man, even though they had never met.

From Glenn and others who were involved in the case, Vincler came away with the impression that Donna was the apple of her father's eye. While Cathy and Little Grady were deformed, Donna was the attractive, normal one. Grady thought she could really make it and was very upset that she had been lured away and was going to marry a guy he thought was a bum.

For his part, Grady had no knowledge that his family was conspiring with the prosecution to put him in jail. He was certain that once enough time had passed, Donna would forgive him. Eventually she would see that he'd done the right thing, the only thing. She would come back to him.

In his conversations with DeCello, Grady made it clear that he was both proud and envious of Donna.

Over and over, DeCello took Grady through the day of the murder to get his story straight so there'd be no inconsistencies when he testified. DeCello found it strange that when they talked about the murder, Grady showed no feelings.

In his practice, DeCello had found that anybody you talk to involved in a murder has feelings about it, either remorse or hate. But Grady just went over the details like he was describing some routine task. Flat. Never once did he express any emotion over killing Jack.

But when it came to discussing his sex life, his voice took on new vigor.

"Everyone I have sex with wants to have sex with my claws. They love it when I use my claws."

He was proud of that fact. Barbara, who was sitting across the room, nodded in agreement.

And as if to prove the point, Grady told DeCello this story.

"One of my daughter's [Donna's] teachers came to the house to discuss her attendance at school."

In fact, Donna had failed to attend school on a regular basis during the fall of 1978 when she met and fell for Jack Layne.

"This teacher, she really liked my claws. So we had sex right in the house and she just kept coming back and back and back because of this."

The lawyer came to realize that it was a source of personal pride for Grady that he was able to have a sexual relationship with someone that was normal. "When he talked about having sex with the teacher, it was like he'd just won the Battle of Bataan. It was like a victory. He wanted you to know he had these accomplishments, no matter how totally insignificant they were," DeCello said.

As for what he did to make a living, carnival to him did not mean sideshow freak. It meant Carnegie Hall. Grady Stiles, Jr., was a famous, dominating figure in the carnival world.

Robert Vincler woke up to a cold day, where snow matted the ground. Traveling to work, breath plumed from his mouth in a cold fog.

By 8:30 A.M., on February 20, 1979, he was in the forty-by-fifty-foot space he shared with two other assistant district attorneys. Each had their own office. Because Vincler's was located not twenty feet behind the reception area, he always had a clear view of who was visiting. He looked up from his work when he heard people in the corridor.

"I knew right away who the people were coming through the door. This girl was rather attractive, young, sixteen years old; followed by her mother, who was also rather attractive, thin, well dressed, and manicured; followed by Mr. Newman who was a midget. It sort of floored me that here was this midget," Vincler recalls.

No one had ever given any indication over the phone that Glenn might not be of normal height.

After recovering his composure, Vincler noted that Donna wore a nice conservative outfit. She'd make a good witness. As for Glenn, he was dressed in a pullover jersey and a pair of slacks. His hair was cut rather long.

"Time to go downstairs," Vincler said.

As the women walked quickly down the corridor to the elevator, Glenn settled down in the young district attorney's office.

The trial was about to begin.

• • •

The courtroom of Common Pleas judge Thomas A. Harper was set up in an old-fashioned way, with the defense and prosecution seated at parallel tables on opposite sides of the courtroom.

The trial started with Vincler's opening statement to the jury. Vincler made it crystal clear that he would seek a first degree murder conviction against Grady Stiles, Jr., on the grounds that the shooting was a premeditated act. To bolster his case, Vincler pointed out the following:

"There are a number of key points on which Anthony DeCello, Mr. Stiles's attorney, and I agree on, including the fact that Mr. Stiles did, in reality, shoot Jack Layne once in the chest and once in the back with a thirty-two-caliber revolver he purchased from an East Ohio Street pawnshop sixteen days before Mr. Layne was murdered."

For his part, Tony DeCello emphatically stated that Grady Stiles had no choice but to kill Jack Layne. Layne had taunted and threatened him to the point where he felt he was in grave danger. Layne had lured his daughter away. To save her, and him, Grady had no choice but to take matters into his own hands.

Vincler then called his star witness: Donna Stiles.

Once again, Donna testified that she was with Grady when he bought the gun and that he told her he was going to "use it on Jack."

After explaining how she ran away for nearly six days, she related how she called her father from the home of Jack's sister.

"If you don't get home in five minutes, I'm going to beat the hell out of you. Then I'm going to kill Jack," Donna quoted Grady.

At the defense table, dressed in the same shabby clothes, and despite DeCello's pleas to wear a tie, all Grady could do was mumble and shake his head in disbelief. Throughout the trial, he continued to drink heavily.

On the stand, Donna told about the shopping trip to buy her dress on the day before the wedding, and what her father's condition was.

"And was your father drunk on the day of the murder?" Vincler questioned.

"My father was fairly drunk," Donna testified. "And he tried to talk me out of the marriage by telling me about the unhappy experiences he'd had with his previous wives."

Donna turned and looked at Grady, her face twisted in hatred.

"She's no good, I can't believe she'd turn on me," Grady mumbled.

Donna claimed her father opposed the marriage because she was underage and that she planned to quit school. As for her living conditions, Donna hated living with her father because, among other things, he "made me baby-sit constantly and didn't let me out enough."

"Damn her, damn her," Grady mumbled.

DeCello had been watching Donna very closely. Like Vincler, he, too, had not had a chance to depose her. This was the first opportunity he had to talk to her. It would be difficult to impeach her testimony. It was obvious that the jury believed the story this attractive girl told.

Donna did concede under DeCello's cross-examination that Grady had purchased the weapon before she and Jack had decided to marry. In the jury's mind, DeCello had just planted a seed that maybe the crime wasn't premeditated after all.

Next on the witness stand was Frank DeSalvo, one of Jack's friends.

"I was watching through the front window of the Stileses' home on the day before the shooting. I saw Mr. Stiles pull a gun from the left side of his wheelchair, point it at Jack, and say, 'I will kill you before you marry my daughter.' "

"He admitted shooting Mr. Layne because he said he had 'no alternative,' " homicide detective Joseph Stottlemyre next testified.

Forensic evidence was offered that inextricably linked the murder weapon to Grady's possession. The autopsy results were entered into evidence.

After a brief few hours of damning testimony, Robert Vincler was satisfied that he had proven his case and the defense rested.

Now, it was DeCello's turn to persuade the jury.

DeCello's tactic was to show that there were real reasons why Grady had opposed the marriage.

Barbara Sanaer, Grady's niece, testified that she had been engaged to Jack Layne and had broken up with him before he'd started dating Donna, and that Jack was prone to violence. "He frequently punched me and pushed me against the wall."

Sanaer and her mother, Sarah, Grady's sister, both testified that they had warned Grady that Jack carried a knife.

Perhaps the most interesting defense testimony came from Barbara Stiles.

Barbara said that Grady purchased the gun at her request after she began receiving obscene and threatening phone calls. Then, "Barbara testified as to their home life. She didn't testify [as to the alleged] threats [Grady made against Jack] because I think even though she feared Grady, she didn't want to get herself in a position where she would have problems herself.

"I think she was relieved, thinking Grady would go to jail and get out of her life. She was in fear of him. You could tell that by the way he treated her," DeCello recalls.

For her part, Donna hated Barbara. She was just glad that she was out of her life.

Things were not looking up for Grady, and he knew it. It was time to bring in the cavalry.

Paul Fishbaugh, The Fat Man, entered the courtroom. Too heavy to fit his six hundred pounds into the witness chair, he was forced to sit in a lotus position on the floor of the courtroom in front of the witness docket.

Fishbaugh, under DeCello's brief questioning, asserted the forthrightness of Grady's character.

The next character witness for Grady was The Bearded Lady, whom Teresa would later identify as Priscilla Bagorno. Bagorno, with her full, dark beard, related what a wonderful human being and credit to the human race Grady was. And by the time the third character witness, a carnival midget—not Glenn— had finished his testimony, spectators of the trial were presented with a portrait of Grady Stiles, Jr., as a caring parent and model citizen.

For his part, Vincler was limited by law in the questions he could ask the character witnesses, just as they were limited in what they could testify to. How do you challenge someone's opinion of another human being? The answer is, you don't. You just assume the jury understands that these are Grady's friends, and their testimony, inherently, is going to be tainted. Hopefully, the weight of evidence will prove to them that Grady Stiles, Jr., is not the paragon of virtue his friends made him out to be.

Grady was a showman, first and foremost. He had cut his teeth performing in front of crowds. Now, he would get to perform for a crowd of twelve, with his life hanging in the balance.

"I call Grady Stiles, Jr., to the witness stand," Tony DeCello announced to the court on the morning of February 21, 1979.

The bailiff wheeled Grady up to the witness stand and turned the wheelchair around. He was sworn in and then, under DeCello's patient questioning, began his testimony.

Grady said he did not recall telling the police that he kept the gun he'd purchased at the East Ohio Street pawnshop by his side for protection when he was alone in the house.

"I bought the gun because my wife Barbara had been receiving threatening phone calls."

Having the gun in the house was just Grady acting in a husband's role, as his wife's protector.

As for Frank DeSalvo's testimony that Grady had pointed the gun with his left hand at Jack the day before the shooting, Grady said DeSalvo was mistaken.

"I cannot support a gun in my left hand," he said, and all attention in the court went to his left claw. It was his weak claw. "It's impossible," he asserted.

As for the testimony of the prosecution witnesses that Grady had previously threatened to kill Layne because he did not want him to marry his daughter, under cross-examination by Vincler, he told the court, "All of them lied on the stand."

Once again, Grady created a public sensation. The *Pittsburgh Post-Gazette* reported, "Some of the jurors were visibly affected by Stiles's account of the fatal shooting of his fifteen-year-old daughter's fiancé. . . ."

"He got up there and traded on his condition," DeCello recalls. "He made a helluva witness for himself."

It was a bravura performance, better than anyone realized. "He had no feelings. Had no love for anyone. He had no fears. He was a very sick man," says DeCello.

Vincler had not been able to shake Grady on cross-examination. He attempted to rebut the character witnesses' testimony by recalling Donna to the stand.

"Did you ever see Mr. Stiles beat his wife?" Vincler asked.

"Yes," Donna replied. "I saw him beat my stepmother on several occasions."

During closing arguments, District Attorney Robert Vincler emphasized that the murder of Jack Layne was a cold, premeditated act of a violent man.

"He asks you to believe that all those people," and the dynamic young attorney waved to the prosecution witnesses in the courtroom, "and the police, got together and fabricated their stories.

"Donna Stiles has been out of town since the incident. How could she have known what anyone else was going to testify to, let alone fabricated her testimony?

"Besides Miss Stiles, several prosecution witnesses indicated that Mr. Stiles frequently promised to kill Mr. Layne rather than allow him to marry his daughter. This was a deliberate act of premeditated murder.

"I would also cite the autopsy report. It clearly contradicts Mr. Stiles's version of the shooting. Mr. Stiles said he was talking to Mr. Layne when the victim came at him and appeared ready to attack him. The defendant also said he could not remember firing a second shot, which struck the victim in the back as he was leaving the living room.

"Well, the autopsy showed that the first bullet, which struck the victim in the chest, traveled in a downward path, after making initial contact with Mr. Layne's body. That shows irrefutably that the victim was seated rather than standing and walking toward him, as Mr. Stiles claimed."

Defense attorney Anthony DeCello countered that "love and compassion" led Grady to defend his daughter and himself, and that the killing of Jack Layne was a pure act of self-defense.

"The greatest hurt and the greatest shame for Mr. Stiles came when his daughter [Donna] told him she'd see him to his grave," DeCello said. "Try and visualize the love and compassion this poor soul has for his children.

My client loved his children so much that he obtained a court order in Florida to assume custody of his two children from his previous wife.

"All Grady has is his family," DeCello concluded with obvious emotion. "He has no real friends because people don't want to have someone as him for a friend."

Judge Harper charged the jury and sent them out to deliberate Grady Stiles's fate. While he had been charged with first degree murder, the jury also had the option of convicting him of second degree murder, an intentional killing without premeditation, or third degree murder, commonly known as voluntary manslaughter. With the exception of the last charge, all were punishable by mandatory prison sentences. First degree murder was also punishable by death.

Three hours later, the jury of six women and six men came out of the jury room. Somber-faced, they took their assigned places in the jury box.

"Mr. Foreman, I understand you've reached a verdict."

"Yes, Your Honor, we have. We find the defendant, Grady Stiles, Jr., guilty of third degree murder."

Grady wept crocodile tears. He sat at the defense table in his wheelchair, the same one he had told Barbara and Donna was stolen the day of the murder, the same one he made them search for while he shot Jack Layne.

"I think the jury felt sorry for him. The bottom line is the jury gave him a break. I felt it was first degree murder then and I still feel it's first degree murder now," says Vincler, who's now in private practice.

"One of the things that we tried to bring out on defense was he [Grady] may have had the gun for protection and he saw the kid coming at him and his reflexes were so poor . . . but that's just not true. He was sitting in the house facing the door when they got home. Grady had that gun pointed exactly where he wanted to hit that kid dead-on.

"Another thing. Grady had told me he had no experience with guns, that it was a lucky shot. I didn't believe him. The reason I didn't believe him because there was another time he was telling me when he was in Florida, there was a place down there that show people frequented, and at one time or another, he would fire a gun there with some of his friends. I knew he had some experience with firearms."

"Still," adds DeCello, who no longer practices law, "he convinced the jury that he was defenseless."

Judge Harper postponed sentencing pending a presentencing report by the county's Adult Probation Office, and Grady was allowed to remain free on the $10,000 bond he had already posted.

The trial had been a draining process for all concerned. Not one person involved in the case, from the police who investigated to the prosecuting attorney, did not feel sorrow at the awful life Grady Stiles had led.

In the presentencing report, the police stated that they had no feelings regarding sentencing. Vincler was even more vague.

"Assistant District Attorney Robert Vincler stated that the present offense was most difficult in terms of sentencing. He stated that the offense was of a very serious nature, however, at the same period of time, he had no statement to make regarding sentencing.

"The present offense is truly a sad case," the report concludes. "It appears that there was some premeditation on the defendant's part and shooting the victim was the only way that the defendant could stop the victim from marrying his daughter. To further complicate the situation, the defendant's physical handicaps would present a problem if the defendant were incarcerated, yet at the same period of time, the present offense is serious enough that a prison sentence might be in order."

Shortly before sentencing, Judge Harper called Vincler.

"Bob, I have gotten a letter from Western Penitentiary [one of the state's penitentiaries] and they've indicated that they did not want him in the system because they'd end up having to put a guard with him all day to take care of him."

"What are we going to do with him, Judge? Realistically, he's wheelchair-bound. And his health's not good."

At Grady's sentencing on April 30, 1979, Grady rose in Judge Harper's courtroom to hear his fate.

Everyone knew Judge Tom Harper, who is now deceased, to be a kind, wise man, and a truly nice guy. He was a man of compassion.

After first noting the difficulties long-term housing of Grady would present to the state prison facilities, Judge Harper got down to the nitty-gritty. He sentenced Grady to fifteen years' probation.

"I'm not so sure that a prison term would not be cruel and unusual punishment in this case. Unquestionably, though, the crime was a serious offense," Harper told the hushed courtroom.

"Society doesn't require vengeance, and I felt a probationary term met the best interests for society and the defendant. In fact, even if the defendant could operate a wheelchair without assistance, prisons in the State of Pennsylvania do not have ramps to facilitate mobility."

Grady would not serve one day behind bars for Jack Layne's cold-blooded murder.

Tony DeCello was happy and thrilled by the verdict and the sentence.

"Judge Harper felt that putting him on probation would accomplish the same effect as putting him in jail," explains DeCello. "By putting him on probation, Grady would dictate his own destiny. If he did something [criminal], he'd go to jail. But he wasn't gonna shoot anyone else. Grady was a [classic bully], to his family especially."

All Grady had to do was report to his probation officer on a regular basis and keep his nose clean, and he would remain free to do as he pleased. He would even be allowed to move to another area of the country as long as he reported to his probation officer in his new habitat.

Immediately after the trial, Grady left Pittsburgh, and never paid DeCello his fourteen-thousand-dollar trial fee. "He never even said thank you. Never," DeCello relates. The money he saved by not paying DeCello helped him organize his own sideshow. No longer would "Lobster Boy" be working for anyone else. Now, he would be the boss of ten acts, presented as one show, that travel together from carnival to carnival. It was the bizarre world Grady felt most in control of, the one place where he didn't have to put his defenses up, where he could be himself.

"You gotta remember all these people were in the same boat. It's their own little protective world. You or I wouldn't associate with them. You'd have nothing in common with them. And they realized that. They are very defensive people. Very defensive," says DeCello.

FROM NIGHTS AT THE CIRCUS

Angela Carter

—British novelist Angela Carter puts an entirely new perspective on the phrase "send in the clowns" in this chapter from her 1984 novel Nights at the Circus.

CLOWN ALLEY, THE GENERIC name of all lodgings of all clowns, temporarily located in this city in the rotten wooden tenement where damp fell from the walls like dew, was a place where reigned the lugubrious atmosphere of a prison or a mad-house; amongst themselves, the clowns distilled the same kind of mutilated patience one finds amongst inmates of closed institutions, a willed and terrible suspension of being. At dinner time, the white faces gathered round the table, bathed in the acrid steam of the baboushka's fish soup, possessed the formal lifelessness of death masks, as if, in some essential sense, they themselves were absent from the repast and left untenanted replicas behind.

Observe, in his behind-the-scenes repose, Buffo the Great, the Master Clown, who sits by rights not at the head but at the magisterial *middle* of the table, in the place where Leonardo seats the Christ, reserving to himself the sacramental task of breaking the black bread and dividing it between his disciples.

Buffo the Great, the terrible Buffo, hilarious, appalling, devastating Buffo with his round, white face and the inch-wide rings of rouge round his eyes, and his four-cornered mouth, like a bow tie, and, mockery of mockeries, under his roguishly cocked, white, conical cap, he wears a wig that does not simulate hair. It is, in fact, a bladder. Think of that. He wears his insides on his outside, and a portion of his most obscene and intimate insides, at that; so that you might think he is bald, he stores his brains in the organ which, conventionally, stores piss.

He is a big man, seven feet high and broad to suit, so that he makes you laugh when he trips over little things. His size is half the fun of it, that he should be so very, very big and yet incapable of coping with the simplest techniques of motion. This giant is the victim of material objects. Things are against him. They wage war on him. When he tries to open a door, the knob comes off in his hand.

At moments of consternation, his eyebrows, black and bushy with mascara, shoot up his forehead and his jaw drops as if brow and jaw were pulled by opposing magnets. Tsking his tongue against his yellow, gravestone teeth, he fits the knob back on again with exaggerated care. Steps back. Approaches the door, again, with a laughably unjustified self-confidence. Grasps the knob, firmly; *this* time, he knows it is secure . . . hasn't he just fixed it himself? But—

Things fall apart at the very shiver of his tread on the ground. He is himself the centre that does not hold.

He specialises in violent slapstick. He likes to burn clown policemen alive. As the mad priest, he will officiate at clown weddings where Grik or Grok in drag is subjected to the most extravagant humiliations. They do a favourite 'Clowns' Christmas Dinner,' in which Buffo takes up his Christ's place at the table, carving knife in one hand, fork in the other, and some hapless august or other is borne on, with a cockscomb on his head, as the bird. (Much play with the links of sausages with which this bird's trousers are stuffed.) But *this* roast, such is the way of Buffo's world, gets up and tries to run away . . .

Buffo the Great, the Clown of Clowns.

He adores the old jokes, the collapsing chairs, the exploding puddings; he says, "The beauty of clowning is, nothing ever changes."

At the climax of his turn, everything having collapsed about him as if a grenade exploded it, he starts to deconstruct himself. His face becomes contorted by the most hideous grimaces, as if he were trying to shake off the very wet white with which it is coated: shake! shake! shake out his teeth, shake off his nose, shake away his eyeballs, let all go flying off in a convulsive self-dismemberment.

He begins to spin round and round where he stands.

Then, when you think, this time, Buffo the Great *must* whirl apart into his constituents, as if he had turned into his own centrifuge, the terrific drum roll which accompanies this extraordinary display concludes and Buffo leaps, shaking, into the air, to fall flat on his back.

Silence.

The lights dim.

Very, very slowly and mournfully, now strikes up the Dead March from *Saul,* led by Grik and Grok, the musical clowns, with bass drum and piccolo, with minuscule fiddle and enormous triangle struck with back-kick of foot, Grik and Grok, who contain within them an entire orchestra. This is the turn called "The Clown's Funeral." The rest of the clowns carry on an exceedingly large coffin draped with the Union Jack. They put the coffin down on the sawdust beside Buffo. They start to put him in it.

But will he fit? Of course he won't! His legs and arms can't be bent, won't be bent, won't be ordered about! Nobody can lay out *this* force of nature, even if it *is* dead! Pozzo or Bimbo runs off to get an axe to hack bits off him, to cut him down to coffin-size. It turns out the axe is made of rubber.

At long, hilarious last, somehow or other they finally contrive to load him into the box and get the coffin lid on top of him, although it keeps on jerking and tilting because dead Buffo can't and won't lie down. The clown attendants heave the coffin up on their shoulders; they have some difficulty coordinating themselves as pall-bearers. One falls to his knees and, when he rises, down goes another. But, sooner or later, the coffin is aloft upon their shoulders and they prepare to process out of the ring with him.

At which Buffo bursts through the coffin lid! Right through. With a great, rending crash, leaving behind a huge, ragged hole, the silhouette of himself, in the flimsy wood. Here he is, again, large as life and white and black and red all over! "Thunder and lightning, did yuz think I was dead?"

Tumultuous resurrection of the clown. He leaps from his coffin even as his acolytes hold it high, performing a double somersault on his way to the ground. (He started out in life as an acrobat.) Roars of applause, cheers. He darts round and round the ring, shaking hands, kissing those babies who are not weeping with terror, tousling the heads of bug-eyed children teetering between tears and laughter. Buffo who was dead is now alive again.

And all bound out of the ring, lead by this demoniac, malign, enchanted reveller.

The other clowns called him the Old Man, as a mark of respect, although he was not yet quite fifty, hovering about the climacteric of his years.

His personal habits were dominated by his tremendous and perpetual thirst. His pockets always bulged with bottles; his drinking was prodigious yet always seemed somehow unsatisfactory to himself, as if alcohol were an inadequate substitute for some headier or more substantial intoxicant, as though he would have liked, if he could, to bottle the whole world, tip it down his throat, then piss it against the wall. Like Fevvers, he was Cockney bred and born; his *real* name was George Buffins, but he had long ago forgotten it, although he was a great patriot, British to the bone, even if as widely travelled as the British Empire in the service of fun.

"We kill ourselves," said Buffo the Great. "Often we hang ourselves with the gaudy braces from which we suspend those trousers loose as the skirts that Muslims wear lest the Messiah be born to a man. Or, sometimes, a pistol may be sneaked from the lion-tamer, his blanks replaced with live bullets. Bang! a bullet through the brain. If in Paris, you can chuck yourself under the Metro. Or, should you have been so lucky as to be able to afford mod. cons, you might gas yourself in your lonely garret, might you not. Despair is the constant companion of the Clown.

"For not infrequently there is no element of the *voluntary* in clowning. Often, d'you see, we take to clowning when all else fails. Under these impenetrable disguises of wet white, you might find, were you to look, the features of those who were once proud to be visible. You find there, per example, the *aerialiste* whose nerve has failed; the bare-back rider who took one tumble too many; the juggler whose hands shake so, from drink or sorrow, that he can no longer keep his balls in the air. And then what is left but the white mask of poor Pierrot, who invites the laughter that would otherwise come unbidden.

"The child's laughter is pure until he first laughs at a clown."

The great white heads around the long table nodded slowly in acquiescence.

"The mirth the clown creates grows in proportion to the humiliation he is forced to endure," Buffo continued, refilling his glass with vodka. "And yet, too, you might say, might you not, that the clown is the very image of Christ." With a nod towards the mildly shining icon in the corner of the stinking kitchen, where night crawled in the form of cockroaches in the corners. The despised and rejected, the scapegoat upon whose stooped shoulders is heaped the fury of the mob, the object and yet—yet! also he is the *subject* of laughter. For what we are, we have *chosen* to be.

"Yes, young lad, young Jack, young First-of-May, we *subject* ourselves to laughter from choice. We are the whores of mirth, for, like a whore, we know what we are; we know we are mere hirelings hard at work and yet those who hire us see us as beings perpetually at play. Our work is their pleasure and so they think our work must be our pleasure, too, so there is always an abyss between their notion of our work as play, and ours, of their leisure as our labour.

"And as for mirth itself, oh, yes, young Jack!" Turning to Walser and waving an admonitory glass at him. "Don't think I haven't very often meditated on the subject of laughter, as, in my all too human rags, I grovel on the sawdust. And you want to know what I think? That they don't laugh in heaven, not even if it were ever so.

"Consider the saints as the acts in a great circus. Catherine juggling her wheel. St Lawrence on his grill, a spectacle from any freak-show. Saint Sebastian, best knife-throwing stunt you ever saw! And St Jerome, with his learned lion with the paw on the book, great little animal act, that, beats the darkie bitch and her joanna hollow!

"And the great ringmaster in the sky, with his white beard and his uplifted finger, for whom all these and many other less sanctified performers put on their turns in the endless ring of fire which surrounds the whirling globe. But never a giggle, never a titter up there. The archangels can call: 'Bring on the clowns!' until they're blue in the face but the celestial band will never strike up the intro to 'The March of the Gladiators' on its harps and trumps, never, no fear—for we are doomed to stay down below, nailed on the endless cross of the humiliations of this world!

"'"The sons of men. Don't you forget, me lad, we clowns are the sons of men."

The others all droned after him, in unison: "We are the sons of men," as in some kind of clerical response.

"You must know," continued Buffo to Walser in his graveyard intonation, "You must know that the word 'clown' derives from the Old Norse, 'klunni,' meaning 'loutish.' 'Klunni,' cognate with the Danish, 'kluntet,' clumsy, maladroit, and the Yorkshire dialect, 'gormless.' You must know what you have become, young man, how the word defines you, now you have opted to lose your wits in the profession of the clown."

"A clown!" they murmured softly, dreamily amongst themselves. "A clown! Welcome to Clown Alley!"

Meanwhile, to the accompaniment of Buffo's sermon, the meal went on. Spoons scraped the bottoms of the earthenware bowls of fish soup; the spatulate, white-gloved hands reached for the shanks of black bread, food sad and dark as the congregation of sorrow assembled at the ill-made table. Buffo, scorning a glass, now tipped vodka straight from the bottle down his throat.

"There is a story told of me, even of me, the Great Buffo, as it has been told of every Clown since the invention of the desolating profession," intoned Buffo. "Told, once, of the melancholy Domenico Biancolette, who had the seventeenth century in stitches; told of Grimaldi; told of the French Pierrot, Jean-Gaspard Deburau, whose inheritance was the moon. This story is not precisely true but has the poetic truth of myth and so attaches itself to each and every laughter-maker. It goeth thus:

"In Copenhagen, once, I had the news of the death of my adored mother, by telegram, the very morning on which I buried my dearly beloved wife who had passed away whilst bringing stillborn into the world the only son that ever sprang from my loins, if 'spring' be not too sprightly a word for the way his reluctant meat came skulking out of her womb before she gave up the ghost. All those I loved wiped out at one fell swoop! And still at matinee time in the Tivoli, I tumble in the ring and how the punters bust a gut to see. Seized by inconsolable grief, I cry: 'The sky is full of blood!' And they laughed all the more. How droll you are, with the tears on your cheeks! In mufti, in mourning, in some low bar between performances, the jolly barmaid says: 'I say, old fellow, what a long face! I know what *you* need. Go along to the Tivoli and take a look at Buffo the Great. He'll soon bring your smiles back!'

"The clown may be the source of mirth, but—who shall make the clown laugh?"

"Who shall make the clown laugh?" they whispered together, rustling like hollow men.

Little Ivan, oblivious to the meaning of the foreign babbling issuing from the blanched, jack-o'-lantern faces that hung over the table, ran round collecting the clinking soup bowls, unnerved yet more and more fascinated by this invasion of glum, painted comedians. The meal, such as it was, was over. All produced pipes, baccy and fresh vodka while the baboushka, kneeling before the samovar, performed the endless, contentless, semi-prayerful gestures of those hands deformed by decades of common toil. Her daughter, the axe-murderess, was far away in Siberia, but, although the baboushka's life was composed of these gestures simulating praying, she no longer possessed sufficient energy to pray for her daughter's soul. The charcoal reddened, blackened, reddened.

"And yet," resumed Buffo, after a pull at a bottle, "we possess one privilege, one rare privilege, that makes of our outcast and disregarded state something wonderful, something precious. We can invent our own faces! We *make* ourselves."

He pointed at the white and red superimposed upon his own, never-visible features.

"The code of the circus permits of no copying, no change. However much the face of Buffo may appear identical to Grik's face, or to Grok's face, or to Coco's face, or Pozzo's, Pizzo's, Bimbo's faces, or to the face of any other joey, carpet clown or august, it is, all the same, a fingerprint of authentic dissimilarity, a genuine expression of my own autonomy. And so my face eclipses me. I have become this face which is not mine, and yet I chose it freely.

"It is given to few to shape themselves, as I have done, as we have done, as you have done, young man, and, in that moment of choice—lingering deliciously among the crayons; what eyes shall I have, what mouth . . . exists a perfect freedom. But, once the choice is made, I am condemned, therefore, to be 'Buffo' in perpetuity. Buffo for ever; long live Buffo the Great! Who will live on as long as some child somewhere remembers him as a wonder, a marvel, a monster, a thing that, had he not been invented, should have been, to teach little children the *truth* about the filthy ways of the filthy world. As long as a child remembers . . ."

Buffo reached out a long arm and purposefully goosed Little Ivan as he passed by with glasses of tea.

". . . some child like Little Ivan," said Buffo, who did not know Little Ivan had watched from the top of the stove as his mother chopped up his father, and assumed the child was both innocent and naive.

"Yet," he went on, "am I this Buffo whom I have created? Or did I, when I made up my face to look like Buffo's, create, *ex nihilo,* another self who is not me? And what am I without my Buffo's face? Why, nobody at all. Take away my make-up and underneath is merely not-Buffo. An absence. A vacancy."

Grik and Grok, the pair of musical clowns, old troupers, always together, the Darby and Joan of the clowns, turned their faces towards

Walser, bending to catch the feeble lamp-light, and he saw those faces were mirror images of one another, alike in every detail save that Grik's face was left-handed and Grok's face was right-handed.

"Sometimes it seems," said Grok, "that the faces exist of themselves, in a disembodied somewhere, waiting for the clown who will wear them, who will bring them to life. Faces that wait in the mirrors of unknown dressing-rooms, unseen in the depths of the glass like fish in dusty pools, fish that will rise up out of the obscure profundity when they spot the one who anxiously scrutinises his own reflection for the face it lacks, *man-eating* fish waiting to gobble up your being and give you another instead . . ."

"But, as for us, old comrades that we are, old stagers that we are," said Grik, "why, do I need a mirror when I put my make-up on? No, sir! All I need to do is look in my old pal's face, for, when we made our face together, we created out of nothing each other's Siamese twin, our nearest and dearest, bound by a tie as strong as shared liver and lights. Without Grik, Grok is a lost syllable, a typo on a programme, a sign-painter's hiccup on a billboard—"

"—and so is he *sans* me. Oh, young man, you First-of-May, we cannot tell you, how would we have sufficient words to tell you just how useless we used to be before Grik and Grok came together and pooled our two uselessnesses, abandoned our separate empty faces for the one face, *our* face, brought to bed the joint child of our impotences, turned into more than the sum of our parts according to the dialectics of uselessness, which is: nothing plus nothing equals something, *once*—"

"—you know the nature of plus."

Having delivered themselves of the equation of the dialectic, they beamed with gratification beneath their impenetrable make-up. But Buffo wasn't having any.

"Bollocks," he said, heavily, belching. "Beg pardon, but balls, me old fruit. *Nothing* will come of nothing. That's the glory of it."

And the entire company repeated after him soft as dead leaves rustling: "That's the glory of it! Nothing will come of nothing!"

Yet the musical clowns, such was their ancient authority within the tribe, stubbornly at once set out to prove they could at least make a little something out of it, for Grik began to hum the softest, tiniest kind of melody, while Grok, his old lover, started to drum, softly, his gloved fingertips against the table top, hum of a drowsy bee and rhythm faint as a pulse but sufficient for the clowns, for the others now rose up from their benches and, in the dim gloom of the Petersburg kitchen, they began to dance.

It was the bergomask, or dance of the buffoons, and if it began with the same mockery of gracefulness as the dance of the rude mechanicals in *A Midsummer Night's Dream,* then soon their measures went sour, turned cruel, turned into a dreadful libel upon the whole notion of dancing.

As they danced, they began rhythmically to pelt one another with leftover crusts of black bread and emptied their vodka bottles over one another's heads, mugged pain, resentment, despair, agony, death, rose up and pelted, emptied, turn and turn about. The baboushka lay drowsing on the stove by now, her ample sorrows forgotten, but little Ivan, entranced, hid in the shadows and fearfully could not forebear to watch, his thumb stuck firmly in his mouth to give him comfort.

The guttering paraffin lamp cast awry shadows on the blackened walls, shadows that did not fall where the laws of light dictated that they should. One by one, each accompanied by his twisted shadow, the clowns climbed up on the table, where Grik and Grok remained seated one at each end, like gravestones, humming and drumming.

One lanky, carrot-haired fellow, whose suit was latticed in prismatic colours like a matador's suit of lights, took firm hold of the window-pane check baggy pants of a tiny creature in a red velvet waistcoat and poured the contents of an entire pint of vodka into the resultant aperture. The dwarf broke out in a storm of silent weeping, and with a backward somersault, attached himself to his aggressor's neck to ride there like the old man of the sea although the harlequin now began to spin round in such a succession of cartwheels he soon disappeared in a radiant blur, to reappear in his turn on the back of the dwarf. At which point, Walser lost sight of this couple in the melee of the savage jig.

What beastly, obscene violence they mimed! A joey thrust the vodka bottle up the arsehole of an august; the august, in response, promptly dropped his tramp's trousers to reveal a virile member of priapic size, bright purple in colour and spotted with yellow stars, dangling two cerise balloons from the fly. At that, a second august, with an evil leer, took a great pair of shears out of his back pocket and sliced the horrid thing off but as soon as he was brandishing it in triumph above his head another lurid phallus appeared in the place of the first, this one bright blue with scarlet polkadots and cerise testicles, and so on, until the clown with the shears was juggling with a dozen of the things.

It seemed that they were dancing the room apart. As the baboushka slept, her too, too solid kitchen fell into pieces under the blows of their disorder as if it had been, all the time, an ingenious prop, and the purple Petersburg night inserted jagged wedges into the walls around the table on which these comedians cavorted with such little pleasure, in a dance which could have invoked the end of the world.

Then Buffo, who had been sitting in his Christ's place all this while with the impassivity of the masked, gestured to Little Ivan—to innocent Little Ivan—to bring to the table that black iron cauldron from which the fish soup had been served and place it before him. And so the tranced child stepped into the act.

Rising ceremoniously to his feet, the Master Clown fished within the cauldron and found there all manner of rude things—knickers, lavatory brushes, and yard upon yard of lavatory paper. (Anality, the one quality that indeed they shared with children.) Chamber-pots appeared from nowhere and soon several wore them on their heads, while Buffo served up more and yet more disgusting tidbits from the magic depths of his pot and dealt them with imperial prodigality about his retinue.

Dance of disintegration; and of regression; celebration of the primal slime.

Little Ivan gaped, near panic, near hysteria, yet all was silent as a summer day—only the drone and pulse of Grik and Grok and, like a sound from another world, the occasional snore and groan of the baboushka on the stove.

FIRST SORROW

Franz Kafka

—"First Sorrow," the story of a solitary trapeze artist, appeared in Franz Kafka's final collection A Hunger Artist, *published in 1924 while Kafka (1883–1924) was on his deathbed.*

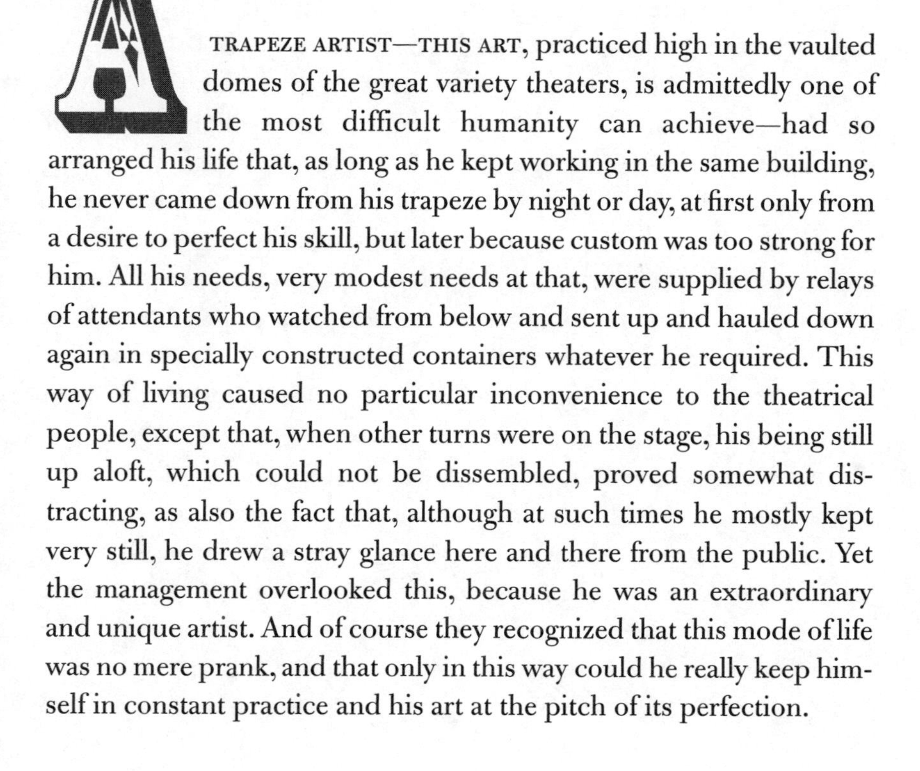

A TRAPEZE ARTIST—THIS ART, practiced high in the vaulted domes of the great variety theaters, is admittedly one of the most difficult humanity can achieve—had so arranged his life that, as long as he kept working in the same building, he never came down from his trapeze by night or day, at first only from a desire to perfect his skill, but later because custom was too strong for him. All his needs, very modest needs at that, were supplied by relays of attendants who watched from below and sent up and hauled down again in specially constructed containers whatever he required. This way of living caused no particular inconvenience to the theatrical people, except that, when other turns were on the stage, his being still up aloft, which could not be dissembled, proved somewhat distracting, as also the fact that, although at such times he mostly kept very still, he drew a stray glance here and there from the public. Yet the management overlooked this, because he was an extraordinary and unique artist. And of course they recognized that this mode of life was no mere prank, and that only in this way could he really keep himself in constant practice and his art at the pitch of its perfection.

Besides, it was quite healthful up there, and when in the warmer seasons of the year the side windows all round the dome of the theater were thrown open and sun and fresh air came pouring irresistibly into the dusky vault, it was even beautiful. True, his social life was somewhat limited, only sometimes a fellow acrobat swarmed up the ladder to him, and then they both sat on the trapeze, leaning left and right against the supporting ropes, and chatted, or builders' workmen repairing the roof exchanged a few words with him through an open window, or the fireman, inspecting the emergency lighting in the top gallery, called over to him something that sounded respectful but could hardly be made out. Otherwise nothing disturbed his seclusion; occasionally, perhaps, some theater hand straying through the empty theater of an afternoon gazed thoughtfully up into the great height of the roof, almost beyond eyeshot, where the trapeze artist, unaware that he was being observed, practiced his art or rested.

The trapeze artist could have gone on living peacefully like that, had it not been for the inevitable journeys from place to place, which he found extremely trying. Of course his manager saw to it that his sufferings were not prolonged one moment more than necessary; for town travel, racing automobiles were used, which whirled him, by night if possible or in the earliest hours of the morning, through the empty streets at breakneck speed, too slow all the same for the trapeze artist's impatience; for railway journeys, a whole compartment was reserved, in which the trapeze artist, as a possible though wretched alternative to his usual way of living, could pass the time up on the luggage rack; in the next town on their circuit, long before he arrived, the trapeze was already slung up in the theater and all the doors leading to the stage were flung wide open, all corridors kept free—yet the manager never knew a happy moment until the trapeze artist set his foot on the rope ladder and in a twinkling, at long last, hung aloft on his trapeze.

Despite so many journeys having been successfully arranged by the manager, each new one embarrassed him again, for the journeys, apart from everything else, got on the nerves of the artist a great deal.

Once when they were again traveling together, the trapeze artist lying on the luggage rack dreaming, the manager leaning back in the opposite window seat reading a book, the trapeze artist addressed his companion in a low voice. The manager was immediately all attention. The trapeze artist, biting his lips, said that he must always in future have two trapezes for his performance instead of only one, two trapezes opposite each other. The manager at once agreed. But the trapeze artist, as if to show that the manager's consent counted for as little as his refusal, said that never again would he perform on only one trapeze, in no circumstances whatever. The very idea that it might happen at all seemed to make him shudder. The manager, watchfully feeling his way, once more emphasized his entire agreement, two trapezes were better than one, besides it would be an advantage to have a second bar, more variety could be introduced into the performance. At that the trapeze artist suddenly burst into tears. Deeply distressed, the manager sprang to his feet and asked what was the matter, then getting no answer climbed up on the seat and caressed him, cheek to cheek, so that his own face was bedabbled by the trapeze artist's tears. Yet it took much questioning and soothing endearment until the trapeze artist sobbed: "Only the one bar in my hands—how can I go on living!" That made it somewhat easier for the manager to comfort him; he promised to wire from the very next station for a second trapeze to be installed in the first town on their circuit; reproached himself for having let the artist work so long on only one trapeze, and thanked and praised him warmly for having at last brought the mistake to his notice. And so he succeeded in reassuring the trapeze artist, little by little, and was able to go back to his corner. But he himself was far from reassured, with deep uneasiness he kept glancing secretly at the trapeze artist over the top of his book. Once such ideas began to torment him, would they ever quite leave him alone? Would they not rather increase in urgency? Would they not threaten his very existence? And indeed the manager believed he could see, during the apparently peaceful sleep which had succeeded the fit of tears, the first furrows of care engraving themselves upon the trapeze artist's smooth, childlike forehead.

THE KNIFE THROWER

Steven Millhauser

—Of Steven Millhauser's 1998 O. Henry Award-winning short story, Mary Gaitskill wrote, "The knife thrower's show has the innocuous grotesquery of a cheap carnival, it has a kind of brutish innocence, it has the ancient allure of cruelty."

WHEN WE LEARNED THAT Hensch, the knife thrower, was stopping at our town for a single performance at eight o'clock on Saturday night, we hesitated, wondering what we felt. Hensch, the knife thrower! Did we feel like clapping our hands for joy, like leaping to our feet and bursting into smiles of anticipation? Or did we, after all, want to tighten our lips and look away in stern disapproval? That was Hensch for you. For if Hensch was an acknowledged master of his art, that difficult and faintly unsavory art about which we knew very little, it was also true that he bore with him certain disturbing rumors, which we reproached ourselves for having failed to heed sufficiently when they appeared from time to time in the arts section of the Sunday paper.

Hensch, the knife thrower! Of course we knew his name. Everyone knew his name, as one knows the name of a famous chess player or magician. What we couldn't be sure of was what he actually did. Dimly we recalled that the skill of his throwing had brought him early attention, but that it wasn't until he had changed the rules entirely that he was taken up in a serious way. He had stepped boldly, some said recklessly, over the line never before crossed by knife throwers, and had managed to make a reputation out of a disreputable thing. Some of us seemed to recall reading that in his early carnival days he had wounded an assistant badly; after a six-month retirement he had returned with his new act. It was here that he had introduced into the chaste discipline of knife throwing the idea of the artful wound, the mark of blood that was the mark of the master. We had even heard that among his followers there were many, young women especially, who longed to be wounded by the master and to bear his scar proudly. If rumors of this kind were disturbing to us, if they prevented us from celebrating Hensch's arrival with innocent delight, we nevertheless acknowledged that without such dubious enticements we'd have been unlikely to attend the performance at all, since the art of knife throwing, for all its apparent danger, is really a tame art, an outmoded art—little more than a quaint old-fashioned amusement in these times of ours. The only knife throwers any of us had ever seen were in the circus sideshow or the carnival ten-in-one, along with the fat lady and the human skeleton. It must, we imagined, have galled Hensch to feel himself a freak among freaks; he must have needed a way out. For wasn't he an artist, in his fashion? And so we admired his daring, even as we deplored his method and despised him as a vulgar showman; we questioned the rumors, tried to recall what we knew of him, interrogated ourselves relentlessly. Some of us dreamed of him: a monkey of a man in checked pants and a red hat, a stern officer in glistening boots. The promotional mailings showed only a knife held by a gloved hand. Is it surprising we didn't know what to feel?

At eight o'clock precisely, Hensch walked onto the stage: a brisk unsmiling man in black tails. His entrance surprised us. For although most of us had been seated since half-past seven, others were still arriving, moving down the aisles, pushing past half-turned knees into squeaking seats. In fact we were so accustomed to delays for late-comers that an 8:00 performance was understood to mean one that began at 8:10 or even 8:15. As Hensch strode across the stage, a busy no-nonsense man, black-haired and top-bald, we didn't know whether we admired him for his supreme indifference to our noises of settling in, or disliked him for his refusal to countenance the slightest delay. He walked quickly across the stage to a waist-high table on which rested a mahogany box. He wore no gloves. At the opposite corner of the stage, in the rear, a black wooden partition bisected the stage walls. Hensch stepped behind his box and opened it to reveal a glitter of knives. At this moment a woman in a loose-flowing white gown stepped in front of the dark partition. Her pale hair was pulled tightly back and she carried a silver bowl.

While the latecomers among us whispered their way past knees and coats, and slipped guiltily into their seats, the woman faced us and reached into her bowl. From it she removed a white hoop about the size of a dinner plate. She held it up and turned it from side to side, as if for our inspection, while Hensch lifted from his box half a dozen knives. Then he stepped to the side of the table. He held the six knives fanwise in his left hand, with the blades pointing up. The knives were about a foot long, the blades shaped like elongated diamonds, and as he stood there at the side of the stage, a man with no expression on his face, a man with nothing to do, Hensch had the vacant and slightly bored look of an overgrown boy holding in one hand an awkward present, waiting patiently for someone to open a door.

With a gentle motion the woman in the white gown tossed the hoop lightly in the air in front of the black wooden partition. Suddenly a knife sank deep into the soft wood, catching the hoop, which hung swinging on the handle. Before we could decide whether or not to applaud, the woman tossed another white hoop. Hensch lifted and threw in a single swift smooth motion, and the second hoop hung swinging from the second knife. After the third hoop rose in the air and hung suddenly on a knife handle, the woman reached into her bowl and held up for our inspection a smaller hoop, the size of a saucer. Hensch raised a knife and caught the flying hoop cleanly against the wood. She next tossed two small hoops one after the other, which Hensch caught in two swift motions: the first at the top of its trajectory, the second near the middle of the partition.

We watched Hensch as he picked up three more knives and spread them fanwise in his left hand. He stood staring at his assistant with fierce attention, his back straight, his thick hand resting by his side. When she tossed three small hoops, one after the other, we saw his body tighten, we waited for the thunk-thunk-thunk of knives in wood, but he stood immobile, sternly gazing. The hoops struck the floor, bounced slightly, and began rolling like big dropped coins across the stage. Hadn't he liked the throw? We felt like looking away, like pretending we hadn't noticed. Nimbly the assistant gathered the rolling hoops, then assumed her position by the black wall. She seemed to take a deep breath before she tossed again. This time Hensch flung his three knives with extraordinary speed, and suddenly we saw all three hoops swinging on the partition, the last mere inches from the floor. She motioned grandly toward Hensch, who did not bow; we burst into vigorous applause.

Again the woman in the white gown reached into her bowl, and this time she held up something between her thumb and forefinger that even those of us in the first rows could not immediately make out. She stepped forward, and many of us recognized, between her fingers, an orange and black butterfly. She returned to the partition and looked at Hensch, who had already chosen his knife. With a gentle tossing gesture she released the butterfly. We burst into applause as the knife drove the butterfly against the wood, where those in the front rows could see the wings helplessly beating.

That was something we hadn't seen before, or even imagined we might see, something worth remembering; and as we applauded we tried to recall the knife throwers of our childhood, the smell of sawdust and cotton candy, the glittering woman on the turning wheel.

Now the woman in white removed the knives from the black partition and carried them across the stage to Hensch, who examined each one closely and wiped it with a cloth before returning it to his box.

Abruptly, Hensch strode to the center of the stage and turned to face us. His assistant pushed the table with its box of knives to his side. She left the stage and returned pushing a second table, which she placed at his other side. She stepped away, into half-darkness, while the lights shone directly on Hensch and his tables. We saw him place his left hand palm up on the empty tabletop. With his right hand he removed a knife from the box on the first table. Suddenly, without looking, he tossed the knife straight up into the air. We saw it rise to its rest and come hurtling down. Someone cried out as it struck his palm, but Hensch raised his hand from the table and held it up for us to see, turning it first one way and then the other: The knife had struck between the fingers. Hensch lowered his hand over the knife so that the blade stuck up between his second and third fingers. He tossed three more knives into the air, one after the other: Rat-tat-tat they struck the table. From the shadows the woman in white stepped forward and tipped the table toward us, so that we could see the four knives sticking between his fingers.

Oh, we admired Hensch, we were taken with the man's fine daring; and yet, as we pounded out our applause, we felt a little restless, a little dissatisfied, as if some unspoken promise had failed to be kept. For hadn't we been a trifle ashamed of ourselves for attending the performance, hadn't we deplored in advance his unsavory antics, his questionable crossing of the line?

As if in answer to our secret impatience, Hensch strode decisively to his corner of the stage. Quickly the pale-haired assistant followed, pushing the table after him. She next shifted the second table to the back of the stage and returned to the black partition. She stood with her back against it, gazing across the stage at Hensch, her loose white gown hanging from thin shoulder straps that had slipped down to her upper arms. At that moment we felt in our arms and along our backs a first faint flutter of anxious excitement, for there they stood before us, the dark master and the pale maiden, like figures in a dream from which we were trying to awake.

Hensch chose a knife and raised it beside his head with deliberation; we realized that he had worked very quickly before. With a swift sharp drop of his forearm, as if he were chopping a piece of wood, he released the knife. At first we thought he had struck her upper arm, but we saw that the blade had sunk into the wood and lay touching her skin. A second knife struck beside her other upper arm. She began to wriggle both shoulders, as if to free herself from the tickling knives, and only as her loose gown came rippling down did we realize that the knives had cut the shoulder straps. Hensch had us now, he had us. Long-legged and smiling, she stepped from the fallen gown and stood before the black partition in a spangled silver leotard. We thought of tightrope walkers, bareback riders, hot circus tents on blue summer days. The pale yellow hair, the spangled cloth, the pale skin touched here and there with shadow, all this gave her the remote, enclosed look of a work of art, while at the same time it lent her a kind of cool voluptuousness, for the metallic glitter of her costume seemed to draw attention to the bareness of her skin, disturbingly unhidden, dangerously white and cool and soft.

Quickly the glittering assistant stepped to the second table at the back of the stage and removed something from the drawer. She returned to the center of the wooden partition and placed on her head a red apple. The apple was so red and shiny that it looked as if it had been painted with nail polish. We looked at Hensch, who stared at her and held himself very still. In a single motion Hensch lifted and threw. She stepped out from under the red apple stuck in the wood.

From the table she removed a second apple and clenched the stem with her teeth. At the black partition she bent slowly backward until the bright red apple was above her upturned lips. We could see the column of her trachea pressing against the skin of her throat and the knobs of her hips pushing up against the silver spangles. Hensch took careful aim and flung the knife through the heart of the apple.

Next from the table she removed a pair of long white gloves, which she pulled on slowly, turning her wrists, tugging. She held up each tight-gloved hand in turn and wriggled the fingers. At the partition she stood with her arms out and her fingers spread. Hensch looked at her, then raised a knife and threw; it stuck into her fingertip, the middle fingertip of her right hand, pinning her to the black wall. The woman stared straight ahead. Hensch picked up a clutch of knives and held them fan-wise in his left hand. Swiftly he flung nine knives, one after the other, and as they struck her fingertips, one after the other, bottom to top, right-left right-left, we stirred uncomfortably in our seats. In the sudden silence she stood there with her arms outspread and her fingers full of knives, her silver spangles flashing, her white gloves whiter than her pale arms, looking as if at any moment her head would drop forward—looking for all the world like a martyr on a cross. Then slowly, gently, she pulled each hand from its glove, leaving the gloves hanging on the wall.

Now Hensch gave a sharp wave of his fingers, as if to dismiss everything that had gone before, and to our surprise the woman stepped forward to the edge of the stage, and addressed us for the first time.

"I must ask you," she said gently, "to be very quiet, because this next act is very dangerous. The master will mark me. Please do not make a sound. We thank you."

She returned to the black partition and simply stood there, her shoulders back, her arms down but pressed against the wood. She gazed steadily at Hensch, who seemed to be studying her; some of us said later that at this moment she gave the impression of a child who was about to be struck in the face, though others felt she looked calm, quite calm.

Hensch chose a knife from his box, held it for a moment, then raised his arm and threw. The knife struck beside her neck. He had missed—had he missed?—and we felt a sharp tug of disappointment, which changed at once to shame, deep shame, for we hadn't come out for blood; only for—well, something else; and as we asked ourselves what we had come for, we were surprised to see her reach up with one hand and pull out the knife. Then we saw, on her neck, the thin red trickle, which ran down to her shoulder; and we understood that her whiteness had been arranged for this moment. Long and loud we applauded, as she-bowed and held aloft the glittering knife, assuring us, in that way, that she was wounded but well, or well-wounded; and we didn't know whether we were applauding her wellness or her wound, or the touch of the master, who had crossed the line, who had carried us, safely, it appeared, into the realm of forbidden things.

Even as we applauded she turned and left the stage, returning a few moments later in a long black dress with long sleeves and a high collar, which concealed her wound. We imagined the white bandage under the black collar; we imagined other bandages, other wounds, on her hips, her waist, the edges of her breasts. Black against black they stood there, she and he, bound now it seemed in a dark pact, as if she were his twin sister, or as if both were on the same side in a game we were all playing, a game we no longer understood; and indeed she looked older in her black dress, sterner, a schoolmarm or maiden aunt. We were not surprised when she stepped forward to address us again.

"If any of you, in the audience, wish to be marked by the master, to receive the mark of the master, now is the time. Is there anyone?"

We all looked around. A single hand rose hesitantly and was instantly lowered. Another hand went up; then there were other hands, young bodies straining forward, eager; and from the stage the woman in black descended and walked slowly along an aisle, looking closely, considering, until she stopped and pointed: "You." And we knew her, Susan Parker, a high school girl, who might have been our daughter, sitting there with her face turned questioningly toward the woman, her eyebrows slightly raised, as she pointed to herself; then the faint flush of realization; and as she climbed the steps of the stage we watched her closely, wondering what the dark woman had seen in her, to make her be the one, wondering too what she was thinking, Susan Parker, as she followed the dark woman to the wooden partition. She was wearing loose jeans and a tight black short-sleeved sweater; her reddish-brown and faintly shiny hair was cut short. Was it for her white skin she had been chosen? or some air of self-possession? We wanted to cry out: sit down! you don't have to do this! but we remained silent, respectful. Hensch stood at his table, watching without expression. It occurred to us that we trusted him at this moment; we clung to him; he was all we had; for if we weren't absolutely sure of him, then who were we, what on earth were we, who had allowed things to come to such a pass?

The woman in black led Susan Parker to the wooden partition and arranged her there: back to the wood, shoulders straight. We saw her run her hand gently, as if tenderly, over the girl's short hair, which lifted and fell back in place. Then taking Susan Parker's right hand in hers, she stepped to the girl's right, so that the entire arm was extended against the black partition. She stood holding Susan Parker's raised hand, gazing at the girl's face—comforting her, it seemed; and we observed Susan Parker's arm looked very white between the black sweater and the black dress, against the black wood of the partition. As the women gazed at each other, Hensch lifted a knife and threw. We heard the muffled bang of the blade, heard Susan Parker's sharp little gasp, saw her other hand clench into a fist. Quickly the dark woman stepped in front of her and pulled out the knife; and turning to us she lifted Susan Parker's arm, and displayed for us a streak of red on the pale forearm. Then she reached into a pocket of her black dress and removed a small tin box. From the box came a ball of cotton, a patch of gauze, and a roll of white surgical tape, with which she swiftly bound the wound: "There, dear," we heard her say. "You were very brave." We watched Susan Parker walk with lowered eyes across the stage, holding her bandaged arm a little away from her body; and as we began to clap, because she was still there, because she had come through, we saw her raise her eyes and give a quick shy smile, before lowering her lashes and descending the steps.

Now arms rose, seats creaked, there was a great rustling and whispering among us, for others were eager to be chosen, to be marked by the master, and once again the woman in black stepped forward to speak.

"Thank you, dear. You were very brave, and now you will bear the mark of the master. You will treasure it all your days. But it is a light mark, do you know, a very light mark. The master can mark more deeply, far more deeply. But for that you must show yourself worthy. Some of you may already be worthy, but I will ask you now to lower your hands, please, for I have with me someone who is ready to be marked. And please, all of you, I ask for your silence."

From the right of the stage stepped forth a young man who might have been fifteen or sixteen. He was dressed in black pants and a black shirt and wore rimless glasses that caught the light. He carried himself with ease, and we saw that he had a kind of lanky and slightly awkward beauty, the beauty, we thought, of a water bird, a heron. The woman led him to the wooden partition and indicated that he should stand with his back against it. She walked to the table at the rear of the stage and removed an object, which she carried back to the partition. Raising the boy's left arm, so that it was extended straight out against the wall at the level of his shoulder, she lifted the object to his wrist and began fastening it into the wood. It appeared to be a clamp, which held his arm in place at the wrist. She then arranged his hand: palm facing us, fingers together. Stepping away, she looked at him thoughtfully. Then she stepped over to his free side, took his other hand, and held it gently.

The stage lights went dark, then a reddish spotlight shone on Hensch at his box of knives. A second light, white as moonlight, shone on the boy and his extended arm. The other side of the boy remained in darkness.

Even as the performance seemed to taunt us with the promise of danger, of a disturbing turn that should not be permitted, or even imagined, we reminded ourselves that the master had so far done nothing but scratch a bit of skin, that his act was after all public and well traveled, that the boy appeared calm; and though we disapproved of the exaggerated effect of the lighting, the crude melodrama of it all, we secretly admired the skill with which the performance played on our fears. What it was we feared, exactly, we didn't know, couldn't say. But there was the knife thrower bathed in blood-light, there was the pale victim manacled to a wall; in the shadows the dark woman; and in the glare of the lighting, the silence, in the very rhythm of the evening, the promise of entering a dark dream.

And Hensch took up a knife and threw; some heard the sharp gasp of the boy, others a thin cry. In the whiteness of the light we saw the knife handle at the center of his bloody palm. Some said that at the moment the knife struck, the boy's shocked face shone with an intense, almost painful joy. The white light suddenly illuminated the woman in black, who raised his free arm high, as if in triumph; then she quickly set to work pulling out the blade, wrapping the palm in strips of gauze, wiping the boy's drained sweating face with a cloth, and leading him off the stage with an arm firmly around his waist. No one made a sound. We looked at Hensch, who was gazing after his assistant.

When she came back, alone, she stepped forward to address us, while the stage lights returned to normal.

"You are a brave boy, Thomas. You will not soon forget this day. And now I must say that we have time for only one more event, this evening. Many of you here, I know, would like to receive the palm mark, as Thomas did. But I am asking something different now. Is there anyone in this audience tonight who would like to make"—and here she paused, not hesitantly, but as if in emphasis—"the ultimate sacrifice? This is the final mark, the mark that can be received only once. Please think it over carefully, before raising your hand."

We wanted her to say more, to explain clearly what it was she meant by those riddling words, which came to us as though whispered in our ears, in the dark, words that seemed to mock us even as they eluded us and we looked about tensely, almost eagerly, as if by the sheer effort of our looking we were asserting our vigilance. We saw no hands, and maybe it was true that at the very center of our relief there was a touch of disappointment, but it was relief nonetheless; and if the entire performance had seemed to be leading toward some overwhelming moment that was no longer to take place, still we had been entertained by our knife thrower, had we not, we had been carried a long way, so that even as we questioned his cruel art we were ready to offer our applause.

"If there are no hands," she said, looking at us sharply, as if to see what it was we were secretly thinking, while we, as if to avoid her gaze, looked rapidly all about. "Oh: yes?" We saw it too, the partly raised hand, which perhaps had always been there, unseen in the half-darkened seats, and we saw the stranger rise, and begin to make her way slowly past drawn-in knees and pulled-back coats and half-risen forms. We watched her climb the steps of the stage, a tall mournful-looking girl in jeans and a dark blouse, with lank long hair and slouched shoulders. "And what is your name?" the woman in black said gently, and we could not hear the answer. "Well then, Laura. And so you are prepared to receive the final mark? Then you must be very brave." And turning to us she said, "I must ask you, please, to remain absolutely silent."

She led the girl to the black wooden partition and arranged her there, unconfined: chin up, hands hanging awkwardly at her sides. The dark woman stepped back and appeared to assess her arrangement, after which she crossed to the back of the stage. At this point some of us had confused thoughts of calling out, of demanding an explanation, but we didn't know what it was we might be protesting, and in any case the thought of distracting Hensch's throw, of perhaps causing an injury, was repellent to us, for we saw that already he had selected a knife. It was a new kind of knife, or so we thought, a longer and thinner knife. And it seemed to us that things were happening too quickly, up there on the stage, for where was the spotlight, where was the drama of a sudden darkening, but Hensch, even as we wondered, did what he always did—he threw his knife. Some of us heard the girl cry out, others were struck by her silence, but what stayed with all of us was the absence of the sound of the knife striking wood. Instead there was a softer sound, a more disturbing sound, a sound almost like silence, and some said the girl looked down, as if in surprise. Others claimed to see in her face, in the expression of her eyes, a look of rapture. As she fell to the floor the dark woman stepped forward and swept her arm toward the knife thrower, who for the first time turned to acknowledge us. And now he bowed: a deep, slow, graceful bow, the bow of a master, down to his knees. Slowly the dark red curtain began to fall. Overhead the lights came on.

As we left the theater we agreed that it had been a skillful performance, though we couldn't help feeling that the knife thrower had gone too far. He had justified his reputation, of that there could be no question; without ever trying to ingratiate himself with us, he had continually seized our deepest attention. But for all that, we couldn't help feeling that he ought to have found some other way. Of course the final act had probably been a setup, the girl had probably leaped smiling to her feet as soon as the curtain closed, though some of us recalled unpleasant rumors of one kind or another, run-ins with the police, charges and countercharges, a murky business. In any case we reminded ourselves that she hadn't been coerced in any way, none of them had been coerced in any way. And it was certainly true that a man in Hensch's position had every right to improve his art, to dream up new acts with which to pique curiosity, indeed such advances were absolutely necessary, for without them a knife thrower could never hope to keep himself in the public eye. Like the rest of us, he had to earn his living, which admittedly wasn't easy in times like these. But when all was said and done, when the pros and cons were weighed, and every issue carefully considered, we couldn't help feeling that the knife thrower had really gone too far. After all, if such performances were encouraged, if they were even tolerated, what might we expect in the future? Would any of us be safe? The more we thought about it, the more uneasy we became, and in the nights that followed, when we woke from troubling dreams, we remembered the traveling knife thrower with agitation and dismay.

WITH FOLDED HANDS FOREVER FROM CIRCUS PARADE

Jim Tully

—Jim Tully (1886–1947) was, among other occupations, a boxer, a publicist for Charlie Chaplin, and a carnival roustabout. This selection appeared in Tully's semi-autobiographical novel Circus Parade *(1927).*

THE STRONG WOMAN'S DEATH had a gloomy effect upon me. Slug Finnerty and Cameron had discovered her. A mark was seen on her throat, as though the string which held her grouch bag had been torn from it. Money, jewelry, finery, everything of possible value had disappeared. We always felt that Cameron and Finnerty had robbed her.

"They'd of skinned her if they could, the measly crooks!" sneered Jock. "Talk about fallin' among thieves."

The coroner was called, and signed the death certificate. There was no money with which to bury her.

"It's a lucky shot for me," said Silver Moon Dugan, "I owed her fifty bucks I won't have to pay. She was a funny dame."

The Moss-Haired Girl said to me after the coroner had gone, "It sure is awful to die in Arkansas with this circus, but then she's just as well off. She was just in wrong, that's all." She walked with me to where the Baby Buzzard sat in front of the musicians' tent.

"Well, she's gone," said the Baby Buzzard as we approached.

"Yes," was Alice's answer.

"It's a hard loss for Bob. She drew a lot of money each week."

"Yes, it's *too bad* for Bob. *Poor Bob,* he does have the *hardest time,*" smiled Alice.

"Yes indeed he do," responded the Baby Buzzard, missing the Moss-Haired Girl's tone of mockery.

"But she has to be buried, you know," continued the Moss-Haired Girl. "There's too much of her to keep above ground. We'd better take up a collection for her. I'll start it with twenty dollars." Just then Cameron appeared. "What will you give?" Alice asked him.

"Well, I think five dollars each among twenty of us will be enough. After all, we can't get a coffin big enough in the town, and it don't matter anyhow. I've got two of the boys makin' a big box and linin' it wit' canvas. The coffins fall apart after three days in the grave anyhow. Them undertakers are the original highway robbers." And Cameron fingered his Elk tooth charm.

The Baby Buzzard disappeared and returned with her glassful of half dollars. She counted ten of the coins and handed them to Alice, who turned them over to Cameron.

"These'll pay her way through purgatory, or start her soul rollin'. That's more'n she'd do for me if I croaked. People 'at croak 'emselves should bury 'emselves. Them's my ways of lookin' at it. I ain't never seen a man yet I'd bump myself off for. You can't do 'em no good when you're dead," half soliloquized the Baby Buzzard.

"May be not," returned the Moss-Haired Girl, looking from Cameron to the Baby Buzzard, "but we can at least shut our mouths and let her rest in peace. Somebody's stole everything she had. Even her silk underwear's gone. And who in the dickens with this circus can wear that?"

"Maybe Goosey stole it to put on the elephants," sneered the old lady.

"Maybe so, but the elephants wouldn't wear it if they knew it was stolen. They're above that."

"Well, well," and Cameron now became reverent, "it's all beyond our power." He pointed heavenward. "He who is above us has called her home."

"He may have called her, but He didn't send her carfare. He probably thought she could bum her way," dryly commented the Baby Buzzard.

"That is not for us to judge," replied Cameron solemnly, "for who are we to question the Great Taskmaster's laws? It is best that we bury her before parade so as not to disturb the even tenor of our ways. I will say a few words and have the band play and sing a few songs. And then we shall take her to the graveyard in one of the elephant's cages. Buddy Conroy is there now makin' arrangements. The wagon with the cage can follow along with the parade, and no one will be the wiser."

The Strong Woman was placed in a square pine canvas-covered box with her blonde head resting on a huge red pillow trimmed in green. Her heavy hands were folded. Her mouth was puckered in a half smile which helped to conceal the cyanide scar at the edge of her lower lip. Her head was buried in the pillow. Her large breasts rose high above everything.

Fourteen men lifted the box.

Cameron's showman instinct prevailed at the last. The calliope was called into service. A man stood upon its platform and played as weird a tune as was ever concocted by the most fantastic human brain.

It seemed to my boyish mind to have been blended with wild wails and screeching laughter. It was followed by:

I had a dream the other night,
Floating on the River of Sin,
I peeped inside of Jordan bright,
Floating on the River of Sin,
And another place I seen inside,
Floating on the River of Sin.
A place where the devil does reside,
Floating on the River of Sin.

Freaks and thieves, trailers and clown acrobats and stake-drivers gathered in front of the Strong Woman's tent.

"Come on now, men, we'll make it snappy," said Slug Finnerty. "Join in the song with the calliope."

He waved his hands.

I seen a band of spirits bright,
Floating on the River of Sin,
Holding church by candle light,
Floating on the River of Sin.
A great big chariot passing by,
Floating on the River of Sin,
Come so close they had to fly,
Floating on the River of Sin.

The crude heavy voices were drowned out by the wail of the calliope.

They drove the chariot down below,
A spirit fell down and hurt his toe,
Floating on the River of Sin.
Then singin' and shoutin' way out loud,
Floating on the River of Sin.
They took her to heaven in a great big cloud,
Floating on the River of Sin.

When the song had died away Silver Moon Dugan, the Boss canvasman, commented.

"Gee, if she ever falls outta heaven there'll be a splash." A few roustabouts laughed. Then Cameron stood before us on a pine box.

"Fellow travelers with Cameron's World's Greatest Combined Shows," he began, and paused—"it is my sad duty to say a few words here. I wish it understood that I come to bury Caesar, not to praise her. She is beyond us now, stripped of everything before God, who takes care of the weary and the worn and calls the wandering lady here home.

"We talk of worldly splendor, yet Solomon in all his gorgeous glory was not arrayed as one of these. She who now lies here before us once held our little world in awe. Now none of us are too procrastinatin' an' poor to show our irreverence, and she recks not at all of it. It is not ours to judge, for we are ever in the Great Taskmaster's eye, and if he should ever blink it ever so slightly we would crumble like the atomic mountains that rise outta the sea.

"Ours is but a little stay here, full of sound and fury, and, if you will pardon the blasphemy, signifying not a hell of a lot.

"It all reminds me of that well-known poem made immortal by Browning, than whom there was no more profound student of the human heart:

There is so much good in the best of us,
And so much bad in the rest of us,
That it little behooves the best of us
To talk about the rest of us.

"Those lines to me have always been a welcoming tocsin. When tired, when weary with the troubles of Cameron's World's Greatest Combined Shows, I often retire to my humble car and solicitate upon them. Feeling the full majesty of them, I have naught but love and understanding for those members of my circus who would fain be ungrateful.

"For are we not the same that our fathers have been? Do we not see the same sights and view the same sun and run in the same blood where our fathers have run?

"A great object-lesson can be received from this. As I have said in preceding, we are ever in our Great Taskmaster's eye. He who rolls the mountains is watching over us.

"God is ever on the side of justice, or as General Robert E. Lee so well said, God marches at the head of the heaviest battalions; and those battalions are imposed of justice and mercy and undying truth."

Cameron took a large red and white kerchief from his pocket. He unfolded it deliberately, then wiped his forehead and eyes, cleared his throat and resumed:

"We have labored in the vineyard with our sleeping friend here—

and that reminds me that she is not dead, but sleepeth." Cameron looked at his audience as one will who feels he has uttered a profound truth. He wiped his eyes again. When he removed the kerchief they suddenly filled with tears. His whole manner changed. "Oh it stabs my heart, this grief before me. He who has loved and has run away may live to love some other day. But what about the victim of this dastardly attempt at liaison? I adjure you . . ." His frame shook, his kerchief rubbed wet eyes. The audience looked bored with piety. Cameron's right hand, holding the kerchief, rose high in the air. He stood on tiptoe. "But friends, do not despair. In that vast circus ground in the other world we shall meet the lady who lies here with folded hands forever."

The crowd dispersed. The Strong Woman was placed in the elephant cage while the calliope played:

Room enough, room enough,
Room enough in heaven for us all—
Oh don't stay away.

It then shifted:

At the cross, at the cross,
Where I first saw light,
And the burden of my heart rolled away,
Rolled away—
It was there by faith
I received my sight,
And now I am happy all the day—
All the day.

The ringmaster's whistle blew. Wagons began to move. The Strong Woman started on her last parade.

FROM DREAMLAND

Kevin Baker

—Kevin Baker's award-winning historical novel Dreamland *(1999) captures the splendor of a bygone era. In this selection, the leader of Coney Island's caucus of little people, Trick the Dwarf, gets what he always wanted—a place to call home.*

OUR CITY WENT UP on a back lot of Dreamland, a treeless, rubbled flat, where the flotsam of the world floated through. It was there that Brinckerhoff had housed his exotic tribes—his Pygmies, and his Esquimaus, his Boers and his Bantocs, and his Dog-eating Igorrotes—all the funny little peoples, with colorful costumes and odd facial hair, who the world had passed by.

Once upon a time there had even been a fairy tale Dutch cottage. There, in the old days, you could find General Piet Cronje sitting out on his porch in the evening, smoking his pipe and stroking his long white muttonchops, contemplating the bygone glories of the veldt, or the day's receipts.

Each afternoon at precisely three-fifteen, Oom Piet rode out straight and true as an acacia tree to surrender his sword to the British again. Brinckerhoff gave out that this was the exact time the Boer War had ended—though in fact it was merely post time over at Big Tim Sullivan's racetrack over at Brighton Beach, and Big Tim didn't care to have any of the fake guns spook his prize horseflesh.

Yet the silence when the old Boer rode out each afternoon was so sudden and startling, he played his role with such immense and impregnable gravity, that his audience was truly awed. A hush fell over the whole grandstand, the only sounds the muted cries from the roller coasters over by the sea and the pounding of the horses' hooves from the track—like some distant echo of the real war, still galloping over the grassy hills of South Africa.

It didn't draw, though, even with real veterans from both sides, and cannons and enormous painted canvases and an ingenious, glistening tin waterfall. Maybe it was the participants—after all, between the Boers and the British, how much of a rooting interest could you take?—but in any case the veterans began to drift off to Central America to find work as mercenaries, until there weren't enough left to contest the issue.

For awhile they tried pitting the remaining white men against an imported tribe of Bantus—black against white always being a surefire draw at the box office. They figured they wouldn't have to pay the Bantus *anything,* just drive a mangy Jersey cow or two into their kraal for them to slaughter and eat right there—an added attraction that drew more paying spectators than the battle itself.

Yet the Bantus surprised them and went on strike; as the *World*'s editorials tsked, it seemed they had been corrupted by the modern world after all. One afternoon, instead of falling in murderous ambush upon the Brits and Boers from behind the potted palm trees Brinckerhoff had dragged in from every ten-cent restaurant in Manhattan, they simply marched out and, with tremendous dignity, laid down their stage spears and sat on the ground.

Naturally, this being America, they were treated like any other strikers. A load of toughs was driven in one night to break their heads and smash up their sham palm huts. Even General Cronje and his mercenaries agreed that this was the only way to deal with the black bastards. But a few nights later, after the parks had shut down, they shucked off their spectacular, sky-blue headdresses, and slipped the plaster chicken bones from their noses, and snuck silently off into the greater city, disguised in the uniforms of pantomime policemen they had found in a storage locker. Of course, no one noticed them—a long line of barefoot black policemen, male and female, without a word of English between them, creeping through the streets of New York together in a long line. They had gone for good, disappeared into the impenetrable vastnesses of San Juan Hill, or Harlem, irrevocably Americanized.

By the time we got there they were long gone—every last remnant of their existence bulldozed to make way for The Little City—their *kraals,* and their grass huts, and even Oom Piet's nostalgic little cottage, all wiped away. Brinckerhoff laid out the plan of the town over their bones, plotting the broad avenues and squares himself with the surveyors. At night he worked ceaselessly in his tower, designing every house, every public building, every stick of furniture.

"Everything has to fit," he commanded. "No slums, no tenements, no delinquency. It must be a model of city planning!"

They went up with breathtaking speed: no flowering Aztec city, but a modern, progressive village behind a gingerbread facade, planned after Nuremberg—for in those days anything clean and orderly had to be modeled after the Germans. There was a lovely little public square, and a clock tower, and livery stables, and even an exquisite miniature railway to draw passengers around and around our town. There was a powerhouse, and a gas works, and a fire station with a real working fire wagon, drawn by a team of Shetland ponies.

It seemed impossible. I had instigated the whole thing, I know. I had set the wheels spinning in Brinckerhoff's head out of my desperation, but nonetheless it was incredible to see it actually taking shape. It emerged like a half-remembered dream the next day—impossible, fantastic, but somehow familiar.

My queen took it all in her royal stride. She liked to saunter out each afternoon and inspect the construction—obviously crazy as a loon, with her royal purple gowns and fake ermine furs flowing behind her. The workers would patronize her, sweeping their hats off in low bows when she approached, barely hiding their grins. They answered whatever lordly question she asked them with elaborate courtesy—"Oh, *yes,* Your Majesty!" "*Certainly,* Your Majesty!" "However you desire it, Your Majesty!" At Coney Island, every day was All Fool's Day, and they were used to mock royalty: African kings, Gypsy princesses, roller coaster attendants dressed up like Teddy Roosevelt.

I scowled back at their sniggering, their insolent, smirking faces. She simply swept on, imperious and impervious, through her incredible new domain.

Which of us was more crazy?

"It's built to last," Brinckerhoff confided, in his quiet, confident way. "Inhabitable all year round. When all the rest of Dreamland—when Luna Park, and Steeplechase, and all the rest of Coney is gone—*this* will still be here."

It *was* perfect, a miniature superior to the original—to the squalid, sprawling behemoth that lay just west of Coney. And with every day Brinckerhoff invented something to make it even more perfect, more complete: a police station, complete with jail cells, and fingerprint pads, and a tiny, windowless third-degree room. A town hall, and a church, and library, with miniature special editions that fit smoothly, easily in our hands. All of it so ingenious, so meticulous and perfect and unique, until only one, final addition remained.

"Don't worry, I haven't forgotten your contribution," Brinckerhoff confided. "You will be the mayor, and live in the palace with your queen."

For that's what we were to be, strange combination: mayor and queen of The Little City. And there was a palace: not so grand as what I had promised her—for when has man not disappointed woman?—but still by far the biggest building in the whole miniature town, three reduced stories high, with red gables and turrets, and a splendid little garden.

Inside was an exquisite little jewel box, just for us. There was a working fireplace, and a library, and a billiards room; the walls hung with old swords and muskets and trophies and even portraits of fabulous, important-looking ancestors. All of it still *reduced;* even the stuffed rhinoceros head, and the moose, and the elephant-foot umbrella stand by the front door—one final, none-too-subtle joke from Matty Brinckerhoff.

"Come, come now," he chided. "You must have the whole world, cut down to size. What is an elephant, compared to a dream?"

He couldn't fool me. The miniature elephant's foot clinched it. The palace, the town, even my poor, mad consort—all this was one more terrific joke. Mockery more terrible than any snickering workman's—mockery worse than anything my father had endured, in his academic gown.

And yet I was seduced. I was seduced the way men usually are seduced, which is not by love, or lovely flesh—but by leather upholstered chairs, and fine thick carpets. By wainscoting, and oak panels, and a liquor cabinet full of the best Madeira. By substantial curtains, and real silver, and a quiet, soothing place to think and rest, and cut the pages of my books.

And for her—for my queen—there was a dressing room, and a bath tiled with leaping, Minosian dolphins. A bedroom that was an exact replica of the old queen's—the real queen, the only real queen there ever would be, ever again, Vicky herself—drawn from a Sunday rotogravure. Perfect right down to the patterns on the wallpaper and the hairbrushes on the dressing table. Save that cut into all of it—into the corners of the mantelpieces, and the frame of the dressing mirror and the bedposts, and the carpets—was an imperial "CR." *Carlotta Regina.*

I saw her then. I saw her go up the stairs the first day we were in the finished palace, while I walked around gaping at the fixings. I saw her walk into what must have been far and away the most luxurious room she had ever seen, and sit herself at the dressing table without a second glance—as if she had been doing it all her life. And if that wasn't the true embodiment of royalty, then I don't know what is.

It was all ready before the season was even half over—all the fine, gingerbread buildings, and the broad, tree-lined streets. Only one thing was missing: the last, living props.

How do you advertise for a freak show? We needed so many, all at once, not just the usual trickle of the outcast and the disinherited. I suggested something in the Help Wanted, a call for your wretched refuse, perhaps, yearning to be tall. Brinckerhoff only smiled his sated, crocodile grin.

"Oh, they'll come, sure enough," he said. "They'll find out, believe me, and when they do we'll have to beat 'em off with sticks."

He was right, as always. As soon as word got around they poured in. Dwarves and midgets. Hunchbacks and freaks, and acrobats and clowns, and jockeys disgraced for doping horses—and children. Real children pulling my disguise in reverse, pasting on false whiskers and trying to lower their voices—posing as little people just in the prospect of steady meals and a warm place to sleep.

My people swarmed in from around the country, and even the Continent, from vaudeville houses, and ten-twenty-thirties, and circuses and bawdy houses and Son-of-Ham shows. They came from the medical schools, where they were trotted out every hour on the hour, as examples of perverted physiology. They came from the attics in their isolated upstate homes, where they'd been stored since the day their parents first understood they were more than just short for their age. They came from working their pickpocket scams or crawling in among the gear wheels of gigantic machinery or serving some particularly delicate inclination in the most exclusive of brothels—in short, from anyplace where a fine hand was needed.

There were thousands of them. They came in by the trainloads, piling off at the New York & Sea Beach terminal. Blinking in the harsh Coney sunlight, sniffing the salt air, wondering if they could make it in the big-little town. They came in all shapes and sizes: There were the big heads and the Pekinese faces, the Chinless Wonders and the Ape Men and the cripples, the almond heads and the pinheads and the mongoloids. And those few, perfectly proportioned midgets, like my Carlotta, who merely had the misfortune to be short—if misfortune is what you could call such beauty in exquisite miniature.

We winnowed them down to four hundred, sorting them day after day through the endless, winding lines. Brinckerhoff had a doctor and a professor of anatomy on hand, to prod and poke at them. Their disqualifications were chalked on the back of their coats: "H" for a hunchback, "F" for freakishness, "T" for talentless, "U" for excessive moles, or hair, or simply overwhelming, repulsive ugliness. The losers were trucked back to the station without so much as a farewell handshake or the train fare—to discover their defects only later, when they happened to take their coats off.

The four hundred chosen ones stood screaming before our palace. The good citizens of our model town—drinking and brawling, frolicking and fondling each other in the town square, where they'd been ordered to assemble. Slobbering obscene ditties up at our palace—

"God save the runt! God save the cunt!"

—giddy with relief, I knew, at having survived another test of their humanity. Goaded by the very idea of a queen, a superior being who was still *one of us.* Taking full advantage of that fool's license which is all we are ever granted.

"Don't go out there," I warned her. "Leave it to tomorrow, at least, when they've sobered up!"

"But We are their queen," she said, beaming as serenely, radiantly as any real monarch, so that even I was overawed. I still thought it was a mistake. Just as she was about to step out onto the balcony a brown blob of some unknown pedigree came flying up from the street, plopping on the balcony like a fish out of water.

"God save the runt—"

She didn't even seem to notice it. She walked right on out—the whole insolent mob of them falling quiet the moment she appeared.

"My good people," she said. "My *good people—*"

—though it wasn't so much what she said, some inane speech, no more or less mad than the palaver of all royals everywhere in the real, big world. It didn't matter what she said, even mad as she obviously was. Standing there on the balcony of our palace in her widow's mantilla, head straight and regal as any European monarch's, and much more beautiful, she had made us a *people* with their own, magnificent queen. Simply by believing in it, all the way, by being the regal creature she was.

"My good people," she said—

—and they were good. And when she finished they burst spontaneously into applause. And when she made that peculiar, chopping, guillotinelike motion that passed for the sign of the cross, they actually knelt, and bowed their heads to receive her blessing.

Then they wandered off to find their wonderful new homes. To live, for once, like real people, in a real place—even if it was wrapped up in a greater flight of fancy. They could ignore all that, for the sake of happiness.

Except for the Big Tent.

The tent was what gave the lie to it all. It was set up just off the main square, painted with clowns, and lions and tigers snarling in their cages. It was here that we all ended up. For in The Little City, everyone—the police and the firemen, the priest and the mayor and the Queen herself—*everyone* worked the Big Tent.

They took a spin or two around town in our miniature train, then they filed inside—all the usual drummers, and the cigar rollers, and the draymen. The hair weighers and the cloth cutters and the soda bottlers, plopping down their nickels to watch us perform.

There were the bona fide circus acts, of course, the jugglers and the clowns and the tiny women who twirled by their teeth from a rope. Real animal trainers who faced down cats able to devour them in a single gulp.

But mostly what they saw was the rest of us—whose everyday existence had become another act, no matter what we did or how well we did it. Every matinee and evening, the alarums would ring out, and The Little City Fire Department would come galloping to the rescue: bells clanging, men clutching stoutly to the back of their cart—a fire department that never answered anything but false alarms. Every day, some midget would swipe a purse from a plant in the crowd—and police whistles would shriek, and The Little City mounted police would come riding in on their ponies to clap the malefactor off to jail.

In The Little City, we could hear God hiccough—and laugh and jeer and spit, every day. A whole gallery full of gods, who changed with each performance.

After each show the spectators were free to wander through our town and peer into our windows. Pushing their way through our doors, stumbling through our walls—leering at every perfect, miniaturized inch, so much superior to anything *they* lived in. We would parade down Main Street, leading them back to the big tent, where the whole town assembled to sing a maudlin farewell song—voices pitched as high as we could make them, until a baritone stepped forward at the very end, dipped to one knee, and sang the chorus again in a voice as deep as the bottom of the sea. It never failed to get a big laugh.

My Carlotta presided over all this with her usual mad aplomb. She made a short welcoming speech at the beginning and the end of every show, never varying so much as a word of it. During the grand tour she would receive guests at tea in our living room, glowering impressively at them if they sat before she did, favoring them with a smile or two if they were particularly obsequious. They ate it up, shaking with laughter behind their hands. She couldn't seem to get enough of it.

I thought she didn't understand: No matter how good our manners, no matter how fine our conversation or how accomplished we were, no matter how much we tried to be like *them*—it didn't matter. It only amused them that we could do such things, like a horse that does arithmetic or a bird that tells your fortune. But she was not bothered by it. "Royalty does not lie in what other people think," was all she would say. "Otherwise, it could never exist. The point is that they come to see Us. They acknowledge We are queen."

I hated it. Can you comprehend what it was like—living in a world where parades were a numbing, daily grind? Where everything you do, no matter how well and how honestly, is the same endless, running joke?

All those tea parties, day after day, with a bunch of snickering shopgirls, and brick masons. Watching them squeeze themselves down onto our miniature chairs and couches, gaping at the size of our tea service. Giggling as they broke the handles of the perfect, tiny china cups off on their pinky fingers. Asking me, again and again, without fail, if I had shot a *baby* elephant to make our umbrella stand—

Not that there was anything else for me to do: I had no real duties; The Little City ran itself. The rest of my subjects didn't mind the intrusions, it sure beat how they had lived before. They even began to take their roles seriously—the firemen working real shifts, maintaining their equipment, their fine garden hoses and three-foot ladders and adorable ponies. The cops walking regular beats, even at night, after the tourists had all gone home. The newsies hawking their papers, despite the fact that there was no news at all in The Little City.

Soon, there were even marriages. They had to be performed in public, by our own Reverend Cherubim, at the delighted Brinckerhoff's insistence. Nobody on the circuit had ever cared whether we were married or not. We were assumed to be like the African slaves, living in a state of nature. But now, matrimonial bliss was the order of the day. Matty Brink even reminded me of our own situation.

"She thinks she's still married to the Emperor Maximilian," I told him.

"So tell her it's a morganatic marriage," he shrugged. "After all, isn't The Little City worth a mass?"

She took to the idea like a trouper, of course. She was a great actress, and there are no actors so mad they can't recognize a great part. In the end we were dragged out beneath the big tent like all the rest, shriven and wed before an overflow Sunday matinee crowd.

Brinckerhoff spared no expense. It was held on the all-important opening weekend of the season. The tent was covered with boughs of lilac and myrtle—my queen in a pure white dress of lace and bows, myself in the general's uniform of an operatic country, sky blue and canary yellow. There were twenty-four bridesmaids to carry her endless white train, a twenty-four-man honor guard to walk beside them up the aisle, toy sabres rattling at their hips.

My poor subjects: They stood around looking as dazed and thrilled as if they were at the coronation of the Czar. The firemen and the police force standing at attention in full uniform, buttons and shoes shining. The ladies-in-waiting hurling white rose petals before us.

We strode majestically up the red-carpeted aisle to Mendelssohn's march, stride by tiny stride—the gallery gods leering and calling out all sorts of predictably lascivious remarks. Up at the altar waited the Reverend Cherubim, standing on a stack of Bibles—a chubby little fool, with rosy cheeks and twinkling eyes, who had played this part for years. He wandered through a leering, pun-strewn ceremony before pronouncing us "half-man and *all* wife"—with a great, burlesque wink at the audience.

This drew a huge laugh, as did each of the wedding presents, also opened before the crowd: a gargantuan rolling pin, right out of Maggie and Jiggs, and nearly as tall as Carlotta herself. A pint-sized bed that was really a trampoline. A tiny touring car, out of which climbed dwarf after dwarf after dwarf.

The crowd loved them all, roaring as each one was unwrapped. But the greatest joke of all was us.

I stood at the altar, dressed in my general's uniform, and lifted the veil of my beautiful beloved. Her eyes closed as she awaited my kiss, while thousands of guests looked on breathlessly—everyone of them ready to roar with derisive laughter.

Can you imagine it? Your silliest, grandest, childhood daydreams—anyone's grandest dreams—transformed into a great public joke. In that moment, while my mad bride stood waiting blindly to receive my kiss, I realized I had been wrong to despise my father. That there was no way, no way after all, to outstrip their mockery.

The grand reception that followed was filled with celebrities, starting with everyone who walked in off the midway and plunked down their two bits. The proprietor, Big Tim Sullivan, was there, broad, fixer's face betraying nothing, congratulating us as warmly and sincerely as if we had been any other two, normal citizens. Even Mayor McClellan came, well-welling and smirking down at us, cruel, aristocratic smile running across his lips, fingering my golden, tinsel epaulettes—

—"If my father had had you on his staff, perhaps he would have swept the field at Antietam!"—

"Yes, then all he would have needed was a spine," I told him, but he was already moving on down the receiving line, my small voice lost among the bigger people. A hand clamped down on my shoulder.

"Very droll, I am sure."

Brinckerhoff swayed sardonically above me, reeking of gin. He staggered, bumping a miniature plaster head of Caligula off a coffee table, to smash on the Persian carpet. He steadied himself on my shoulder, and patted me knowingly:

"You are such a funny fellow. Well, now you can get busy on the issue," he slurred.

"Whatta you mean?"

"Oh, you were right," he nodded. "She's a real queen. Now it's time for you to be fruitful and multiply—or can't you manage that?"

I flung his hand off my shoulder, left him stumbling over his damned elephant foot—but I suppose I should have anticipated it: The royal wedding would draw only one day's play, two at the most, in the dailies. There were too many other rough miracles in this town.

So there would be children, skipping and singing on the sidewalks of The Little City—if not our royal progeny, then someone else's. But what would happen if they turned out to be Big? Would they be banished from our magic kingdom, along with their dwarf parents? Or would they become one more addition to the act—the tiny parents spanking the recalcitrant schoolboy who towered over them? The schoolboy turning around and spanking the parents? Oh, the possibilities were limitless!

And what would happen when there were too many children, big or small? For our model city was a contained place, circumscribed by its toy railway. There was no room to expand, and the excess would have to be pushed out into the carny streets, and the unplanned world, and how would such decisions be made?

None of my constituents seemed to care. Theirs had always been a hand-to-mouth existence; they weren't about to start worrying now. They went on personalizing their model homes, adding on rooms, planting trees and flowers and bushes, acting like regular people.

Looking forward to the winter, when the winds would rake the beach, and the breakers would roll huge and gray out beyond the piers. When all the visitors would leave, and the parks would shut down, and it would be just us, alone in our own world at the spit end of a continent.

I couldn't stand it. That was when I started sneaking back up to the watery world of the Bowery again, after hours. Not that anyone would miss me. Carlotta was the attraction; out-and-out madness always sells better than the more subtle kind. Brinckerhoff kept harping on my failure to come up with some kind of act to match her: another tiny general's uniform, perhaps, or maybe a stovepipe hat so I could be a pint-sized Abe Lincoln.

"If you're not goin' to be a proper consort, why then you'd better consort," he warned again.

But I was tired of Carlotta's act myself. There is no aphrodisiac like madness, but it wears off quickly. Not that she ever reneged on our unspoken bargain: I had complete access to all that perfectly proportioned beauty. Soon, though, it had no more appeal to me than the matching oak pistols or the miniature Velázquez copy above our fireplace.

She could feel her allure diminishing: Like all great actors, she was sensitive to the slightest fluctuation in how she was adored.

"Do you want Us to dance for you?" she volunteered one night, surprising me, dragging her costume, wooden knee clogs and all, into the study where I was sipping brandy in my smoking jacket and pyjamas, cutting my way through Roosevelt's latest tome about slaughtering gazelles on the Serengeti.

"We have not danced for you for a long time," she said, and I was so touched by her offer that I let her.

It was the same, strangely mesmerizing dance she had performed for the Baxter Street Dudes that night in the Grand Duke's Theatre. The magical transformation from mechanical doll to living beauty, back to doll again, performed as perfectly as ever, without music, and an audience of one. So moving that when she had finished, falling woodenly to her knees, I leapt out of my chair and went to her, lifting her up by her hand.

"Doesn't it . . . don't you feel . . . it *humbles* you?" I asked her, mortified now that she would do such a thing for me.

"Nothing humbles a queen," she informed me. "Haven't you learned that by now?"

I picked her up, fragile china package that she was, and carried her right back to her imperial bed in her royal bedroom, and ravished her thoroughly. But it was never the same: The queen in exile, the queen in chains, dancing for a gang of orphaned toughs was one thing. The queen at her duties, presiding over our sequestered, sideshow world was another, and I no longer wanted any part of it.

I returned to my Bowery dives, hunting for—what? Another such fantasy? It was foolish, I knew: a mindless debauch of drinking and voyeurism. I didn't care. I went too far, was far too careless—which was how I came to be dangled on that monster's knee at the dog pit, my back nearly cracked open like a lobster's.

The thing was, I still preferred the old dream, the old pretense, to this new, fantastic existence: the one where I pretended to be a boy. Nobody else wanted to see that act. I could walk, invisible, through the nighttime streets, and I would be the only witness to my depravation. That was how it had to be.

I had decided: There would be no issue. No fruitful marriage, no happy, make-believe existence in our gingerbread city. The joke had gone on long enough, and it was an iron law of vaudeville—every gag must have its end.

BOREDOM

Maxim Gorky

—Maxim Gorky (1868–1936) visited Coney Island during his 1907 tour of America. This brilliant essay, which appeared in the Independent *the same year, shows Gorky to be alternately disgusted and amused by America's legendary nickel heaven.*

WITH THE ADVENT OF night a fantastic city all of fire suddenly rises from the ocean into the sky. Thousands of ruddy sparks glimmer in the darkness, limning in fine, sensitive outline on the black background of the sky, shapely towers of miraculous castles, palaces and temples. Golden gossamer threads tremble in the air. They intertwine in transparent, flaming patterns, which flutter and melt away in love with their own beauty mirrored in the waters. Fabulous and beyond conceiving, ineffably beautiful, is this fiery scintillation. It burns but does not consume. Its palpitations are scarce visible. In the wilderness of sky and ocean rises the magic picture of a flaming city. Over it quiver the reddened heavens, and below the water reflects its contours, blending them into a whimsical blotch of molten gold.

Strange thoughts fill the mind at the sight of this play of fire. In the halls of the palaces, in the radiant gleam of flaming mirth, methinks, strains of music float, soft and proud, such as mortal ear has never heard. On the melodious current of their sounds the best thoughts of the world are carried along like sailing stars. The stars meet in a sacred dance, they throw out dazzling sparks, and as they clasp in a momentary embrace, they give birth to new flames, new thoughts.

I see a huge cradle, marvelously wrought of golden tissue, flowers and stars rocking yonder in the soft darkness, upon the trembling bosom of the ocean.

There at night rests the sun.

But the sun of the day brings man nearer to the truth of life. Then the fiery magic castles are tall white buildings.

The blue mist of the ocean vapors mingles with the drab smoke of the metropolis across the harbor. Its flimsy white structures are enveloped in a transparent sheet, in which they quiver like a mirage. They seem to beckon alluringly, and offer quiet and beauty.

The city hums with its constant insatiate, hungry roar. The strained sound, agitating the air and the soul, the ceaseless bellow of iron, the melancholy wail of life driven by the power of gold, the cold, cynical whistle of the Yellow Devil scare the people away from the turmoil of the earth burdened and besmirched by the ill-smelling body of the city. And the people go forth to the shore of the sea, where the beautiful white buildings stand and promise respite and tranquility.

The buildings huddle close together on a long, sandy strip of land, which, like a sharp knife, plunges deep into the dark water. The sand glitters in the sun with a warm, yellow gleam, and the transparent buildings stand out on its velvety expanse like thin white silk embroidery. The effect is as of rich garments thrown carelessly on the bosom of the island by some bather before plunging into the waters.

I turn my gaze wistfully upon this island. I long to nestle in its downy texture. I would recline on its luxurious folds, and from there look out into the wide spaces, where white birds dart swiftly and noiselessly, where ocean and sky lie drowsing in the scorching gleam of the sun.

This is Coney Island.

On Monday the metropolitan newspapers triumphantly announce:

"Three Hundred Thousand People in Coney Island Yesterday. Twenty-three Children Lost."

"There's something doing there," the reader thinks.

First a long ride by trolley thru Brooklyn and Long Island amid the dust and noise of the streets. Then the gaze is met by the sight of dazzling, magnificent Coney Island. From the very first moment of arrival at this city of fire, the eye is blinded. It is assailed by thousands of cold, white sparks, and for a long time can distinguish nothing in the scintillating dust round about. Everything whirls and dazzles, and blends into a tempestuous ferment of fiery foam. The visitor is stunned; his consciousness is withered by the intense gleam; his thoughts are rented from his mind; he becomes a particle in the crowd. People wander about in the flashing, blinding fire, intoxicated and devoid of will. A dull-white mist penetrates their brains, greedy expectation envelopes their souls. Dazed by the brilliancy the throngs wind about like dark bands in the surging sea of light, pressed upon all sides by the black bournes of night.

Everywhere electric bulbs shed their cold, garish gleam. They shine on posts and walls, on window easings and cornices; they stretch in an even line along the high tubes of the power-house; they burn on all the roofs, and prick the eve with the sharp needles of their dead, indifferent sparkle. The people screw up their eyes, and smiling disconcertedly crawl along the ground like the heavy line of a tangled chain.

A man must make a great effort not to lose himself in the crowd, not to be overwhelmed by his amazement—an amazement in which there is neither transport nor joy. But if he succeeds in individualizing himself, he finds that these millions of fires produce a dismal, all-revealing light. Tho they hint at the possibility of beauty, they everywhere discover a dull, gloomy ugliness. The city, magic and fantastic from afar, now appears an absurd jumble of straight lines of wood, a cheap, hastily constructed toyhouse for the amusement of children. Dozens of white buildings, monstrously diverse, not one with even the suggestion of beauty. They are built of wood, and smeared over with peeling white paint, which gives them the appearance of suffering with the same skin disease. The high turrets and low colonnades extend in two dead-even lines insipidly pressing upon each other.

Everything is stripped naked by the dispassionate glare. The glare is everywhere, and nowhere a shadow. Each building stands there like a dumbfounded fool with wide-open mouth, and sends forth the glare of brass trumpets and the whining rumble of orchestions. Inside is a cloud of smoke and the dark figures of the people. The people eat, drink and smoke.

But no human voice is heard. The monotonous hissing of the arc lights fills the air, the sounds of music, the cheap notes of the orchestrions, and the thin, continuous sputtering of the sausage-frying counters. All these sounds mingle in an importunate hum, as of some thick, taut chord. And if the human voice breaks into this ceaseless resonance, it is like a frightened whisper. Everything 'round about glitters insolently and reveals its own dismal ugliness.

The soul is seized with a desire for a living, beautiful fire, a sublime fire, which should free the people from the slavery of varied boredom. For this boredom deafens their ears and blinds their eyes. The soul would burn away all this allurement, all this mad frenzy, this dead magnificence and spiritual penury. It would have a merry dancing and shouting and singing; it would see a passionate play of the motley tongues of fire; it would have joyousness and life.

The people huddled together in this city actually number hundreds of thousands. They swarm into the cages like black flies. Children walk about, silent, with gaping mouths and dazzled eyes. They look around with such intensity, such seriousness, that the sight of them feeding their little souls upon this hideousness, which they mistake for beauty, inspires a pained sense of pity. The men's faces, shaven even to the mustache, all strangely like one another, are grave and immobile. The majority bring their wives and children along, and feel that they are benefactors of their families, because they provide not only bread, but also magnificent shows. They enjoy the tinsel, but, too serious to betray their pleasure, they keep their thin lips pressed together, and look from the corners of their screwed-up eyes, like people whom nothing can astonish. Yet, under the mask of indifference simulated by the man of mature experience, a strained desire can be detected to take in all the delights of the city. The men with the serious faces, smiling indifferently and concealing the satisfied gleam of their sparkling eyes, seat themselves on the backs of the wooden horses and elephants of the merry-go-round and, dangling their feet, wait with nervous impatience for the keen pleasure of flying along the rails. With a whoop they dart up to the top, with a whistle they descend again. After this stirring journey they draw their skin tight on their faces again and go to taste of new pleasures.

The amusements are without number. There on the summit of an iron tower two long white wings rock slowly up and down. At the end of each wing hang cages, and in these cages are people. When one of the wings rises heavily toward the sky the faces of the occupants of the cages grow sadly serious. They all look in round-eyed silence at the ground receding from them. In the cages of the other wing, then carefully descending, the faces of the people are radiant with smiles. Joyous screams are heard, which strangely remind one of the merry yelp of a puppy let to the floor after he has been held up in the air by the scruff of his neck.

Boats fly in the air around the top of another tower, a third keeps turning about and impels some sort of iron balloon, a fourth, a fifth—they all move and blaze and call with the mute shouts of cold fire. Everything rocks and roars and bellows and turns the heads of the people. They are filled with contented *ennui*, their nerves are racked by an intricate maze of motion and dazzling fire. Bright eyes grow still brighter, as if the brain paled and lost blood in the strange turmoil of the white, glittering wood. The *ennui*, which issues from under the pressure of self-disgust, seems to turn and turn in a slow circle of agony. It drags tens of thousands of uniformly dark people into its somber dance, and sweeps them into a will-less heap, as the wind sweeps the rubbish of the street. Then it scatters them apart and sweeps them together again.

Inside the buildings the people are also seeking pleasure, and here, too, all look serious. The amusement offered is educational. The people are shown hell, with all the terrors and punishments that await those who have transgressed the sacred laws created for them.

Hell is constructed of papier maché and painted dark red. Everything in it is on fire—paper fire—and it is filled with the thick, dirty odor of grease. Hell is very badly done. It would arouse disgust in a man of even modest demands. It is represented by a cave with stones thrown together in chaotic masses. The cave is penetrated by a reddish darkness. On one of the stones sits Satan, clothed in red. Grimaces distort his lean, brown face. He rubs his hands contentedly, as a man who is doing a good business. He must be very uncomfortable on his perch, a paper stone, which cracks and rocks. But he pretends not to notice his discomfort, and looks down at the evil demons busying themselves with the sinners.

A girl is there who has just bough a new hat. She is trying it on before a mirror, happy and contented. But a pair of little fiends, apparently very greedy, steal up behind her and seize her under the armpits. She screams, but it is too late. The demons put her into a long, smooth trough, which descends tightly into a pit in the middle of the cave. From the pit issue a gray vapor and tongues of fire made of red paper. The girl, with her mirror and her new hat, goes down into the pit, lying on her back in the trough.

A young man has drunk a glass of whisky. Instantly the devils clutch him, and down he goes thru that same hole in the floor of the platform.

The atmosphere in hell is stifling. The demons are insignificant looking and feeble. Apparently they are greatly exhausted by their work and irritated by its sameness and evident futility. When they fling the sinners unceremoniously into the trough like logs of wood, you feel like crying out:

"Enough, enough nonsense, boys!"

A girl extracts some coins from her companion's purse. Forthwith the spies, the demons, attack her, to the great satisfaction of Satan, who sits there snickering and dangling his crooked legs joyfully. The demons frown angrily up at the idle fellow, and spitefully hurl into the jaws of the burning pit everybody who enters hell by chance, on business or out of curiosity.

The audience looks on these horrors in silence with serious faces.

The hall is dark. Some sturdy fellow with curly hair holds forth in a lugubrious voice while he points to the stage.

He says that if the people do not want to be victims of Satan with the red garments and the crooked legs, they should not kiss girls to whom they are not married, because then the girls might become bad women. Women outcasts ought not to steal money from the pockets of their companions, and people should not drink whisky or beer or other liquors that arouse the passions; they should not visit saloons, but the churches, for churches are not only more beneficial to the soul, but they are also cheaper.

He talks monotonously, wearily. He himself does not seem to believe in what he was told to preach.

You involuntarily apostrophize the owners of this corrective amusement for sinners:

"Gentlemen, if you wish morality to work on men's souls with the force of castor oil, you ought to pay your preachers more."

At the conclusion of the terrible story a nauseatingly beautiful angel appears from a corner of the cavern. He hangs on a wire, and moves across the entire cave, holding a wooden trumpet, pasted over with gilt paper, between his teeth. On catching sight of him, Satan dives like a fish into the pit after the sinners. A crash is heard, the paper stones are hurled down, and the devils run off cheerfully to rest from their labor. The curtain drops. The public rises and leaves. Some venture to laugh. The majority, however, seem absorbed in reflection. Perhaps they think:

"If hell is so nasty, it isn't worth sinning."

They proceed further. In the next place they are shown "The World Beyond the Grave." It is large, and also made of papier maché. Here the souls of the dead, hideously garbed, wander in confusion. You may wink at them, but you may not touch them. This is a fact. They must feel greatly bored in the dusk of the subterranean labyrinth, shut up within rugged walls, in a cold, damp atmosphere. Some souls cough disagreeably, others silently chew tobacco, spitting yellow saliva on the ground. One soul, leaning in a corner against the wall, smokes a cigar.

When you pass by them they look into your face with colorless eyes. They compress their lips tightly, and shiver with cold as they thrust their hands into the gray folds of their rags of the other world. They are hungry, these poor souls, and many of them evidently suffer from rheumatism. The public looks at them silently. It breathes in the moist air, and feels its soul with dismal *ennui*, which extinguishes thought, as a wet, dirty cloth extinguishes the fire of a smoldering coal.

In another place again "The Flood" is displayed. The flood, you know, was brought on to punish the inhabitants of the earth for their sins.

And all the spectacles in this city have one purpose: to show the people how they will be punished after death for their sins, to teach them to live upon earth humbly, and to obey the laws.

Everywhere the one commandment is repeated:

"Don't!"

For it helps to crush the spirit of the majority of the public—the working people.

But it is necessary to make money, and in the commodious corners of the bright city, as everywhere in the world, depravity laughs disdainfully at hypocrisy and falsehood. Of course the depravity is hidden, and, of course, it's a wearying, tiresome depravity, but it also is "for the people." It is organized as a paying business, as a means to extract their earnings from the pockets of the people. Fed by the passion for gold it appears in a form vile and despicable indeed in this marsh of glittering boredom.

The people feed on it.

The people are always constrained. As yet they have never acted as free men. So they permit the enslavement of their bodies and their souls: for this alone are they to blame.

They pour in thick streams between two lines of dazzlingly illuminated houses, and the houses snap them up with their hungry jaws. On the right they are intimidated by the terrors of eternal torture.

"Do not sin!" they are warned. "Sin is dangerous!"

On the left, in the spacious dancing hall, women slowly waltz about, and here everything cries out to them:

"Sin! For sin is pleasant!"

Blinded by the gleam of the light, lured by the cheap, but glittering sumptuousness, intoxicated by the noise, they turn about in a slow dance of weary boredom. To the left they go willingly and blindly to Sin, to the right to hear exhortations to Holy Living.

This aimless straying stupefies the people. But for that very reason it is profitable both to the traders in morality and the vendors of depravity.

Life is made for the people to work six days in the week, sin on the seventh, and pay for their sins, confess their sins, and pay for the confession.

The fires hiss like thousands of excited serpents, dark swarms of insects buzz feebly and dismally, and the people slowly wind about in the dazzling cobwebs of the amusment halls. Without haste, without a laugh or a smile on their smoothly shaven faces, they lazily crowd thru all the doors, stand long before the animal cages and chew tobacco and spit.

In one huge cage a man chases Bengal tigers with shots from a revolver and the merciless blows of a thin whip. The handsome beasts maddened by terror, blinded by the lights, deafened by the music and revolver shots, fling themselves about between the iron bars, and snort and roar. Their green eyes flash, their lips tremble; they gnash their teeth in fury, and menacingly raise now one forepaw now the other. But the man keeps shooting straight into their eyes and the loud report of the blank cartridges and the smart blows of the whip, drive one powerful, supple creature into a corner of the cage. All in a tremble of revolt, seized with the impotent anguish of the powerful, choking with the sharp pang of humiliation, the imprisoned beast sinks down for a moment, and looks on with dazed eyes, his serpentine tail writhing nervously.

The elastic body rolls itself into a firm ball, and twitches, ready to leap into the air, to bury its claws in the flesh of the man with the whip, rend him, annihilate him.

The hind legs of the animal quiver like a spring, his neck stretches, the green irises flash blood-red sparks. The watchful, waiting eyes that blaze in the vindictive countenance confront beyond the bars the dim, coppery blotch of a thousand colorless eyes, set in uniform, yellow faces, coldly expectant.

The face of the crowd, terrible in its dead immobility, waits. The crowd, too, hankers for blood and it waits, not out of revengefulness, but from curiosity, like a satiated, long-subdued beast.

The tiger draws his head in his shoulders and looks out sadly with his wide-open eyes. His whole body sinks back softly, and his skin wrinkles up, as if an icy rain had fallen on a surface heated by the passion for vengeance.

The man runs about the cage, shoots his pistol and cracks his whip, and shouts like a madman. His shouts are intended to hide his painful dread of the animals. The crowd regards the capers of the man, and waits in suspense for the fatal attack. They wait; unconsciously the primitive instinct is awakened in them. They crave fight, they want to feel the delicious shiver produced by the sight of two bodies intertwining, the splutter of blood and pieces of torn, steaming human flesh flying thru the cage and falling on the floor. They want to hear the roar, the cries, the shrieks of agony.

But the brain of the throng is already infected by the poison of various prohibitions and intimidations. Desiring blood, the crowd is afraid. It wishes, yet does not wish. In this struggle within itself it experiences a sharp gratification—it lives.

The man has frightened all the animals. The tigers softly withdraw into a corner of the cage, and the man, all in a sweat, satisfied that he has remained alive that day, bows to the coppery face of the crowd, as to an idol. He endeavors to conceal the tremor on his pale lips with a smile.

The crowd shouts and claps its hands and sighs—is it relief or is it regret?

Then the crowd breaks into dark pieces, and disperses over the slimy marsh of boredom.

Having delighted their eyes with the picture of man's rivalry with beasts, the human animals go in search of other amusements. There is a circus. In the center of the arena a man tosses two children into the air with his long legs. The children dart over them like two white doves with broken wings. Sometimes they fall to the ground. Then they cautiously look into the blood-suffused face of their father or master, and again ascend into the air. The crowd have disposed themselves about the arena, and look on. When the children slip from the performer's legs, a thrill of animation passes over all the countenances, as a wind sends a light ripple over the slumbering waters of a stagnant pool.

You long to see a drunken man with a jovial face, who would push and sing and bawl, happy because he is drunk, and sincerely wishing all good people the same.

The music rends the air. The orchestra is poor, the musicians worn out. The sounds of the brass instruments stray about as if they limped, as if no even course were possible for them. Even the circus horses, who are used to everything, turn cautiously aside, and nervously twitch their sharp ears, as if they wanted to shake off the rasping tin sounds. This music of the poor for the amusement of slaves puts strange notions into your head. You would like to tear the very largest brass trumpet from the musician's hand, and blow into it with all the power of your lungs, long and loud, so terribly that all the people would run from this prison, driven by the fury of the mad sounds.

No far from the orchestra is a cage with bears. One of them, a stout brown bear with little, shrewd eyes, stands in the middle of the cage, and shakes his head deliberately. Apparently he thinks:

"All this is sensible only if it's contrived to blind, deafen, and mutilate the people. Then, of course, the end justifies the means. But if people come here to be amused, I have no faith in their sanity."

Two other bears sit opposite each other, as if playing chess. Another is busy raking up straw in a corner of the cage. He knocks his claws against the bars. His snout is disappointedly calm. He seems to expect nothing from this life and has made up his mind to go to bed.

The animals arouse the keenest interest. The waiting eyes of the spectators follow them steadily and minutely. The people appear to be searching for something long forgotten in the free and powerful movements of the beautiful bodies of the lion and panther. They thrust sticks thru the gratings, and silently experimenting prod the animals' stomachs and sides and tickle their paws, and look to see what will happen.

The animals that have not yet become familiarized with the character of human beings are angry. They thrust their paws against the bars, and roar. This pleases the spectators. Protected from the beast by the iron grill, and assured of their safety, the people look calmly into the blood-shot eyes and smile contentedly. But the majority of the animals pay no heed to the people. When they receive a blow with a stick, or are spat upon, they slowly rise, and without looking at the insulter retire into a distant corner of the cage. There the lions, ligers, panthers, and leopards couch their beautiful, powerful bodies. In the darkness their round irises burn with the green fire of scorn for mankind. And the people glancing at them once again walk away, saying:

"Uninteresting!"

A brass band plays desperately at a semi-circular entrance, a kind of dark, wide-gaping jaw, within which the backs of chairs stare like a row of teeth. In front of the musicians is a post to which a pair of monkeys are tied by a thin chain. It is a mother and her child. The child presses closely against the mother's breast, and its long, thin hands, with their little fingers cross over the mother's back. The mother encircles the baby in a firm embrace with one arm. The other is cautiously extended forward, its fingers nervously crooked, ready to seize, to scratch, to strike. The mother's strained, wide-open gaze clearly bespeaks impotent despair, the anguished expectation of unavoidable insult and injury, melancholy rage. The child has nestled its cheek against its mother's breast and looks slantwise at the people with cold terror, motionless, hopeless. Apparently it has been filled with dread from the first day of its life, and the dread has frozen and congealed in it for all days to come. Displaying her white teeth the mother, without for a second removing the hand that clasps the child of her flesh, continually rebuffs the canes, the umbrellas, the hands of the onlookers, her tormentors.

The spectators are many. They are all white-skinned savages, men and women in straw hats and hats with feathers. It is fearfully amusing for all of them to see how skillfully the monkey mother shields her child from the blows they aim at its little body.

The mother quickly turns on a smooth space the size of a plate. She risks falling any second under the feet of the crowd, but she tirelessly repels everything that threatens to come in contact with her child. Sometimes she does not succeed in warding off a blow, and then she shrieks out pitifully. Her arm quickly cuts the air like a lash, but the onlookers are so many, and every one desires so much to pinch, to strike, to pull the monkey by the tail or by the chain around its neck, that sometimes she misses. Her eyes blink thoughtlessly, and radiate wrinkles of injury and distress appear around her mouth.

The child's hands squeeze her bosom. It clasps her so firmly that its hands are almost hidden in her thin hair. It has sunk down motionless, and its eyes stare fixedly at the coppery blotch of the faces all around.

Sometimes one of the musicians turns the stupid, brass bellow of his instrument upon the monkey, and overwhelms the animal with a deafening noise. The little baby timidly clasps the mother's body still harder, shows its teeth and looks at the musician sharply.

The people laugh and nod their heads approvingly to the musician. He is satisfied and a minute later repeats the feat.

Among the spectators are women, some apparently mothers. But no one utters a word of protest against this cruel fun. All are satisfied.

Man is nurtured on terror, so he endeavors to inspire others with terror of himself. But he arouses only disgust, the poor, unfortunate wretch!

This torture continues thru the whole long night and part of the morning.

Alongside the orchestra is the cage of an elephant. He is an elderly gentleman with a worn, glossy skin. He thrusts his trunk thru the grating and swings it with serious mien. He looks at the public, and, good wise animal that he is, he thinks:

"Of course, these scoundrels, swept together by the dirty broom of tedium, are capable of making sport even of their prophets. So I've heard old elephants tell. But I'm sorry for the monkey, anyway. I've heard also that human beings, like jackals and hyenas, sometimes tear one another to pieces. But that's no consolation to the monkey."

You look at the pair of eyes in which is depicted the grief of a mother powerless to protect her child, and at the eyes of the baby, in which the deep, cold, dread of man has congealed into immobile rigidity. You look at the people capable of deriving amusement from the torture of a living creature, and turning to the monkey, you say:

"Little beast, forgive them! They know not what they do. They will become better in time."

Thus, when night comes, a fantastic magic city, all of fire, suddenly blazes up from the ocean. Without consuming, it burns long against the dark background of the sky, its beauty mirrored in the broad, gleaming bosom of the sea.

In the glittering gossamer of its fantastic buildings, tens of thousands of gray people, like patches on the ragged clothes of a beggar, creep along with weary faces and colorless eyes.

Mean panderers to debased tastes unfold the disgusting nakedness of their falsehood, the *naïveté* of their shrewdness, the hypocrisy and insatiable force of their greed. The cold gleam of the dead fire bares the stupidity of it all. Its pompous glitter rests upon everything 'round about the people.

But the precaution has been taken to blind the people, and they drink in the vile poison with silent rapture. The poison contaminates their souls. Boredom whirls about in an idle dance, expiring in the agony of its inanition.

One thing alone is good in the garish city: You can drink in hatred to your soul's content, hatred sufficient to last thruout life, hatred of the power of stupidity!

THE BIG FERRIS WHEEL

Robert Graves

—Upon its unveiling at the 1893 Chicago World's Fair, the Ferris wheel was seen as a landmark achievement in machine-age ingenuity. This article from the now-defunct Alleghenian *recounts the excitement.*

It Is the Chief Sensation of the World's Fair.
Inventor Declared a Genius.
When He First Broached His Plans to the Directors of the World's Fair They Thought He Was Crazy—A Description of the Wheel As It Stands in Midway Plaisance.
From The Alleghenian, *1 July 1893.*
World's Fair, June 28.—Special. By Robert Graves.

There is nothing in the World's Columbian exposition that compares in genuine novelty and sensationalism with the great vertical wheel which stands in the very center of Midway plaisance. In these letters I long ago predicted that this giant structure would be the chief sensation of the World's fair, just as the Eiffel tower was the chief sensation of the Paris exposition, and my prediction has been verified. Though the wheel has been in operation to the public but a few days, vast crowds of people constantly surround it watching its movements, and thousands more pay their half dollar apiece for the privilege of going around upon it.

Considered from the engineering standpoint as well as from that of popular interest this is a greater marvel than the Eiffel tower, which earned a great reputation for its builder and a small fortune for its owners. Whereas the Eiffel tower was simply a bridge a thousand feet long erected upon a strong foundation and placed on end, a simple construction like a couple of Chicago's tall steel buildings stood one upon the other and resting upon a tall foundation of sufficient strength to hold them, the vertical wheel is a bridge 825 feet long, 30 feet wide and constructed of steel, twisted into a circle and hung upon an axle round which it revolves by means of the force given it by powerful steam engines. The Eiffel tower involved no new engineering principle, and when finished was a thing dead and lifeless. The wheel, on the other hand, has movement, grace, the indescribable charm possessed by a vast body in action.

What the genesis of the vertical wheel was in the brain of its inventor is an interesting thought. Undoubtedly it had its origin in the horizontal merry-go-round, and that started in the whirligig which country boys used to make with a post and a plank set across the top of it, pinioned at its middle. From the whirligig to the flying horses or merry-go-round was but a step. The merry-go-round has had its greatest development at the sea shore resorts of Coney Island and Atlantic City. At the latter place the owner of the merry-go-round owns also a good share of the town. The nimble nickels flowing into his coffers in an uninterrupted stream all summer long have enabled him to buy no end of corner lots and erect brick blocks thereon.

Someone saw that the horizontal wheel was coining money and concluded to go it one better by building a vertical wheel. There are vertical wheels at the sea shore, and some of their kind have been brought to the World's fair and may be seen outside the fair gates taking passengers round at the old rate of a nickel a ride. These small vertical wheels must have been the suggestion to Ferris, the bridge builder and engineer. He said he would build a wheel that would astonish the world, and by the side of the little wheels of the sea shore be as the ocean itself to a mill pond.

He prepared his plans and came to Chicago to ask permission to erect his wheel within the World's fair grounds. At first the fair directors only laughed at him. They thought he was crazy, that he was a crank. Then they granted him a concession, but without any thought that he would ever build his wheel. After a time they concluded that it was not wise to bother themselves further with such a visionary individual, and they cancelled the concession. They were not going to have a wild-eyed man with wheels in his head lumbering up the center of the plaisance with his contraptions. But Ferris, confident of success and backed by ample capital, stuck to the scheme and induced the directors, after a time, to again reconsider their action and again permit him to go ahead. This is the brief history of the struggle this genius had to secure recognition even from such progressive and wide-awake men as the directors of the World's fair. Such has been the history of genius ever.

It is almost impossible either by picture or description in words to give you an idea of what this wheel is like. A mere statement of its dimensions, 250 feet in diameter, 825 feet in circumference, 30 feet broad and weight more than 4,000 tons, does not mean much to the average mind. It may help the reader to understand what the structure is like if I say that the highest point of the wheel is as far from the ground as the top of one ten-story building would be if it were put on the roof of another building of equal height.

When you look at this wheel as it stands on the plaisance you are struck by the resemblance it bears to some mighty bicycle. It has the same sort of a hub, the same rods and struts running therefrom to the periphery, the same light airiness [of] model. In truth, it seems too light. One fears the slender rods which must support the whole enormous weight are too puny to fulfill their office. One cannot avoid the thought of what would happen if a high wind should come sweeping across the prairie and attack this structure broadside. Would the thin rods be sufficient to sustain not only the enormous weight of the structure and that of the 2,000 passengers who might chance to be in the cars but the pressure of the wind as well? Engineer Ferris says the wheel is strong enough to do all this. Other engineers, some of them men of eminence in their profession, say the same thing. Therefore the public seems content to take it for granted that the wheel is not only the greatest novelty of the age, but that riding upon it is as safe as riding over a bridge that is placed horizontally on masonry piers.

There are thirty-six cars on the wheel. Each is 27 feet long, 9 feet high and 13 feet broad. It is like an enormous bird cage. Human beings are to be the inhabitants. The doors are closed when the passengers are within, and locked. The windows are covered with a strong wire netting. There is a conductor to each car to look after the comfort of the passengers. No crank will have an opportunity commit suicide from this wheel, no hysterical woman shall jump from a window. From platforms built on the ground six cars are loaded at one time. Each car will seat, on revolving chairs, forty passengers. Therefore the thirty-six cars will seat 1,440 passengers. But with standing room occupied the wheel has a capacity of 2,000 persons.

As soon as the first six cars are loaded the man in charge gives the signal and the steam is turned into cylinders of the thousand horse-power engine which moves the vast machine. Slowly, with just enough trembling and oscillating to make the nerves of passengers quiver, the wheel must make one entire revolution. By this time the occupants of the coaches have become somewhat accustomed to the novel situation. They have ceased to think of the possible danger and are occupied with the beauty of the panorama which lies far below them.

Now comes the most interesting feature of the trip. The wheel is set in motion at a more rapid pace, though still not very fast, and is not stopped until a complete revolution is made. It is an indescribable sensation, that of revolving through such a vast orbit in a bird cage, that of swinging in a circle far out over the plaisance in one direction, then turning in the other direction, and still higher, and finally beginning the descent from such a great height. People wonder what would happen if the pinions which hold the cars through their roofs should break, or refuse to revolve. They wonder how they would get down if the machinery should break and the engineer be unable to further revolve the wheel, thus leaving them dangling in mid air. While they are thinking of these things the movement ceases, then starts up again, and finally it becomes their turn to step out on the wooden platform and down again to mother earth.

I have no desire to advertise the wheel when I tell you a trip upon it is worth taking. You cannot advertise the wheel, anyway, any more than you can advertise the fair, or the Atlantic ocean. They are all too big. They are their own advertisement. The novel sensation, the opportunity to study a great engineering work, the beauty of the scene presented from the great altitude, all combine to make the trip on this structure fully worth the time and the cost.

As yet there is not the slightest reason to fear the safety of the machine. The steel towers which support the vast bicycle wheel are bedded and bolted into thirty feet of concrete. They are calculated to support five times the weight and the wind pressure produced by a tornado of a hundred and fifty miles an hour. Motion is imparted to the mass by means of huge cogs in which a link belt fits. If anything should break and it be desirable to stop the machinery there is a powerful brake operated by compressed air. The axle which runs from the top of one tower to the other, 140 feet in the air, is the greatest steel forging ever made, being 82 inches in diameter and 45 feet long, weighing fifty-six tons. How Ferris ever got it up there is a mystery to me, but he did it. The cars are so attached to the wheel, it is said, that it is impossible for them to fail to turn so as to preserve the center of gravity.

What is the principle, the chief principle, on which the wheel is constructed? It is that of a bicycle wheel, as I have said, except that this wheel does not rest upon the surface but depends from the steel axle. The lower half of the wheel simply hangs from the mighty axle, and this lower half supports the upper half by means of the steel framework of its two rims. That is the whole thing in a nut shell. The wheel, though apparently rigid in its construction, has just enough elasticity to make this method of support possible, and yet not enough elasticity to produce any appreciable trembling or slipping effect.

Now the World's fair directors are glad they changed their minds and decided to recognize this genius. Not only have they thereby secured the greatest sensation of the fair, but without a dollar of outlay on their part have made certain of an enormous revenue. The exposition gets one-half the earnings of the wheel, and it is estimated the total receipts will average something like $10,000 a day during the remainder of the summer. The cost of the wheel complete, was about $250,000. Engineer Ferris is likely to reap a rich reward for his boldness and enterprise.

FROM CARNIVAL

Arthur H. Lewis

—Arthur H. Lewis traveled with a number of carnivals during what is arguably the industry's twilight years, the late 1960s. This chapter from Carnival *(1970) offers a wistful look at the significance of the carrousel in carnival culture.*

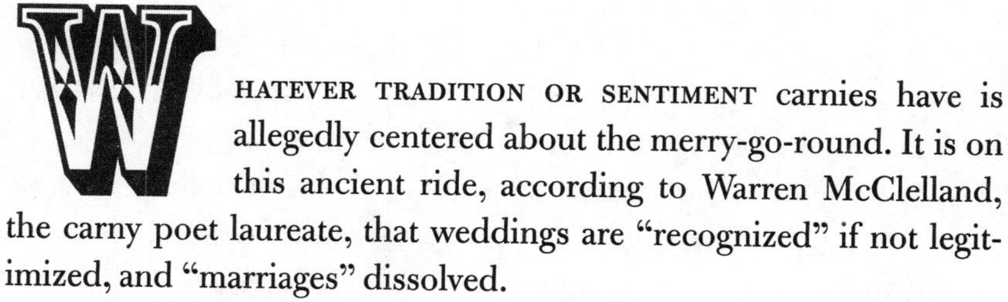

HATEVER TRADITION OR SENTIMENT carnies have is allegedly centered about the merry-go-round. It is on this ancient ride, according to Warren McClelland, the carny poet laureate, that weddings are "recognized" if not legitimized, and "marriages" dissolved.

"One turn for a carny couple," explained Warren, "is sufficient to notify rivals of both sexes that 'holy' bands of matrimony have been tied. Contrariwise, a spouse has only to say to his or her mate, 'I'm going to get on the carrousel.' They have then been given the equivalent of a divorce."

In the light of such importance attached to merry-go-rounds, it is no wonder that Morris Hannum was proud to own the world's only one that runs backward.

"Take a spin," Morris urged. "You'll see what I mean."

On my first ride I detected not a whit of difference between it and others. Not until I talked to Ralph Murdoch, Hannum's carrousel operator, did I become aware of its rarity. At Ralph's suggestion I mounted a white horse, and as the electric calliope regaled me with nostalgic tunes, I made a few dozen circles.

Actually, from what Morris had said, I expected the rear end of my horse to lead the stallion's head in backward flight, and I'd be moving in the wrong direction. When this didn't occur, and the horses, lions, tigers and leopards traveled forward, I was convinced Hannum had been pulling my leg.

"Not so," said Ralph. "You were going clockwise. All the others everywhere in the world go counterclockwise. Look at the horses' manes. They're on the inside, not on the outside where they should be."

I looked at "my" white horse now being ridden by a gleeful little boy. What Ralph had said was true.

"Started this way," Ralph, a tall, handsome man in his early thirties, explained. "As carrousels go, Mr. Hannum's is practically new. You should see some of them built before the turn of the century and still working. Ours was made in 1954.

"It went on the fritz a few seasons back. We sent to the factory up in Buffalo for parts. As a matter of fact, they were quite expensive—cost twelve hundred dollars. But somehow the factory failed to include a vital 'organ' or else sent us a defective one. When I reassembled the motor, the damned thing ran ass-backward.

"No matter what I did I couldn't reverse it. Since I've been working with this particular ride for the past twelve summers I considered myself an expert."

Ralph said he took up the problem with his boss.

"When Mr. Hannum saw it traveling in the wrong direction and I admitted there was nothing I could do, he burst out laughing. 'The damned thing's hexed,' he said. So I asked him did he want a company expert to come down from Buffalo.

" 'No,' he told me. 'Somebody's cast a spell on the poor thing and it might be bad luck for mortal interference. Turn the animals around; nobody'll notice the difference.' That's what I did. But Mr. Hannum was wrong about no one noticing the difference. Every once in a while I'll see someone, usually a carny, standing there looking at it in a puzzled fashion. He'll scratch his head, perhaps walk away and come back again. He knows something is screwy, but he can't quite figure out what.

"Then suddenly he'll grin and shake his head. He'll come to me and I'll tell him what went wrong."

I asked Ralph, who is somewhat of a philosopher, why merry-go-rounds fascinate him. He removed his heavy horn-rimmed glasses and thoughtfully stroked his beardless chin.

"I suppose," he replied slowly, "it's an escape to a world within a world where everyone is happy if only for a fragment of time. I listen to the calliope wheezing out a gay tune and watch the kids scramble aboard. They're all gleeful, their stomachs tingling with excitement, and they got that tiny but essential touch of fear.

"I see the bigger kids, the six- and seven-year-olds, leap on their 'mounts,' convinced, of course, that the horses are real and ready to obey riders' commands. And I see mothers, fathers and grandmothers and grandfathers strap four- and five-year-olds securely in lion- and tiger-drawn carriages, then step down and wave to them every turn of the wheel.

"I *know* these parents and grandparents are recalling their own childhood pleasures. Sometimes, more often than you'd imagine, there'll be an old gentleman accompanying a child, pretending he's taking a ride to protect his grandson or granddaughter. But it's only pretense. He's trying to recapture a segment of his own childhood.

"At least two or three times a season I'll see an elderly couple whispering to each other in front of the booth, then finally buying a pair of tickets for themselves."

Ralph smiled.

"Sentimental? Of course it is. The merry-go-round's the heart of the carnival. That's why every midway *must* have one, even if it doesn't make enough money to justify the cost of a privilege."

Ralph did not want to discuss his off-season work. All he'd admit was that he is in a profession he practices in the Chicago area.

"When the first of May comes and I 'get sawdust in my shoes,' " he said, "off I am for the ten weeks. That's as long as I dare stay away."

I asked Ralph if it were true about the romantic functions merry-go-rounds are supposed to play in midway marriages and divorces. He shook his head.

"That's for the birds! Participants in carnival 'romances' couldn't care less about 'formal' or 'informal' acquisition or disposal of a mate. When they want to change partners for the night or for the season they just up and change them. Carnies are *not* sentimental."

One outstanding exception is Mr. Oscar C. Buck, carnival owner and whittler of carrousel animals. Mr. Buck has a favorite, a huge black stallion christened King, lovingly carved by Oscar and his late father, another Oscar C. Buck, more than half a century ago. It has been in almost continuous use ever since. The number of children who've sat astride this magnificent beast's broad back since 1916 must be staggering.

"Not only kids," said Mr. Buck, "but their children and grandchildren. Last year in Gastonia, North Carolina, he was ridden by the great-grandson of a youngster who was on King a couple days after the horse left our shop in Jamaica, Long Island, June, 1916.

"Come up to me afterward and told me. I shook his hand and wrote out a lifetime pass good for the man himself, his great-grandson and for *his* great-grandson. I won't be around then. Chances are King won't be, either. But you can bet there'll still be merry-go-rounds and they'll still be popular, even with kids comin' back to earth after spendin' vacations on the moon."

From his office trailer window, Oscar can and frequently does look out on his clean midway and see the merry-go-round, never set up at a distance of more than a hundred feet. Every time the ride comes to a halt, King is in his owner's direct line of vision. This is no accident. It's an unwritten, yet strictly observed rule, no matter where the carnival is set up.

I rode King myself on a cool, autumn night at Carthage, North Carolina. A few hours later Oscar told me something of the black stallion's history and a bit of his own as well.

"My father," recalled Oscar, a large, pleasant-spoken, clean-shaven man, "came from Hohensellen, Germany, in the Black Forest region where the best wood-carvers are from. He was one of the finest, his attention to detail was nearly unbelievable. I inherited a little of that.

"He emigrated to the United States sometime around 1890 and

settled on Long Island where he had his shop. I was born there in 1896. When I was old enough, my father and I went into business together. We got a contract to make merry-go-round animals for the Luff Company which assembled and sold them to carnivals and amusement parks all over the country.

"Until 1932 every horse, every lion, every tiger, every leopard and every other animal was hand-carved. They were beautiful, each one different, real works of art."

He sighed.

"Not like today, everything machine-tooled and turned out on a beltline. Well, to go on, my father and I worked side by side for many, many years until he died. Between us we created hundreds of wonderful animals. But my favorite is the first one I used on my own merry-go-round. It took the pair of us more than a week to carve it. That was fifty-two years ago."

Oscar smiled.

"We called him King. I saw you mount him a little while ago and I guess my ride boy told you all about it."

I shook my head; the ride boy had been far too busy to tell me anything. But I did admit that Lou Pease, who runs the Buck kootch shows, had briefed me.

My host, despite a large, bright red sign reading: POSITIVELY NO SMOKING ANYWHERE IN THIS TRAILER and hung in a prominent position on the wall, lit a cigarette from the butt of a smoldering one and continued.

"I was twenty-one years old and I got itchy pants. Bought a merry-go-round and another couple rides and started out in the carnival business. 'Course, off-season when I wasn't on the road I went back to work with my father.

"King went with me all the time. By 1941 my carnival had gotten pretty big and I said to myself I'd better get a new carrousel. The original looked pretty shabby compared to all the other new rides I'd bought.

"So I stored it in a barn up in Keene, New Hampshire, and 'retired' King. When the 1942 season began, I bought a brand-new merry-go-round, a forty-foot, two abreast, from the Alan Hershel Company. It was a beauty and damned expensive, but I missed my black stallion.

"After the season was over I returned to Keene and went out to that barn with my trucks to pick up King and reassemble the old carrousel. I got sick when I saw what happened meantime. The barn had been struck by lightning and most of the merry-go-round caught on fire.

"I felt almost like a part of me was burned, too. When I poked through the ruins, there was King, a bit scorched but in good condition otherwise, ready to go to work again. And the ride wasn't in as bad a shape as I thought it would be.

"We'd closed the Long Island shop years before, right after my father died. Our quarters were in Florida, where they still are. Well, that winter I stopped almost everything else and went to work on the old merry-go-round. I repainted King, repaired the other animals and carved a few new ones just like I used to out in Jamaica with my father.

"Then I reassembled the ride and took it on the road. Been with me ever since. That's what you see out there now. I've done all right in this business and I got a Sky Diver costs over a hundred thousand dollars, plus a couple others cost near as much. But nothing, believe me, mister, is ever gonna persuade me to 'retire' King again."

KEELA, THE OUTCAST INDIAN MAIDEN

Eudora Welty

—Eudora Welty's (1909–2001) short story "Keela, the Outcast Indian Maiden" was originally published in the 1941 collection A Curtain of Green and Other Stories. *It was Welty's first book.*

NE MORNING IN SUMMERTIME, when all his sons and daughters were off picking plums and Little Lee Roy was all alone, sitting on the porch and only listening to the screech owls away down in the woods, he had a surprise.

First he heard white men talking. He heard two white men coming up the path from the highway. Little Lee Roy ducked his head and held his breath; then he patted all around back of him for his crutches. The chickens all came out from under the house and waited attentively on the steps.

The men came closer. It was the young man who was doing all of the talking. But when they got through the fence, Max, the older man, interrupted him. He tapped him on the arm and pointed his thumb toward Little Lee Roy.

He said, "Bud? Yonder he is."

But the younger man kept straight on talking, in an explanatory voice.

"Bud?" said Max again. "Look, Bud, yonder's the only little club-footed nigger man was ever around Cane Springs. Is he the party?"

They came nearer and nearer to Little Lee Roy and then stopped and stood there in the middle of the yard. But the young man was so excited he did not seem to realize that they had arrived anywhere. He was only about twenty years old, very sunburned. He talked constantly, making only one gesture—raising his hand stiffly and then moving it a little to one side.

"They dressed it in a red dress, and it ate chickens alive," he said. "I sold tickets and I thought it was worth a dime, honest. They gimme a piece of paper with the thing wrote off I had to say. That was easy. 'Keela, the Outcast Indian Maiden!' I call it out through a pasteboard megaphone. Then ever' time it was fixin' to eat a live chicken, I blowed the sireen out front."

"Just tell me, Bud," said Max, resting back on the heels of his perforated tan-and-white sport shoes. "Is this nigger the one? Is that him sittin' there?"

Little Lee Roy sat huddled and blinking, a smile on his face. . . . But the young man did not look his way.

"Just took the job that time. I didn't mean to—I mean, I meant to go to Port Arthur because my brother was on a boat," he said. "My name is Steve, mister. But I worked with this show selling tickets for three months, and I never would of knowed it was like that if it hadn't been for that man." He arrested his gesture.

"Yeah, what man?" said Max in a hopeless voice.

Little Lee Roy was looking from one white man to the other, excited almost beyond respectful silence. He trembled all over, and a look of amazement and sudden life came into his eyes.

"Two years ago," Steve was saying impatiently. "And we was travelin' through Texas in those ole trucks.—See, the reason nobody ever come clost to it before was they give it a iron bar this long. And tole it if anybody come near, to shake the bar good at 'em, like this. But it couldn't say nothin'. Turned out they'd tole it it couldn't say nothin' to anybody ever, so it just kind of mumbled and growled, like a animal."

"Hee! hee!" This from Little Lee Roy, softly.

"Tell me again," said Max, and just from his look you could tell that everybody knew old Max. "Somehow I can't get it straight in my mind. Is this the boy? Is this little nigger boy the same as this Keela, the Outcast Indian Maiden?"

Up on the porch, above them, Little Lee Roy gave Max a glance full of hilarity, and then bent the other way to catch Steve's next words.

"Why, if anybody was to even come near it or even bresh their shoulder against the rope it'd growl and take on and shake its iron rod. When it would eat the live chickens it'd growl somethin' awful—you ought to heard it."

"Hee! hee!" It was a soft, almost incredulous laugh that began to escape from Little Lee Roy's tight lips, a little mew of delight.

"They'd throw it this chicken, and it would reach out an' grab it. Would sort of rub over the chicken's neck with its thumb an' press on it good, an' then it would bite its head off."

"OK," said Max.

"It skint back the feathers and stuff from the neck and sucked the blood. But ever'body said it was still alive." Steve drew closer to Max and fastened his light-colored, troubled eyes on his face.

"OK."

"Then it would pull the feathers out easy and neat-like, awful fast, an' growl the whole time, kind of moan, an' then it would commence to eat all the white meat. I'd go in an' look at it. I reckon I seen it a thousand times."

"That was you, boy?" Max demanded of Little Lee Roy unexpectedly.

But Little Lee Roy could only say, "Hee! hee!" The little man at the head of the steps where the chickens sat, one on each step, and the two men facing each other below made a pyramid.

Steve stuck his hand out for silence. "They said—I mean, I said it, out front through the megaphone, I said it myself, that it wouldn't eat nothin' but only live meat. It was supposed to be a Indian woman, see, in this red dress an' stockin's. It didn't have on no shoes, so when it drug its foot ever'body could see. . . . When it come to the chicken's heart, it would eat that too, real fast, and the heart would still be jumpin'."

"Wait a second, Bud," said Max briefly, "Say, boy, is this white man here crazy?"

Little Lee Roy burst into hysterical, deprecatory giggles. He said, "Naw suh, don't think so." He tried to catch Steve's eye, seeking appreciation, crying, "Naw suh, don't think he crazy, mista."

Steve gripped Max's arm. "Wait! Wait!" he cried anxiously. "You ain't listenin'. I want to tell you about it. You didn't catch my name—Steve. You never did hear about that little nigger—all that happened to him? Lived in Cane Springs, Miss'ippi?"

"Bud," said Max, disengaging himself, "I don't hear anything. I got a juke box, see, so I don't have to listen."

"Look—I was really the one," said Steve more patiently, but nervously, as if he had been slowly breaking bad news. He walked up and down the bare-swept ground in front of Little Lee Roy's porch, along the row of princess feathers and snow-on-the-mountain. Little Lee Roy's turning head followed him. "I was the one—that's what I'm tellin' you."

"Suppose I was to listen to what every dope comes in Max's Place got to say, *I'd* be nuts," said Max.

"It's all me, see," said Steve. "I know that. I was the one was the cause for it goin' on an' on an' not bein' found out—such an awful thing. It was me, what I said out front through the megaphone."

He stopped still and stared at Max in despair.

"Look," said Max. He sat on the steps, and the chickens hopped off. "I know I ain't nobody but Max. I got Max's Place. I only run a place, understand, fifty yards down the highway. Liquor buried twenty feet from the premises, and no trouble yet. I ain't ever been up here before. I don't claim to been anywhere. People come to my place. Now. You're the hitchhiker. You're tellin' me, see. You claim a lot of information. If I don't get it I don't get it and I ain't complainin' about it, see. But I think you're nuts, and did from the first. I only come up here with you because I figured you's crazy."

"Maybe you don't believe I remember every word of it even now," Steve was saying gently. "I think about it at night—that an' drums on the midway. You ever hear drums on the midway?" He paused and stared politely at Max and Little Lee Roy.

"Yeh," said Max.

"Don't it make you feel sad. I remember how the drums was goin' and I was yellin', 'Ladies and gents! Do not try to touch Keela, the Outcast Indian Maiden—she will only beat your brains out with her iron rod, and eat them alive!' " Steve waved his arm gently in the air, and Little Lee Roy drew back and squealed. " 'Do not go near her, ladies and gents! I'm warnin' you!' So nobody ever did. Nobody ever come near her. Until that man."

"Sure," said Max. "That fella." He shut his eyes.

"Afterwards when he come up so bold, I remembered seein' him walk up an' buy the ticket an' go in the tent. I'll never forget that man as long as I live. To me he's a sort of—well—"

"Hero," said Max.

"I wish I could remember what he looked like. Seem like he was a tallish man with a sort of white face. Seem like he had bad teeth, but I may be wrong. I remember he frowned a lot. Kept frownin'. Whenever he'd buy a ticket, why, he'd frown."

"Ever seen him since?" asked Max cautiously, still with his eyes closed. "Ever hunt him up?"

"No, never did," said Steve. Then he went on. "He'd frown an' buy a ticket ever' day we was in these two little smelly towns in Texas, sometimes three-four times a day, whether it was fixin' to eat a chicken or not."

"OK, so he gets in the tent," said Max.

"Well, what the man finally done was, he walked right up to the little stand where it was tied up and laid his hand out open on the planks in the platform. He just laid his hand out open there and said, 'Come here,' real low and quick, that-a-way."

Steve laid his open hand on Little Lee Roy's porch and held it there, frowning in concentration.

"I get it," said Max. "He'd caught on it was a fake."

Steve straightened up. "So ever'body yelled to git away, git away," he continued, his voice rising, "because it was growlin' an' carryin' on an' shakin' its iron bar like they tole it. When I heard all that commotion—boy! I was scared."

"You didn't know it was a fake."

Steve was silent for a moment, and Little Lee Roy held his breath, for fear everything was all over.

"Look," said Steve finally, his voice trembling. "I guess I was supposed to feel bad like this, and you wasn't. I wasn't supposed to ship out on that boat from Port Arthur and all like that. This other had to happen to me—not you all. Feelin' responsible. You'll be OK, mister, but I won't. I feel awful about it. That poor little old thing."

"Look, you got him right here," said Max quickly. "See him? Use your eyes. He's OK, ain't he? Looks OK to me. It's just you. You're nuts, is all."

"You know—when that man laid out his open hand on the boards, why, it just let go the iron bar," continued Steve, "let it fall down like that—bang—and act like it didn't know what to do. Then it drug itself over to where the fella was standin' an' leaned down an' grabbed holt onto that white man's hand as tight as it could an' cried like a baby. It didn't want to hit him!"

"Hee! hee! hee!"

"No sir, it didn't want to hit him. You know what it wanted?"

Max shook his bead.

"It wanted him to help it. So the man said, 'Do you wanna get out of this place, whoever you are?' An' it never answered—none of us knowed it could talk—but it just wouldn't let that man's hand a-loose. It hung on, cryin' like a baby. So the man says, 'Well, wait here till I come back.' "

"Uh-huh?" said Max.

"Went off an' come back with the sheriff. Took us all to jail. But just the man owned the show and his son got took to the pen. They said I could go free. I kep' tellin' 'em I didn't know it wouldn't hit me with the iron bar an' kep' tellin' 'em I didn't know it could tell what you was sayin' to it."

"Yeh, guess you told 'em," said Max.

"By that time I felt bad. Been feelin' bad ever since. Can't hold on to a job or stay in one place for nothin' in the world. They made it stay in jail to see if it could talk or not, and the first night it wouldn't say nothin'. Some time it cried. And they undressed it an' found out it wasn't no outcast Indian woman a-tall. It was a little clubfooted nigger man."

"Hee! hee!"

"You mean it was this boy here—yeh. It was him."

"Washed its face, and it was paint all over it made it look red. It all come off. And it could talk—as good as me or you. But they'd tole it not to, so it never did. They'd tole it if anybody was to come near it they was comin' to git it—and for it to hit 'em quick with that iron bar an' growl. So nobody ever come near it—until that man. I was yellin' outside, tellin' 'em to keep away, keep away. You could see where they'd whup it. They had to whup it some to make it eat all the chickens. It was awful dirty. They let it go back home free, to where they got it in the first place. They made them pay its ticket from Little Oil, Texas, to Cane Springs, Miss'ippi."

"You got a good memory," said Max.

"The way it *started* was," said Steve, in a wondering voice, "the show was just travelin' along in ole trucks through the country, and just seen this little deformed nigger man, sittin' on a fence, and just took it. It couldn't help it."

Little Lee Roy tossed his head back in a frenzy of amusement.

"I found it all out later. I was up on the Ferris wheel with one of the boys—got to talkin' up yonder in the peace an' quiet—an' said they just kind of happened up on it. Like a cyclone happens: it wasn't nothin' it could do. It was just took up." Steve suddenly paled through his sunburn. "An' they found out that back in Miss'ippi it had it a little bitty pair of crutches an' could just go runnin' on 'em!"

"And there they are," said Max.

Little Lee Roy held up a crutch and turned it about, and then snatched it back like a monkey.

"But if it hadn't been for that man, I wouldn't of knowed it till yet. If it wasn't for him bein' so bold. If he hadn't knowed what he was doin'."

"You remember that man this fella's talkin' about, boy?" asked Max, eying Little Lee Roy.

Little Lee Roy, in reluctance and shyness, shook his head gently.

"Naw suh, I can't say as I remembas that ve'y man, suh," he said softly, looking down where just then a sparrow alighted on his child's shoe. He added happily, as if on inspiration, "Now I remembas *this* man."

Steve did not look up, but when Max shook with silent laughter, alarm seemed to seize him like a spasm in his side. He walked painfully over and stood in the shade for a few minutes, leaning his head on a sycamore tree.

"Seemed like that man just studied it out an' knowed it was somethin' wrong," he said presently, his voice coming more remotely than ever. "But I didn't know. I can't look at nothin' an' be sure what it is. Then afterwards I know. Then I see how it was."

"Yeh, but you're nuts," said Max affably.

"You wouldn't of knowed it either!" cried Steve in sudden boyish, defensive anger. Then he came out from under the tree and stood again almost pleadingly in the sun, facing Max where he was sitting below Little Lee Roy on the steps. "You'd of let it go on an' on when they made it do those things—just like I did."

"Bet I could tell a man from a woman and an Indian from a nigger though," said Max.

Steve scuffed the dust into little puffs with his worn shoe. The chickens scattered, alarmed at last.

Little Lee Roy looked from one man to the other radiantly, his hands pressed over his grinning gums.

Then Steve sighed, and as if he did not know what else he could do, he reached out and without any warning hit Max in the jaw with his fist. Max fell off the steps.

Little Lee Roy suddenly sat as still and dark as a statue, looking on.

"Say! Say!" cried Steve. He pulled shyly at Max where he lay on the ground, with his lips pursed up like a whistler, and then stepped back. He looked horrified. "How you feel?"

"Lousy," said Max thoughtfully. "Let me alone." He raised up on one elbow and lay there looking all around, at the cabin, at Little Lee Roy sitting cross-legged on the porch, and at Steve with his hand out. Finally he got up.

"I can't figure out how I could of ever knocked down an athaletic guy like you. I had to do it," said Steve. "But I guess you don't understand. I had to hit you. First you didn't believe me, and then it didn't bother you."

"That's all OK, only hush," said Max, and added, "Some dope is always giving me the low-down on something, but this is the first time one of 'em ever got away with a thing like this. I got to watch out."

"I hope it don't stay black long," said Steve.

"I got to be going," said Max. But he waited. "What you want to transact with Keela? You come a long way to see him." He stared at Steve with his eyes wide open now, and interested.

"Well, I was goin' to give him some money or something I guess, if I ever found him, only now I ain't got any," said Steve defiantly.

"OK," said Max. "Here's some change for you, boy. Just take it. Go on back in the house. Go on."

Little Lee Roy took the money speechlessly, and then fell upon his yellow crutches and hopped with miraculous rapidity away through the door. Max stared after him for a moment.

"As for you"—he brushed himself off, turned to Steve and then said, "When did you eat last?"

"Well, I'll tell you," said Steve.

"Not here," said Max. "I didn't go to ask you a question. Just follow me. We serve eats at Max's Place, and I want to play the juke box. You eat, and I'll listen to the juke box."

"Well . . ." said Steve. "But when it cools off I got to catch a ride some place."

"Today while all you all was gone, and not a soul in de house," said Little Lee Roy at the supper table that night, "two white mens come heah to de house. Wouldn't come in. But talks to me about de old times when I use to be wid de circus—"

"Hush up, Pappy," said the children.

A TEMPLE OF THE HOLY GHOST

Flannery O'Connor

—Master short story writer and peacock farmer Flannery O'Connor (1925–1964) always maintained a healthy fascination with God's less desirable creatures. It is no surprise then, that, in this story from 1955's A Good Man is Hard to Find, *O'Connor would peek under the sideshow tent in her search for divinity.*

LL WEEKEND THE TWO girls were calling each other Temple One and Temple Two, shaking with laughter and getting so red and hot that they were positively ugly, particularly Joanne who had spots on her face anyway. They came in the brown convent uniforms they had to wear at Mount St. Scholastica but as soon as they opened their suitcases, they took off the uniforms and put on red skirts and loud blouses. They put on lipstick and their Sunday shoes and walked around in the high heels all over the house, always passing the long mirror in the hall slowly to get a look at their legs. None of their ways were lost on the child. If only one of them had come, that one would have played with her, but since there were two of them, she was out of it and watched them suspiciously from a distance.

They were fourteen—two years older than she was—but neither of them was bright, which was why they had been sent to the convent. If they had gone to a regular school, they wouldn't have done anything but think about boys; at the convent the sisters, her mother said, would keep a grip on their necks. The child decided, after observing them for a few hours, that they were practically morons and she was glad to think that they were only second cousins and she couldn't have inherited any of their stupidity. Susan called herself Su-zan. She was very skinny but she had a pretty pointed face and red hair. Joanne had yellow hair that was naturally curly but she talked through her nose and when she laughed, she turned purple in patches. Neither one of them could say an intelligent thing and all their sentences began, "You know this boy I know well one time he . . ."

They were to stay all weekend and her mother said she didn't see how she would entertain them since she didn't know any boys their age. At this, the child, struck suddenly with genius, shouted, "There's Cheat! Get Cheat to come! Ask Miss Kirby to get Cheat to come show them around!" and she nearly choked on the food she had in her mouth. She doubled over laughing and hit the table with her fist and looked at the two bewildered girls while water started in her eyes and rolled down her fat cheeks and the braces she had in her mouth glared like tin. She had never thought of anything so funny before.

Her mother laughed in a guarded way and Miss Kirby blushed and carried her fork delicately to her mouth with one pea on it. She was a long-faced blonde schoolteacher who boarded with them and Mr. Cheatam was her admirer, a rich old farmer who arrived every Saturday afternoon in a fifteen-year-old baby-blue Pontiac powdered with red clay dust and black inside with Negroes that he charged ten cents apiece to bring into town on Saturday afternoons. After he dumped them he came to see Miss Kirby, always bringing a little gift—a bag of boiled peanuts or a watermelon or a stalk of sugar cane and once a wholesale box of Baby Ruth candy bars. He was bald-headed except for a little fringe of rust-colored hair and his face was nearly the same color as the unpaved roads and washed like them with ruts and gulleys. He wore a pale green shirt with a thin black stripe in it and blue galluses and his trousers cut across a protruding stomach that he pressed tenderly from time to time with his big flat thumb. All his teeth were backed with gold and he would roll his eyes at Miss Kirby in an impish way and say, "Haw haw," sitting in their porch swing with his legs spread apart and his hightopped shoes pointing in opposite directions on the floor.

"I don't think Cheat is going to be in town this weekend," Miss Kirby said, not in the least understanding that this was a joke, and the child was convulsed afresh, threw herself backward in her chair, fell out of it, rolled on the floor and lay there heaving. Her mother told her if she didn't stop this foolishness she would have to leave the table.

Yesterday her mother had arranged with Alonzo Myers to drive them the forty-five miles to Mayville, where the convent was, to get the girls for the weekend and Sunday afternoon he was hired to drive them back again. He was an eighteen-year-old boy who weighed two hundred and fifty pounds and worked for the taxi company and he was all you could get to drive you anywhere. He smoked or rather chewed a short black cigar and he had a round sweaty chest that showed through the yellow nylon shirt he wore. When he drove all the windows of the car had to be open.

"Well there's Alonzo!" the child roared from the floor. "Get Alonzo to show em around! Get Alonzo!"

The two girls, who had seen Alonzo, began to scream their indignation.

Her mother thought this was funny too but she said, "That'll be about enough out of you," and changed the subject. She asked them why they called each other Temple One and Temple Two and this sent them off into gales of giggles. Finally they managed to explain. Sister Perpetua, the oldest nun at the Sisters of Mercy in Mayville, had given them a lecture on what to do if a young man should—here they laughed so hard they were not able to go on without going back to the beginning—on what to do if a young man should—they put their heads in their laps—on what to do if—they finally managed to shout it out—if he should "behave in an ungentlemanly manner with them in the back of an automobile." Sister Perpetua said they were to say, "Stop sir! I am a Temple of the Holy Ghost!" and that would put an end to it. The child sat up off the floor with a blank face. She didn't see anything so funny in this. What was really funny was the idea of Mr. Cheatam or Alonzo Myers beauing them around. That killed her.

Her mother didn't laugh at what they had said. "I think you girls are pretty silly," she said. "After all, that's what you are—Temples of the Holy Ghost."

The two of them looked up at her, politely concealing their giggles, but with astonished faces as if they were beginning to realize that she was made of the same stuff as Sister Perpetua.

Miss Kirby preserved her set expression and the child thought, it's all over her head anyhow. I am a Temple of the Holy Ghost, she said to herself, and was pleased with the phrase. It made her feel as if somebody had given her a present.

After dinner, her mother collapsed on the bed and said, "Those girls are going to drive me crazy if I don't get some entertainment for them. They're awful."

"I bet I know who you could get," the child started.

"Now listen. I don't want to hear any more about Mr. Cheatam," her mother said. "You embarrass Miss Kirby. He's her only friend. Oh my Lord," and she sat up and looked mournfully out the window, "that poor soul is so lonesome she'll even ride in that car that smells like the last circle in hell."

And she's a Temple of the Holy Ghost too, the child reflected. "I wasn't thinking of him," she said. "I was thinking of those two Wilkinses, Wendell and Cory, that visit old lady Buchell out on her farm. They're her grandsons. They work for her."

"Now that's an idea," her mother murmured and gave her an appreciative look. But then she slumped again. "They're only farm boys. These girls would turn up their noses at them."

"Huh," the child said. "They wear pants. They're sixteen and they got a car. Somebody said they were both going to be Church of God preachers because you don't have to know nothing to be one."

"They would be perfectly safe with those boys all right," her mother said and in a minute she got up and called their grandmother on the telephone and after she had talked to the old woman a half an hour, it was arranged that Wendell and Cory would come to supper and afterwards take the girls to the fair.

Susan and Joanne were so pleased that they washed their hair and rolled it up on aluminum curlers. Hah, thought the child, sitting cross-legged on the bed to watch them undo the curlers, wait'll you get a load of Wendell and Cory! "You'll like these boys," she said. "Wendell is six feet tall ands got red hair. Cory is six feet six inches talls got black hair and wears a sport jacket and they gottem this car with a squirrel tail on the front."

"How does a child like you know so much about these men?" Susan asked and pushed her face up close to the mirror to watch the pupils in her eyes dilate.

The child lay back on the bed and began to count the narrow boards in the ceiling until she lost her place. I know them all right, she said to someone. We fought in the world war together. They were under me and I saved them five times from Japanese suicide divers and Wendell said I am going to marry that kid and the other said oh no you ain't I am and I said neither one of you is because I will court marshall you all before you can bat an eye. "I've seen them around is all," she said.

When they came the girls stared at them a second and then began to giggle and talk to each other about the convent. They sat in the swing together and Wendell and Cory sat on the banisters together. They sat like monkeys, their knees on a level with their shoulders and their arms hanging down between. They were short thin boys with red faces and high cheekbones and pale seed-like eyes. They had brought a harmonica and a guitar. One of them began to blow softly on the mouth organ, watching the girls over it, and the other started strumming the guitar and then began to sing, not watching them but keeping his head tilted upward as if he were only interested in hearing himself. He was singing a hillbilly song that sounded half like a love song and half like a hymn.

The child was standing on a barrel pushed into some bushes at the side of the house, her face on a level with the porch floor. The sun was going down and the sky was turning a bruised violet color that seemed to be connected with the sweet mournful sound of the music. Wendell began to smile as he sang and to look at the girls. He looked at Susan with a dog-like loving look and sang,

"I've found a friend in Jesus,
He's everything to me,

He's the lily of the valley,
He's the One who's set me free!"

Then he turned the same look on Joanne and sang,

"A wall of fire about me,
I've nothing now to fear,
He's the lily of the valley,
And I'll always have Him near!"

The girls looked at each other and held their lips stiff so as not to giggle but Susan let out one anyway and clapped her hand on her mouth. The singer frowned and for a few seconds only strummed the guitar. Then he began "The Old Rugged Cross" and they listened politely but when he had finished they said, "Let us sing one!" and before he could start another, they began to sing with their convent-trained voices,

"Tantum ergo Sacramentum
Veneremur Cernui:
Et antiquum documentum
Novo cedat ritui:"

The child watched the boys' solemn faces turn with perplexed frowning stares at each other as if they were uncertain whether they were being made fun of.

"Praestet fides supplementum
Sensuum defectui.
Genitori, Genitoque
Laus et jubilatio

Salus, honor, virtus quoque . . ."

The boys' faces were dark red in the gray-purple light. They looked fierce and startled.

"Sit et benedictio;
Procedenti ab utroque
Compar sit laudatio.
Amen."

The girls dragged out the Amen and then there was a silence.

"That must be Jew singing," Wendell said and began to tune the guitar.

The girls giggled idiotically but the child stamped her foot on the barrel. "You big dumb ox!" she shouted. "You big dumb Church of God ox!" she roared and fell off the barrel and scrambled up and shot around the corner of the house as they jumped from the banister to see who was shouting.

Her mother had arranged for them to have supper in the back yard and she had a table laid out there under some Japanese lanterns that she pulled out for garden parties. "I ain't eating with them," the child said and snatched her plate off the table and carried it to the kitchen and sat down with the thin blue-gummed cook and ate her supper.

"Howcome you be so ugly sometime?" the cook asked.

"Those stupid idiots," the child said.

The lanterns gilded the leaves of the trees orange on the level where they hung and above them was black-green and below them were different dim muted colors that made the girls sitting at the table look prettier than they were. From time to time, the child turned her head and glared out the kitchen window at the scene below.

"God could strike you deaf dumb and blind," the cook said, "and then you wouldn't be as smart as you is."

"I would still be smarter than some," the child said.

After supper they left for the fair. She wanted to go to the fair but not with them so even if they had asked her she wouldn't have gone. She went upstairs and paced the long bedroom with her hands locked together behind her back and her head thrust forward and an expression, fierce and dreamy both, on her face. She didn't turn on the electric light but let the darkness collect and make the room smaller and more private. At regular intervals a light crossed the open window and threw shadows on the wall. She stopped and stood looking out over the dark slopes, past where the pond glinted silver, past the wall of woods to the speckled sky where a long finger of light was revolving up and around and away, searching the air as if it were hunting for the lost sun. It was the beacon light from the fair.

She could hear the distant sound of the calliope and she saw in her head all the tents raised up in a kind of gold sawdust light and the diamond ring of the Ferris wheel going around and around up in the air and down again and the screeking merry-go-round going around and around on the ground. A fair lasted five or six days and there was a special afternoon for school children and a special night for niggers. She had gone last year on the afternoon for school children and had seen the monkeys and the fat man and had ridden on the Ferris wheel. Certain tents were closed then because they contained things that would be known only to grown people but she had looked with interest at the advertising on the closed tents, at the faded-looking pictures on the canvas of people in tights, with stiff stretched composed faces like the faces of the martyrs waiting to have their tongues cut out by the Roman soldier. She had imagined that what was inside these tents concerned medicine and she had made up her mind to be a doctor when she grew up.

She had since changed and decided to be an engineer but as she looked out the window and followed the revolving searchlight as it widened and shortened and wheeled in its arc, she felt that she would have to be much more than just a doctor or an engineer. She would have to be a saint because that was the occupation that included everything you could know; and yet she knew she would never be a saint. She did not steal or murder but she was a born liar and slothful and she sassed her mother and was deliberately ugly to almost everybody. She was eaten up also with the sin of Pride, the worst one. She made fun of the Baptist preacher who came to the school at commencement to give the devotional. She would pull down her mouth and hold her forehead as if she were in agony and groan, "Fawther, we thank Thee," exactly the way he did and she had been told many times not to do it. She could never be a saint, but she thought she could be a martyr if they killed her quick.

She could stand to be shot but not to be burned in oil. She didn't know if she could stand to be torn to pieces by lions or not. She began to prepare her martyrdom, seeing herself in a pair of tights in a great arena, lit by the early Christians hanging in cages of fire, making a gold dusty light that fell on her and the lions. The first lion charged forward and fell at her feet, converted. A whole series of lions did the same. The lions liked her so much she even slept with them and finally the Romans were obliged to burn her but to their astonishment she would not burn down and finding she was so hard to kill, they finally cut off her head very quickly with a sword and she went immediately to heaven. She rehearsed this several times, returning each time at the entrance of Paradise to the lions.

Finally she got up from the window and got ready for bed and got in without saying her prayers. There were two heavy double beds in the room. The girls were occupying the other one and she tried to think of something cold and clammy that she could hide in their bed but her thought was fruitless. She didn't have anything she could think of, like a chicken carcass or a piece of beef liver. The sound of the calliope coming through the window kept her awake and she remembered that she hadn't said her prayers and got up and knelt down and began them. She took a running start and went through to the other side of the Apostle's Creed and then hung by her chin on the side of the bed, empty-minded. Her prayers, when she remembered to say them, were usually perfunctory but sometimes when she had done something wrong or heard music or lost something, or sometimes for no reason at all, she would be moved to fervor and would think of Christ on the long journey to Calvary, crushed three times on the rough cross. Her mind would stay on this a while and then get empty and when something roused her, she would find that she was thinking of a different thing entirely, of some dog or some girl or something she was going to do some day. Tonight, remembering Wendell and Cory, she was filled with thanksgiving and almost weeping with delight, she said, "Lord, Lord, thank You that I'm not in the Church of God, thank You Lord, thank You!" and got back in bed and kept repeating it until she went to sleep.

The girls came in at a quarter to twelve and waked her up with their giggling. They turned on the small blue-shaded lamp to see to get undressed by and their skinny shadows climbed up the wall and broke and continued moving about softly on the ceiling. The child sat up to hear what all they had seen at the fair. Susan had a plastic pistol full of cheap candy and Joanne a pasteboard cat with red polka dots on it. "Did you see the monkeys dance?" the child asked. "Did you see that fat man and those midgets?"

"All kinds of freaks," Joanne said. And then she said to Susan, "I enjoyed it all but the you-know-what," and her face assumed a peculiar expression as if she had bit into something that she didn't know if she liked or not.

The other stood still and shook her head once and nodded slightly at the child. "Little pitchers," she said in a low voice but the child heard it and her heart began to beat very fast.

She got out of her bed and climbed onto the footboard of theirs. They turned off the light and got in but she didn't move. She sat there, looking hard at them until their faces were well defined in the dark. "I'm not as old as you all," she said, "but I'm about a million times smarter."

"There are some things," Susan said, "that a child of your age doesn't know," and they both began to giggle.

"Go back to your own bed," Joanne said.

The child didn't move. "One time," she said, her voice hollow-sounding in the dark, "I saw this rabbit have rabbits."

There was a silence. Then Susan said, "How?" in an indifferent tone and she knew that she had them. She said she wouldn't tell until they told about the you-know-what. Actually she had never seen a rabbit have rabbits but she forgot this as they began to tell what they had seen in the tent.

It had been a freak with a particular name but they couldn't remember the name. The tent where it was had been divided into two parts by a black curtain, one side for men and one for women. The freak went from one side to the other, talking first to the men and then to the women, but everyone could hear. The stage ran all the way across the front. The girls heard the freak say to the men, "I'm going to show you this and if you laugh, God may strike you the same way." The freak had a country voice, slow and nasal and neither high nor low, just flat. "God made me thisaway and if you laugh He may strike you the same way. This is the way He wanted me to be and I ain't disputing His way. I'm showing you because I got to make the best of it. I expect you to act like ladies and gentlemen. I never done it to myself nor had a thing to do with it but I'm making the best of it. I don't dispute hit." Then there was a long silence on the other side of the tent and finally the freak left the men and came over onto the women's side and said the same thing.

The child felt every muscle strained as if she were hearing the answer to a riddle that was more puzzling than the riddle itself. "You mean it had two heads?" she said.

"No," Susan said, "it was a man and woman both. It pulled up its dress and showed us. It had on a blue dress."

The child wanted to ask how it could be a man and woman both without two heads but she did not. She wanted to get back into her own bed and think it out and she began to climb down off the footboard.

"What about the rabbit?" Joanne asked.

The child stopped and only her face appeared over the footboard, abstracted, absent. "It spit them out of its mouth," she said, "six of them."

She lay in bed trying to picture the tent with the freak walking from side to side but she was too sleepy to figure it out. She was better able to see the faces of the country people watching, the men more solemn than they were in church, and the women stern and polite, with painted-looking eyes, standing as if they were waiting for the first note of the piano to begin the hymn. She could hear the freak saying, "God made me thisaway and I don't dispute hit," and the people saying, "Amen. Amen."

"God done this to me and I praise Him."

"Amen. Amen."

"He could strike you thisaway."

"Amen. Amen."

"But he has not."

"Amen."

"Raise yourself up. A temple of the Holy Ghost. You! You are God's temple, don't you know? Don't you know? God's Spirit has a dwelling in you, don't you know?"

"Amen. Amen."

"If anybody desecrates the temple of God, God will bring him to ruin and if you laugh, He may strike you thisaway. A temple of God is a holy thing. Amen. Amen."

"I am a temple of the Holy Ghost."

"Amen."

The people began to slap their hands without making a loud noise and with a regular beat between the Amens, more and more softly, as if they knew there was a child near, half asleep.

The next afternoon the girls put on their brown convent uniforms again and the child and her mother took them back to Mount St. Scholastica. "Oh glory, oh Pete!" they said. "Back to the salt mines." Alonzo Myers drove them and the child sat in front with him and her mother sat in back between the two girls, telling them such things as how pleased she was to have had them and how they must come back again and then about the good times she and their mothers had had when they were girls at the convent. The child didn't listen to any of this twaddle but kept as close to the locked door as she could get and held her head out the window. They had thought Alonzo would smell better on Sunday but he did not. With her hair blowing over her face she could look directly into the ivory sun which was framed in the middle of the blue afternoon but when she pulled it away from her eyes she had to squint.

Mount St. Scholastica was a red brick house set back in a garden in the center of town. There was a filling station on one side of it and a firehouse on the other. It had a high black grillework fence around it and narrow bricked walks between old trees and japonica bushes that were heavy with blooms. A big moon-faced nun came bustling to the door to let them in and embraced her mother and would have done the same to her but that she stuck out her hand and preserved a frigid frown, looking just past the sister's shoes at the wainscoting. They had a tendency to kiss even homely children, but the nun shook her hand vigorously and even cracked her knuckles a little and said they must come to the chapel, that benediction was just beginning. You put your foot in their door and they got you praying, the child thought as they hurried down the polished corridor.

You'd think she had to catch a train, she continued in the same ugly vein as they entered the chapel where the sisters were kneeling on one side and the girls, all in brown uniforms, on the other. The chapel smelled of incense. It was light green and gold, a series of springing arches that ended with the one over the altar where the priest was kneeling in front of the monstrance, bowed low. A small boy in a surplice was standing behind him, swinging the censer. The child knelt down between her mother and the nun and they were well into the *"Tantum Ergo"* before her ugly thoughts stopped and she began to realize that she was in the presence of God. Hep me not to be so mean, she began mechanically. Hep me not to give her so much sass. Hep me not to talk like I do. Her mind began to get quiet and then empty but when the priest raised the monstrance with the Host shining ivory-colored in the center of it, she was thinking of the tent at the fair that had the freak in it. The freak was saying, "I don't dispute hit. This is the way He wanted me to be."

As they were leaving the convent door, the big nun swooped down on her mischievously and nearly smothered her in the black habit, mashing the side of her face into the crucifix hitched onto her belt and then holding her off and looking at her with little periwinkle eyes.

On the way home she and her mother sat in the back and Alonzo drove by himself in the front. The child observed three folds of fat in the back of his neck and noted that his ears were pointed almost like a pig's. Her mother, making conversation, asked him if he had gone to the fair.

"Gone," he said, "and never missed a thing and it was good I gone when I did because they ain't going to have it next week like they said they was."

"Why?" asked her mother.

"They shut it on down," he said. "Some of the preachers from town gone out and inspected it and got the police to shut it on down."

Her mother let the conversation drop and the child's round face was lost in thought. She turned it toward the window and looked out over a stretch of pasture land that rose and fell with a gathering greenness until it touched the dark woods. The sun was a huge red ball like an elevated Host drenched in blood and when it sank out of sight, it left a line in the sky like a red clay road hanging over the trees.

THE CIRCUS EIGHTY YEARS AGO

The Wages of Sin Is Death
An Escapade That Was Spoiled by a Tragedy

Susan Dickinson

—As the subtitle suggests, this story by Susan Dickinson (1830–1913), Emily Dickinson's sister, describes a seemingly harmless night out rife with possibility as it descends into horror following the unsightly death of a clown.

ONE OF THE JOYS of my girlhood was to hear a most attractive aunt, well on in years, relate, in a style and manner worthy a De Maupassant, her runaway experience in attending a travelling circus. With her pretty head set off by a dainty and becoming widow's cap of tarleton, a snowy lace folded about her neck, she would smooth down her satin gown with a deprecating touch and relate her escapade with a delightful sense of her own youthful daring and narrow escape from eternal torment. O ye fathers—heads of families, good, saved church folks, ministers in regular standing—as you genially gather your bright groups about you and flock to the circus tent nowadays, to see the animals mentioned in the Bible, and laugh at the fun without formula, and sentiments not exactly of the most strictly Matthew Arnold type, urged upon you by the clown—have you heard, do you know, that this same circus was once held the very gate of hell, as its white tents were spread upon the green fields of our decorous valley towns and villages?

Perhaps all goodness and joy would be easier were it not for the "Thou shalt nots" of the Jewish interdictions, even today, for human nature loves a challenge, a hurdle—or why else did this high-spirited, refined offshoot of New England's best, long for and surreptitiously plan to be one of the wicked, abandoned number who crowded "Van Deusen's greatest circus and menagerie in the world," in Geneva, N.Y., on a summer night—well—two lifetimes at least ago? In her own words, as I remember it, the story ran thus:

"My brother, with whom I had a temporary home at that time, was already pledged to attend a religious meeting at a friend's house, with his wife, leaving the coast clear for my departure at 7 o'clock with my escort, a very nice young man, who was received as a recognized caller in the home. Besides being quite handsome, he was not overaddicted to the strictest religious observances. That is, he was sensitive to the pleasant aromas of life. It was a hazardous enterprise we were undertaking, for he admitted we could not possibly get back before 9:30—or perhaps even as late as 10.

"So far in my life my excitements had been in rather a minor key, the wildest of all culminating in my brother's commencement at Yale college, before there were any balls or other diversions from education and religion. The mere anticipation of this adventure took my breath away. The start was easy and favored by circumstances. It was arranged that the return of the family should precede ours, and I trusted to luck that my sister would think me in bed and asleep on her return, and no difficulties would arise from that cause to betray the secrecy of our plan. As there were no street cars or stages, the walk to the dreary, empty fields, well out of the village, took more time than we had counted upon. We missed the triumphal entree, which, as shown by the posters, must have been most impressive, but got good seats in the very front row, everything else having been filled earlier. Of course there was not one familiar face near me, and as I was dressed very plainly, with my cottage bonnet tied closely under my chin, I felt sure I should not be easily recognized in any case. My excitement was intense beyond description. I think the animals of Noah's ark that had been so strenuously advertised as an apology, or cover, for the wicked pleasure of the circus, must have been quite feeble and moth-eaten. There was only one elephant, and he was so languid and subdued there could have been little thrill in the chariot race around the ring, 'freely offered to all!'

"The queer, dismal sounds from the cages of course lent an almost frightful suggestion of jungles, and wild places and things far away, as did the strange chokings and squawking of foreign feathered things behind their bars. The one white bear from Greenland fascinated me, until a voice near my elbow insisted that it was probably a black one painted, and a sudden twinge of guilt pierced me as the old line of that chill region, so often sung in my childhood, rang in my ears—

From Greenland's icy mountains.

The highly trained animals vividly promised in the bills resulted in a few Shetland ponies, and two superannuated monkeys full of repulsive tricks, and in their looks fiends incarnate.

"As I said, we had missed the grand entree, but when the bareback riders, the Ladies Francesca de Moro and Syringa del Spagna, rode into the ring, they more than made up for our loss. Their short, stiff, spangled skirts and pink silk tights, with dainty slippers to match their handsome arms and necks, their red cheeks and black hair and staring eyes filled me with delight. I had never seen anything like them. With utter ease and grace they sat their gorgeously caparisoned black 'Arabian steeds,' and rode slowly around the ring of sawdust at first, as if to accustom us to their wonder, while the ringmaster, elegantly dressed, as if to give a dinner to the mayor in Main street today, curved and uncurved his long, fancy whiplash in the air, to excite the gentle, broken-willed horses, and recited the marvelous performances of these dazzling creatures about to be beheld. Back and forth they rode and whirled and danced to a music completely taking, if not classic. The drum blared out as if to dare us all to dashing feats. Donna Syringa del Spagna came out alone for a climax, riding quite without bridle, standing while her horse ran at full speed, or clinging to its flowing mane, reversing every known habit of the saddle as she leapt over bars held high, and through hoops, till, tossing kisses and smiles to everyone in the tent, she disappeared in the calico curtains.

"I was radiantly happy, and forgot my brother and sister at prayer-meeting. The clown was as yet unseen. Soon a noisy applause roused us almost to fright, and a great, gay, painted creature came shambling into the ring. And this was a circus clown! That low, awful thing of which I had heard hints—and, sad to say, I was perfectly carried away with him! He ran about the ring in a wild fashion, imitating the pompous ringmaster with every imaginable amusing grimace and quip. With what audacity he asked: 'Mr. Sheldon, did you ever see so many homely men as are here to-night? But, oh, such lovely ladies! I should think you would want to marry them all!' 'Can't you dance for them, sing for them, or do something to please them?' suggested the fine Mr. Sheldon. 'Oh, yes, certainly, just watch me!' was the reply, and then followed every conceivable antic and joke, ending with the old song, 'How I loved Annie Lee!'

"Two delicate limbed tumblers then hopped from behind the curtains into the ring to most exciting flourishes of the band, turning somersaults and standing on their heads. Our jolly painted friend now convulsed the people by following them in derisive attempts to perform their agile feats. Back and forth, up and down, here and there he flew, at least outdoing them all and fairly astonishing to see. When some bars were placed for a display of leaping, he flew quickly over them, under them, still a point higher, while the band urged louder to up and on! Over and beyond the best he went in his grotesque red and yellow bravery. The crowd yelled their joy with the craze of the clown—exciting him to more. But he does not get up. He is shamming now. He is waiting to do something funnier yet. Of a sudden it is still—still—he does not move. He has broken his neck. Without any word, light careless feet ran behind the curtains with the pallid creature of fun. He was dead. I was scared beyond control and clutched my friend's arm, burying my face on his shoulder and crying like a child, brokenly imploring 'O take me home, take me home!'

"Poor fellow, he did take me home but I ran almost every step of the way, sobbing in a shaken fashion. I clambered in the rose trellis, refusing his tender offers of assistance, sprang through my open window, and threw myself on my bed where I cried until dawn; while over and over my young conscience urged, 'It would not have happened if I had not gone!'

"My eyes were red at breakfast, confirming my life of a bad headache, but for that I cared nothing. Only the poor, dead clown was grieving me to death. In proper time my escort—I will only call him Mr. B., for his own sake, since he is a Sunday-school superintendent now and his early life must not be traduced—called to inquire for me. But as others were calling, too, we were obliged to carry on our conversation in cipher. A letter received from him soon after brought the climax of my circus woes. It was a proposal of marriage, a very nice, manly love letter, asking me to let him care for me through all life's woes and sorrows—and so on. I was very young and very much more scared than even when I saw the poor clown fall. I again locked myself in my room, and wrote my refusal of his life guard. I remember only one sentence verbatim—wishing to seem gentle and throw in a touch of sentiment, at the close of the note, I exclaimed, 'How can you be such a very foolish man, as to let the ivy of your affections twine around such a stubborn oak as I am.' "

Here, my aunt, a tiny little body, always covered her roguish face with her slender white fingers, laughing heartily. After which she would sometimes add—"There are some verses about a clown that impress me deeply. Are we not always saddest when we sing?" And she would recite in her soft staccata voice the following lines:

Fool in the day! But when alone at night
Swift comes the right;
Cooling the fevered fancy for the time,
Changing to God's own soul the mime—
Shall I not thankful be—
Rejoice in ecstasy?

High thought the nonce! To-morrow can and bells!
O hell of hells!
Hush, hush again! I tell thee fevered soul
Cometh a day, when thou i' faith all whole,

Shall clasp the Father's hand,
Shall know and understand.

At the end there was never a gleam of mischief left on her face, and the brilliant dark eyes held a hint of real tragedy, as if the years had set her back in that fatal night of her girlhood again.

FROM THE FINAL CONFESSION OF MABEL STARK

Robert Hough

—The real-life Mabel Stark was the most sought-after female tiger trainer in circus history. This selection from Robert Hough's 2001 fictional memoir recounts Mabel's early encounters inside the cage.

SEE, CAT TRAINING WAS supposed to be the thing that was going to give me purpose and options, two things you need plenty of at any age but most particularly when you're young. After a few minutes of walking around aimlessly, I figured I might as well head back to the menage, if only to give myself something to do before the evening show.

To make a long story short I kept on helping the menage boys with the tigers, no cherry pie asked for and none received, though it's true I'd lost a little of my vim now I was doing it just to kill time during lulls. Whenever I saw Louis I'd say good-morning or good-afternoon and then get out of his way pronto (though surely he must've noticed how the tigers purred every time I got near the cage? How they'd come over to me and rub their sides against the bars? How they hardly ever tried to hook their claws in my arm and pull?) The most I ever got out of Louis was a terse nod, and then the sound made by those knee-high leather boots stomping away from me.

When I next spoke with Al G., he told me to pay Louis no mind, that he had a sharpness about him and there was nothing I or anyone else could do to change that. Only time would bring him around.

This went on for weeks: my doing my goat act and my high-school riding act and my Slide for Life and in my off-hours hanging around the cats (while generally feeling logy and on the neurasthenic end of things). It might've even been months. Then one day I was in my corner, opposite King and Queen and Toby, reading a book though finding it hard to concentrate for I was thinking maybe I'd quit and try to worm my way onto another menage show. Louis came tramping down the aisle between the cages. The ground was damp that day, and his heels hit the earth so hard he kicked up divets.

He stopped in front of me and held out a twisted willow whip.

"Here."

Was the first whip I'd ever held, a long piece of leather smooth and comfortable and with a smell halfway between worn wood and Louis Roth. He led me outside, through the backyard, and into an empty stretch of dirt beyond the lot. It was a hot day, sun blazing. Louis was wearing his meat belt, and he reached in and grabbed a hunk of horse and dropped it on the ground. Then he walked me a dozen feet back and said, "Wait for ze flies to come and when zay do start flicking zem off. When you can flick off one fly so zat another is not disturbed, vee can haff a talk. Are you understanding me?"

I nodded yes and he walked off. I stood there, alone, with a whip and a piece of meat fixing to turn rank, which in the noon sun wasn't going to be a long process. After a bit I started contemplating the thing in my hand, impressed mostly by how it managed to be so smooth and rigid at the same time. I shifted hands and noticed how my sweat had seeped colour out of the handle, leaving a copper smear running diagonal over my palm. I put it back in my right hand and squeezed, and by God its firmness reminded me of Dimitri the day I sponge bathed him, by which I mean dead stiff though with a hint of sponginess.

By this point, the meat was starting to turn a dull grey green and a trio of flies were doing a zigzag dance in the air above it; it looked like they were deciding which one got the honour of being the first to make a landing. I waited, it being a measure of my desire to follow Louis's directions to a T. I didn't even think of practising until those flies were on the meat. One landed, and another. I raised my right hand, circled the whip dramatically over my head and let loose, snapping my wrist at what I figured was the perfect moment for wrist snapping, the idea being the force of that snap would travel down the length of the braid and translate so hard into the popper it'd make a snap could be heard on the far side of the lot. Instead, that long, long whip unrolled like a carpet on a hill. By the time my wrist snap wound its way to the tip it'd pretty much worn itself out, the popper flopping silent into the dust, a full ten feet from the target. It didn't disturb the flies' business one iota.

I cursed that nervous little Hungarian, for it occurred to me he'd given me the biggest whip in the business and the last thing someone would ever learn on. Basically he was putting me off, thinking I'd get discouraged and forget the tigers. Had this not occurred to me it might've even worked, but the plain fact was I was mad, and anger's always motivated me about as well as anything else. I spent all afternoon trying to make that damn thing snap, quitting only when I had to go eat and then get ready for the evening show.

That night we jumped over the Colorado border to New Mexico. When everyone was bunking down for a midday nap, I found Louis polishing his boots in the menage tent. A pint of Tennessee sipping whisky was beside him.

"Can I get another piece of horsemeat?"

Naturally I could've gotten my own piece of horsemeat—could've borrowed a slab from a cage boy or bugged the cookhouse staff or visited the butcher in town, for that matter. The point was, I wanted him to know I hadn't given up yet. He looked at me, surprised I was going to miss my sleep a second day in a row, and sighed.

"All right," he finally said. "Tell Red I said it vass okay."

Around the end of *that* day's whipping session, the meat gamey and green and so ridden with flies it hummed, I started to get that popper to snap. Not powerfully, mind you, not the way Louis could, but a snap nonetheless. I'd been thinking a lack of strength in my arms was the problem when in fact it was my technique: The arm-circling has to be tight and purposeful, the wrist snap coming at the exact moment the power generated by all that arm circling is at its maximum (and not a tenth of a second earlier or a tenth of a second later, a mistake not difficult to make). The first time the popper actually popped I practically jumped out of my boots—I thought some rubes with pistols had wandered on the lot looking for trouble (which was something that happened all the time back then, especially if the workingmen had been out stealing shirts off clotheslines the night before). When I realized what had really happened, I grinned.

I made the whip crack a few more times before having to quit. Next day, I was at it again, forgoing my sleep, giving Louis the may-I-have-another-piece-of-horsemeat? act, spending a hot two hours twirling a whip over my head and yelling, "Yah!" That day I figured out a good way to get the popper to go off more ferociously was to jerk the whip back just as it was about to snap. While this certainly did add a zing, it was also a little dangerous; midway through the session I misfired and the whip end rebounded and caught me on the cheek, leaving a red welt that burned for days. Was lucky I didn't put my eye out.

My main problem now was accuracy: I couldn't get close enough to those flies so they'd so much as get nervous, never mind leave their supper. Season ended and we came back to Venice and I got myself a room at the St. Mark's, and like many of the women who didn't get jobs over the winter I danced a little burlesque in town to keep myself fed. But only a little. During the day I devoted myself to whip training and staying near the three tigers I hoped to work. Day after day after day, I practised. If Al G. was interested in what I was doing, he didn't show it—in fact, he never once came round to check my progress or offer encouragement or tell me what I was doing wrong, something I attributed to his being so busy with skirt-chasing and running a circus.

Instead he sent Dan. One day, with no warning or footfalls approaching, he was there, watching me, mouth parted, till finally I lost my composure and said, "You got something to say, Dan, then say it."

His hands got lost quick in his pockets and his shoulders shrugged up and he watched his own foot make a pattern in the dirt, until finally he upped and outed with "I knows what you doin' wrong, Miss Stark."

"Well then Dan why don't you tell me what that is?"

"Gots to aim two feet behind the piece of meat. Gots to pretend like its in the *way*. Gots to whip through the target, ma'am. Not at it."

"Is that a fact?"

"Natural-born fact. I seen Al G. do it. Back on the dog-and-pony. He may not look it now, but that man he's got the gift too."

We looked at each other.

"Was that all, Dan?"

"Yes ma'am," he said before walking off.

Standing alone with my whip and my stinking meat I saw a little red, for Dan's advice sounded so ridiculous I wondered if it was something Al G. had told him to say so as to put me even further off track. Still, I wasn't having much luck my own way, which was to stare at that putrid meat for a good five seconds before letting fly. So I gave it a whirl Dan's way. Didn't even really try, seeing as I had no confidence in his suggestion, just delivered the whip in that general direction, wrist snapping at some imaginery spot of dirt maybe two feet behind.

The meat bounced skyward and set the flies to buzzing.

After that, it was a matter of me wanting to hit that piece of meat every time and therefore not being able to do so, no way nohow, and wasting three more days before realizing the secret of doing anything artful is to try as hard as you can while at the same time not trying at all. With this bit of swami knowledge under my belt, I soon got so eight times out of ten I could send those flies into a commotion, though I'd long figured out that no one, and that included Louis Roth, could ever hit one specific fly while leaving another be.

So I went and got Louis. Rapped on the door of his parked Pullman car and told him I had something he needed to see. Immediately I knew he'd been drinking, for his accent was thicker than usual, almost to the point I couldn't understand him: "Vell vell vell, ze girl she hass somessing to show ze boss, mmmmmmm?" We headed through the backyard, Louis walking stiff and rapid-fire as always though with the occasional off-course sidestep. Every few feet, I had to skip a little just to keep up. We reached my training space, out in an empty yard behind the menage tent. There he watched as I picked up the whip and aimed and not-aimed at the same time. After a quick arm twirl, I let loose a wrist snap that was a millisecond tardy. A dozen feet away, a pair of flies were sniffing and dancing over the target. One was way over on the left, one was way over on the right, and the fact my slightly off-course lashing got close enough to scare the right-side fly only I put down to sheer fluke.

Louis's mouth went to hang open, though he stopped himself just as his lower lip cleared his teeth. I watched his jaw muscles grind beneath tight skin as he looked at that day's meat being bothered by a single silent fly. Just kept looking at it, he did, until finally he turned to me and barked, "Come."

So what did I, twenty-four-year-old Mary Haynie of West Kentucky slash Mary Aganosticus of Louisville slash Mary Williams from East Texas slash Mabel Stark of the St. Mark's Hotel do? Followed him, best as I was able, for Louis practically bolted through the backyard, across the midway and into the training barn. Without benefit of a cage boy, he started shifting cages so his two best lions, Humpy and Bill, connected to the tunnel leading into the steel arena. This exertion made him sweat, and this caused him to give off the scent of alcohol gone sweet with exertion: was like camphor lozenges, though stronger. He yanked the tunnel door rope and the lions filed into the tunnel. He opened the second tunnel door and they entered the ring. Then he brushed by me—not so much as an *excuse me*—and stepped inside. Humpy roared and Bill flopped on his side and Louis barked, "Children! Seats!"

Humpy took the pedestal to the left and Bill the pedestal to the right. Louis stood between them, dropping his whip on the floor. Then he reached out and pressed a hand against each lion's throat, both arms disappearing to their elbows in tawny mane. With this, the lions lifted their heads and placed their chins on Louis's shoulders. Louis turned to his right and pressed his lips up against Bill's mouth and he kissed the lion for five or ten seconds. Then he turned to Humpy and kissed him even harder than he 'd kissed Bill, his hand furrowing through Humpy's mane to the back of Humpy's head before grabbing up a handful of cat hair and pulling, so that Humpy's gums and lips and tongue were forced over the lower half of Louis Roth's face, smearing it with saliva and hay bits and fragments of horse. Then, as man and animal kissed, Louis slipped his hands into the sides of the animal's mouth and, with a steady pressure, craned it wide open. Head then followed hands, Louis now inside a lion from the neck up, the tips of Humpy's incisors making pointy-shaped impressions in the skin of Louis's neck.

In a second Louis was out, not a hair mussed though his face was dampened and speckled with mouth debris. He walked out of the ring and stood beside me, smelling of cat and whisky. We were both silent. His jaw muscles worked and he folded his arms tight over his stomach. The *things* that man could say without speaking.

I opened the cage door and stepped inside and walked to the point between the pedestals. I was shaking inside, half from fear and half from wanting to do this so bad. Humpy grinned and Bill growled, a deep distant-thunder rumble that got inside and roped up and down my spine and got turned into my own voice once it reached the inside of my head. *Go back*, was what it said.

Instead I craned my neck and kissed the lion as he was still growling and maybe thinking of having himself a kill, though he calmed with my lips against his and my hand tickling his neck. When his growling stopped I turned and put my lips to Humpy and kissed him too, the big cat lolling his tongue out of his mouth so it lathered my tongue and teeth and gums before parting his jaws a little to signal he expected hands to slip inside. Taking this cue I pulled his jaws apart and put my head in the animal's mouth, and it was while inside Humpy's head I felt myself go dead calm, for at that moment there was no question what was going to get me—was going to be the jaws of a lion, reeking of tartar and animal flesh going to rot between molars, and in this certainty there was a warmth difficult to describe. Fact was, I didn't even want to pull my head back out.

After a bit Humpy widened his jaws. When I felt the point of his teeth leave my neck I pulled out. I left the cage and stood beside Louis, and for the next thirty or forty seconds we had ourselves a conversation without one word being passed. Humpy and Bill had both flopped and were flicking at flies with their tails. When Louis finally spoke, was for the record only.

"All right," he said. "Tomorrow vee start."

That night I went back to my room and did a curious thing. I'd kept some mementoes from my pre-Stark life, cards and letters and even a menu from the Continental in San Francisco. I was sitting on my cot, looking at them, when a hopeful feeling came over me and the next thing you know I had out scissors and was cutting and cutting and cutting.

Next morning, I met Louis bright and early. He had huge grey wells under his eyes and wrinkles in his face that weren't ordinarily there, but otherwise he looked impeccable: hair combed and boots polished and training suit pressed. The cage boy, Red, met us too, the three of us shifting tiger cages until they connected with the steel arena. Red went inside and shifted three pedestals so they were in a row, calling "Props ready!" when finished.

Louis darted off, back bobbing ramrod stiff. I looked to Red for an explanation, and he shrugged. A minute later, Louis returned with a pair of overalls on his arm. "Here," he said, "put ziss on. If zey catch a nail in your skirt zey will keep on tearing. Zey luff the sound of things tearing."

I ducked behind a tool shed to change, and while I was doing so Red and Louis released the tunnel doors. The tigers slunk into the ring, looking shaggy and consternated. Toby roared, and I trembled, for it wasn't the roar of a lion showing off but of a tiger indicating displeasure, and there's a world of seriousness separating the two. This roar bothered King, who took a swipe at Toby, and in a second the two tigers were at each other, on their hind legs and exchanging a flurry of quick clawless blows before crankily taking steps backward. Queen peered at Louis and me, her gaze slowly taking it all in.

I slipped into the ring with a buggy whip and stayed close to the bars. The tigers had seen me outside the ring for the past six months, and I had to give them a chance to get used to the idea of bars no longer separating us. Queen stayed still, watching me, while the other two paced around the far side of the ring. After a minute, King flopped on his belly and Queen rolled on him and it was only Toby who was still fixed on figuring out what I was doing in there. So he came close. Came within four feet and then stopped and peered at me through green slits. He was panting loudly enough the liquid gurgling in the back of his throat sounded like its own deep voice. He could've been thinking about killing me or he could've been thinking about that day's weather, for all he showed.

It was then I focused my gaze on his eyes and time froze and I knew. I knew exactly what that animal was thinking, would've mistaken it for my own thoughts had I not seen it written across his kelp-green pupils.

I'll test her, that tiger was thinking. *I'll just see.*

So he came forward another foot. The crowd gathered outside the steel arena hushed. I cracked my whip and my voice rang clear in the silence of the menage—"Seat!"

Toby stood his ground and I cracked the whip again and issued the command again, until finally he slunk back toward the pedestal but to show he couldn't be cowed he lay beside the pedestal instead of taking his seat, all of which is tiger for *Fuck you.* Still, I was encouraged he hadn't taken a swipe and that he was even halfway near where he should be. I called Queen's name, followed by the seat command, and was surprised when she actually did it, looking happy with the activity. I did the same with King, only he got serious-looking and he came toward me. Again, I looked into a tiger's mind like it was a shelf in a grocery store, and again I knew exactly what it was he was planning. Which was, *Think I'll act as if nothing's concerning me and then rip her stomach clear out, just to see the look of surprise on her face.*

In other words, I jumped before that forepaw shot out, sprang clear out of its path and watched it sail by. I could see muscles reticulating beneath the surface, like a fit man's, only it was covered in orange-and-black fur and ended in a fluffy white dangerousness. Then it was my turn for surprises, so I brought the whip down hard on his nose. This froze him—not the pain of the whip but the shock caused by my being able to read his thoughts, which is the only real way to get the word *vulnerable* rumbling through the head of a tiger. I hit him again, this time harder because he was still and I had more opportunity to wind up. He hissed and swiped the air one more time and with a rumble of disgust slunk to his pedestal and took his seat.

By this point, I had two cats seated and one sprawled on the arena floor, which is more than anyone expected I'd get done, seeing as how the cats had gone half rogue since killing their trainer a year and a half previous. As for me, I was bathed in sweat and trembling from having tensed my muscles too hard, so I nodded to Red and he roped open the tunnel door. Each cat rushed toward the exit, and after some nasty pawing at the gummed-up opening they left in the following order: King, Toby, Queen.

On the outside I towelled off. Truth was, I felt like I'd taken a Chinaman bottle, meaning numb and euphoric and seeing stars. Louis could do nothing but shake his head, not believing. Around us people were chattering, workingmen mostly, and though their words bedspreaded all over one another I knew they were talking about what they'd just seen.

That night, Louis Roth invited me to dinner.

I'd never seen a man eat so precisely. He cut each piece of roast with a sawing rhythm that lasted exactly eight saws, even if it took only six to get through, the last two squeaking against china. He'd then lay his knife at a forty-five-degree angle across the top of his plate—carefully, so as not to make a clatter—before returning his fork to his right hand and then putting the morsel of food into his mouth. Then he'd chew exactly eighteen times. Count, I did, for he wasn't a man who needed to hear the sound of his own voice, or the voice of anybody else for that matter, meaning there were pauses in the conversation. Every third bite he'd take a swallow of red wine, which he drank too much of, more than a bottle and a half, though you'd never know he was drunk except his accent thickened and his movements got a little less darting.

Otherwise, the meal was businesslike as businesslike gets, Louis willing to discuss only tigers and what my plans with them were. So I informed him I wanted to go straight to the top, and he told me the top was a good place to be if you could wrap your head around the fact there was only one place to go afterwards. I had soup, salad, fish and potatoes, and a slice of chocolate cake. Later that evening he dropped me off at the St. Mark's before heading back to his own car on the lot. He didn't try to kiss me, there being nothing during dinner to predict it, our first touch being a handshake on the street outside the lobby, my fingers disappearing in a big sinewy hand that looked out of place on such a wiry little frame.

"Good evening" were his last words before heading down the darkened street. I was left puzzling, though over the next few days I figured out that dinner had been his way of saying he was going to take me on without actually out-and-out saying he was going to take me on. Once it sank in that Louis Roth was going to mentor me, and maybe I was finding myself out of the mess my life had been for ten years . . . well. The sheer *relief* of it. Was a feeling infected everything I did over the next couple of days. Sometimes I'd look at myself in the mirror and see how happy I was and I'd actually say, "Can't you wipe that grin off your face, Mabel? Can't you? Go ahead, *try*," and there I'd be, wrestling with my mouth muscles, the lunacy of which would make me break out laughing, and I'd be giggling at nothing but my own reflection and it'd occur to me, *Jesus Mabel, you really are crackers* and it'd be this thought that'd sober me up quick. (The worst part of being sent to a nuthouse? For the rest of your days, every time you have a purity of emotion, you worry, *Uh-oh here I go again.*)

My education started the very next day, around eleven. And what an education it was. Remember, back then Pavlov hadn't yet been invented, so no one was really sure what it was made an animal do anything. Most trainers got their way by battering the animal until it did what it was supposed to, the reward being if the cat stepped on the pedestal he'd stop getting his hind end flogged with a cane whip.

Problem was, the animal didn't learn much more than how to get out of the way, the tricks full of miscues and inaccuracies and those errors in movement trainers call splash. Plus over time the animal usually developed a keen interest in killing his trainer, which is a foolhardy relationship to have with any animal that kills by seizing your shoulders and pulling you on top, at which point anything not protected by rib cage gets torn out by a single swipe of hind-leg claws. You die watching the tiger feed on your mess. It isn't even particularly quick.

It was Louis who figured instead you should give the cat something good when he did something right. He called his method "gentling" and it was "gentling" he taught me throughout January and February. Whenever King or Toby or Queen did what I wanted, or anything close to it, I'd hum, "Good little kittie," or scratch their throats or drop a piece of horseflesh at their feet or purr in their ears until they started purring right along, a sound like a motor idling. I worked this way with the tigers for five weeks, rewarding every time they came close (and then closer) to doing what I wanted, giving them a wake-up smack if they got ornery, jumping out of the way whenever my sixth sense flared. If I made a mistake Louis let me know about it pretty quick. He was good at that, though after a while it also got so if I did something good his jaws would flex and he'd say, "Yess yess, that iss it."

By the end of that time Toby could do a sit-up and a rollover, and the three cats could lie side by side without slashing at each other. For a finale, they'd move into a pyramid in the middle of the ring, Toby on the high pedestal, wearing an expression that looked like pride but was actually a cat waiting for a hunk of meat and knowing he was going to get it. Seeing this, Louis not only said "Yess yess, that iss it," but grinned while he said it, for putting three tigers in a pyramid was what passed for something in 1913.

One night about two weeks prior to the start of the season, Toby started convulsing. For the next half-hour, I held his head in my lap while I spoke softly and stroked the spot low on a tiger's belly where they feel a keenness of pleasure. He was so sick he didn't even try to bite or claw, normally the first thing an ailing tiger will do. Finally he arfed weakly and his body shook and a film of white spread over his eyes. I bawled like a little girl, Louis and Al G. and Dan standing off to one side with their hands in their pockets, feeling bad and wondering what they were going to do vis-a-vis the photo of newcomer Mabel Stark and her "Pyramid of Fearsome Feline Ferocity!!!," which was now on Barnes circus paper all up and down the West Coast. This'd been Al G.'s idea, his opinion being nothing but nothing styled a tiger act like a blonde, especially considering how everyone knew the last woman trainer on the Barnes show had been pulled down forward and fed on. Only problem was, all the styling in the world wouldn't make a pyramid out of just two cats.

Was it my bawling? Was it the gravity of the situation? Or was it that Louis Roth took this moment to notice his protégée was young and lithe and looked at him with crossed eyes through curly blonde bangs? All I know is when Louis Roth, a man not known for kindnesses or human considerations, offered up his two best lions for a mixed act, I could only blink a few times and think to myself, *Hmmmmmmmmmm.*

We started by putting King and Queen in a cage next to Humpy and Bill so they could get used to the sight and the smell of each other. This phase lasted a week, though longer would've been better. Then we put them all together in the cage, the lion pedestals and the tiger pedestals as far away as the cage diameter allowed. Over the next week, we kept moving their seats closer and closer, rewarding every time they took them, until the day came when we flanked the lions with King and Queen. No one liked this but Louis and me; the lions roared and pawed and growled and put on all the fake bluster lions are famous for putting on. The tigers went silent, which was worse, for if you looked carefully you could see their muscles were tensed and their ears were shifted backward ever so slightly.

I needed the twisted willow that day, along with a lot of imitation purring and "Good kitties" and lower-belly scratching. I threw down a lot of horsemeat, too. This went on for several more days before I tried kissing the lions with the two tigers looking on, a move truly nervous-making for I had to drop my whip to do it and I wondered if the tigers would interpret this as a signal feeding time had commenced. Louis advised if a tiger stalked I kick it hard in the whiskers with a boot heel and then pull back quick so a claw didn't take hold.

We opened March 8 in Santa Monica. Three rings, with thirteen displays, all of them animal acts. I rode high school in the fourth display, and put on my mixed act in the tenth, a centre-ring attraction flanked by dog acts in rings one and three and a performing bear doing a hind leg around the hippodrome. Was a good little act for its time: After marching the cats around the cage perimeter I got them on their seats and had King, my performing tiger, run through his sit-up and rollover. Then I kissed Humpy and Bill and for a finale moved the two tigers down and close, forming a four-cat pyramid.

The applause? Was like music. Was like the crescendo of an orchestra. You hear applause like that and for as long as it lasts everything you ever thought about yourself thins and gets blanketed with *Hey, you're a person people clap at.* Only problem is, it can and will turn you foolish: the moment the applause started to dim I was dizzied with a need to stretch it out, so right off I lost my head and turned my back on those cats and took a bow, something no one had ever done before in the circus and a piece of foolhardiness that got written up next day in the papers. Louis was furious, Al G. delighted. A week later, Al G. issued new paper, his posters announcing "Mabel Stark Subjugates to Her Will the Most Dangerous Killers Ever Recruited from Mountain Fastness and Jungle Lair." Was a claim followed by five exclamation points.

Following Santa Monica, we played six days at a Shriners' convention in Los Angeles, a rarity for we mostly jumped every night. From there we moved into the Mojave and then crossed the Tehachapi Mountains to get to Bakersfield, Porterville, Reedly, Selma, Tulare and Coalinga before drifting Oregon way. Houses were good, it being the tail end of what they call the Golden Age of the Circus, before roads and cars offered people in small towns choices. When we came to town, banks closed, as did all schools and businesses. Attendence was routinely more than 80 percent of the people in any given town.

There were two shows daily, plus a Tom Mix–style Wild West in place of a concert after the show. In addition to my horse and cat acts, I rode in the lion cage during parade, behind bars with four of Louis's gentlest. Al G. got a new goat trainer and Slide for Lifer, his feeling being that either act would've destroyed my mystique. Soon I got used to signing autographs and dealing with reporters, most of the questions having to do with, *Is it true women are more able to soothe the savage beast?* or *Do you really hypnotize your animals?* or *How's it feel filling the shoes of Marguerite Haupt, seeing as how she got killed wearing them herself?* Imagine what this was like for a little orphan from the homely end of Kentucky: encircled by men in trench coats, press cards tucked in Fedora bands, scribbling every word you care to utter, then fighting to get the next question in.

Well.

Was lovely and exciting and nerve-wracking all rolled into one, my being a woman who's always found pure happiness a commodity difficult to deal with. Course, I suppose that's why I was drawn to the tigers in the first place. No matter how well things're going, you always know it's only a matter of time before a claw catches, or a tooth snags, or a forepaw lashes, and your contentment feels bearable again.

THE GREAT SHOWMAN DEAD

—Huckster, genius, con artist, the world's first advertising wizard: Quite a bit has been said about P. T. Barnum; here's what the "Old Gray Lady" had to say upon his death in 1891.

LAST HOURS OF THE LIFE OF PHINEAS T. BARNUM
THE VETERAN MANAGER SINKS INTO A PEACEFUL SLEEP THAT KNOWS NO WAKING—THE FUNERAL TO BE PRIVATE AT HIS EXPRESS DESIRE
The New York Times

RIDGEPORT, CONN., APRIL 7.—At 6:22 o'clock tonight the long sickness of P. T. Barnum came to an end by his quietly passing away at Marina, his residence in this city.

Shortly after midnight there came an alarming change for the worse. Drs. Hubbard and Godfrey, who were in attendance, saw at once that the change was such as to indicate that the patient could not long survive. The weakened pulse, more difficult respiration, and lower temperature showed that the action of the heart had become so feeble as to presage the collapse which was the beginning of the end. Mr. Barnum seemed to realize that he could not live much longer, and spoke of his approaching end with calmness. Through the night he suffered much pain. Mrs. Barnum remained at the bedside during the night.

One of the requests made by Mr. Barnum was that, when all hope was gone, sedatives which would make his passage to the next world more peaceful be administered. About 4 o'clock this morning the veteran showman spoke his last words. He was asked if he wished a drink of water, and answered, "Yes." Soon after he sank into a lethargy. It was difficult to arouse him from this state, and on opening his eyes a faint gleam of recognition alone indicated that he had knowledge of his surroundings, or knew those about him. All day long Mr. Barnum lay in a semi-unconscious state. About 10 o'clock the first sedative was administered, and repeated several times during the day.

When it became certain that the end was but a few hours distant, telegrams to relatives were sent out, and among the sorrowing group in the sick room this evening when the final moments came were Mrs. Barnum, the Rev. L. B. Fisher, pastor of the Universalist church of this city, of which Mr. Barnum was a member; Mrs. D. W. Thompson, Mr. Barnum's daughter; Mrs. W. H. Buchtelle of New York, another daughter; C. Barnum Seeley, his grandson; Drs. Hubbard and Godfrey, his physicians; C. B. Olcutt, a trained nurse from Bellevue Hospital, and W. D. Roberts, his faithful colored valet. The scene at the deathbed was deeply pathetic. All were in tears. Although Mrs. Barnum has stood up bravely under the strain, the closing moments were too much for her and she gave way at times. For an hour or two before his death those at the bedside watched for some sign of recognition or a word from the dying man, but in vain. His end was peaceful and apparently perfectly painless.

Although no arrangements have as yet been perfected for the funeral, it is known that it will take place Friday. The Rev. Mr. Collyer of New York, a lifelong friend of Mr. Barnum, will assist the Rev. Mr. Fisher in the services, which will be private. In accordance with the expressed wish of the deceased he will be buried in Mountain Grove Cemetery, where he recently had erected a massive granite monument.

As has been repeatedly published, Mr. Barnum makes provision in his will for the continuance as a permanent institution of the great show with which his name is associated. For his wife, his daughters, and other relatives, he has made handsome provision, but the bulk of his property goes to C. Barnum Seeley, his only grandson. Mr. Seeley lives in New York. He is a member of the Stock Exchange, Mr. Barnum having purchased a seat for him a short time ago.

Mr. Barnum had been sick since Nov. 6. Several times he rallied, but only twice during his illness had he left the sick room. Death was due to degeneration of the muscles of the heart. Throughout the city tonight there is the deepest sorrow. The Post Office, City Hall, business houses, and many private residences are draped in mourning. Many telegrams of condolence have already been received at Marina. Day before yesterday Mr. Barnum was eighty years and nine months of age. None but the family and near relatives will be allowed to see the remains. It was a request of Mr. Barnum and will be carried out.

Mr. Barnum's Life Story

The great American showman will never again plan or manage a museum, circus, or other exhibition. For more than forty years he toiled to amuse the public. He has now gone to his final rest. His life was filled with many noteworthy incidents and remarkable adventures—so many, indeed, that to give but the heads of each would occupy far more space than it is possible for a newspaper to devote to such a subject. For this reason it is obvious that the sketch which follows can only be regarded as an outline of the principal events in his most eventful career.

Phineas Taylor Barnum was born in the town of Bethel, in Connecticut, on July 5, 1810, his name, Phineas Taylor, being derived from his maternal grandfather, one of the oldest settlers of New England. His father, Philo Barnum, the son of Ephraim Barnum, who served as a Captain in the Revolutionary war, was a tailor, a farmer, at times a tavern keeper, and ever on the lookout to turn a quick penny by any honorable means. Born of such ancestors and with such surroundings, it is hardly necessary to say that the boy was early taught that if he would succeed in the world he must work hard. That lesson he never forgot. When little more than a child he was obliged to do his share toward the support of himself and his family. So when he was only six years of age he drove cows to and from pasture, weeded the kitchen garden at the back of the humble house in which he was born, shelled corn, and as he grew older rode the plow horse, and whenever he had an opportunity attended school. From the first he was a quick if not a very regular student.

In arithmetic and every form of calculation he was particularly apt, and one of his earliest recollections, and one which he always mentioned with much pleasure, was that in his tenth year he was called out of bed by his teacher, who had wagered with an acquaintance that in less than five minutes he (the boy) could calculate the number of feet in a given load of wood. After obtaining the dimensions, half asleep as he was, Phineas, much to the delight of his teacher and the discomfiture of the doubting acquaintance, correctly figured out the result in less than two minutes. Nor was this knowledge of figures the only marked trait which was early developed by the boy. He was also at a remarkably early age fully aware of the value of money. He never was known to squander or foolishly spend a penny. When he was six years old he had saved coppers enough to exchange for a silver dollar. This he "turned" as rapidly as he could with safety, and by peddling home-made molasses candy, gingerbread, and at times a species of liquor made by himself and called cherry rum, he had accumulated when he was not quite twelve years of age a sum sufficient to buy and pay for a sheep and a calf. Indeed, to use an expression subsequently employed by him when relating these early experiences, he was rapidly becoming a small Croesus, when his father very kindly gave him permission to buy his own clothing with his own money. Of course, this permission materially reduced his little store.

So, living the life of a country boy, his career being diversified by one visit to New York as an assistant to a cattle drover, and numerous small business transactions, in which he nearly always displayed an ability to make a good bargain, the young Phineas continued in Bethel until he was far advanced in his teens. At this time he became a prominent member of the Bible class in the local Sunday school, and among other scholars was, upon certain occasions, required to answer questions from the Bible. The following answer to such a question which was written by him may well serve as an illustration of his bent of mind, as well as of the progress which he had made as a scholar. The text which he drew in accordance with the custom of the Sunday school was, "But one thing is needful and Mary hath chosen the good part, which shall not be taken away from her." Based upon this was the question. "What is the one thing needful?" This was young Barnum's written answer: "This question, 'What is the one thing needful?' is capable of receiving various answers, depending much upon the persons to whom it is addressed. The merchant might answer that the one thing needful is plenty of customers to buy liberally without beating down, and to pay cash for all their purchases. The farmer might reply that the one thing needful is large harvests and high prices. The physician might answer that it is plenty of patients. The lawyer might be of opinion that it is an unruly community always engaged in bickerings and litigations. The clergyman might reply, 'It is a fat salary, with multitudes of sinners seeking salvation and paying large pew rents.' The sensible bachelor might exclaim, 'It is a pretty wife, who loves her husband, and who knows how to sew on buttons.' The maiden might answer, 'It is a good husband who will love, cherish, and protect me while life shall last.' But the proper answer and, doubtless, that which applied to the case of Mary, would be, 'The one thing needful is to believe in the Lord Jesus Christ, follow in His footsteps, love God, and obey His commandments, love our fellow-men, and embrace every opportunity of administering to their necessities.' In short, the one thing needful is to live a life that we can always look back upon with satisfaction and be enabled ever to contemplate its termination with trust in Him who has so kindly vouchsafed it to us, surrounded us with innumerable blessings if we have but the heart and the wisdom to receive them in a proper manner."

For many years after those quiet days in the Bethel Sunday school the life of young Barnum was one of hard and constant struggle. His father died when he was fifteen years of age, and he was left almost penniless to make his own way in the world. To gain a respectable living he tried all sorts of trades, and it can with all truth be said that whatever he found to do he always did with all his might. He was by turns a peddler and trader in a small way, a clerk in Brooklyn and New York, the keeper of a small porter house, the proprietor of a village store, and editor of a country newspaper, for writing alleged libels in which he was imprisoned only to be liberated with a grand flourish of trumpets and the congratulations of a crowd. After this he kept a boarding house, did more trading with varying success, was in the lottery business, made a trip to Philadelphia, then regarded as a far distant city, and was married to a young tailoress, whom he many years after described as "the best woman in the world, well suited to his disposition, admirable and valuable in every character as a wife, a mother, and a friend."

For more than five years after taking this most important and, as the result proved, satisfactory step, Mr. Barnum continued with varying success to struggle with the world until, in 1835, he at last found the calling for which he seems to have been born. In short, he went into "the show business," in which he afterward became so famous. Regarding this period in his life he in after years wrote as follows: "By this time it was clear to my mind that my proper position in this busy world was not yet reached. The business for which I was destined and, I believe, made had not yet come to me. I had not found that I was to cater for that insatiate want of human nature—the love of amusement; that I was to make a sensation in two continents, and that fame and fortune awaited me so soon as I should appear in the character of a showman. The show business has all phases and grades of dignity, from the exhibition of a monkey to the exposition of that highest art in music or the drama which secures for the gifted artists a world-wide fame Princes well might envy. Men, women, and children who cannot live on gravity alone need something to satisfy their gayer, lighter moods and hours, and he who ministers to this want is, in my opinion, in a business established by the Creator of our nature. If he worthily fulfills his mission and amuses without corrupting, he need never feel that he has lived in vain. As for myself, I can say that the least deserving of all my efforts in the show line was the one which introduced me to the business, a scheme in no sense of my own devising, one which had been for some time before the public, and which had so many vouchers for its genuineness that at the time of taking possession of it I honestly believed it to be genuine."

The first venture to which Mr. Barnum thus refers was a remarkable negro woman, who was said to have been 161 years old and a nurse of Gen. George Washington—the first of a long line. The wonders of this person are found fully set forth in the following notice, cut from the *Pennsylvania Inquirer* of July 15, 1835:

> "CURIOSITY.—The citizens of Philadelphia and its vicinity have an opportunity of witnessing at Masonic Hall one of the greatest natural curiosities ever witnessed, viz., Joice Heth, a negress, aged 161 years, who formerly belonged to the father of Gen. Washington. She has been a member of the Baptist Church 116 years, and can rehearse many hymns and sing them according to former custom. She was born near the old Potomac River, in Virginia, and has for 90 or 100 years lived in Paris, Ky., with the Bowling family. All who have seen this extraordinary woman are satisfied of the truth of the account of her age. The evidence of the Bowling family, which is respectable, is strong that the original bill of sale of Augustine Washington, in his own handwriting, and other evidence which the proprietor has in his possession will satisfy even the most incredulous."

For $1,000, some of which was borrowed and the rest raised by the sale of a grocery store in the possession of which he happened to be at the moment, Mr. Barnum bought the "wonderful negress," and, making money by the venture, he ever afterward, with only short intermissions, continued to follow the business of a showman.

During the years which followed he traveled all over this country and in many other parts of the world, and was interested in some of the most important undertakings for the amusement of the public of which recent history furnishes any record. Of all his enterprises, however, he regarded his connection with the American Museum and his management of Jenny Lind and Tom Thumb as the most important. It was on the 27th of December, 1841, that by a shrewd stroke of business he obtained control of the American Museum, on the corner of Ann Street and Broadway in New York, and for years afterward he continued to conduct that establishment. Under his management it became one of the most famous places of amusement in the world. In it, as it is hardly necessary to state, were exhibited "the Feejee Mermaid," "the original bearded woman," "the woolly horse," giants and dwarfs almost without end, and, to use Mr. Barnum's own expression, "innumerable other attractions of a minor though nevertheless a most interesting, instructive, and moral character." In addition to these "other attractions" Mr. Barnum's plan also embraced the performance in the museum of such moral dramas, so called, as "Uncle Tom's Cabin," "Moses in Egypt," "The Drunkard," and "Joseph and His Brethren." It is noticeable in this connection that Mr. Barney Williams and Miss Mary Gannon, afterward so famous, commenced their careers under his management at very small salaries. E. A. Sothern and many other actors who subsequently became celebrated were also from time to time members of the museum dramatic company. It was in November, 1842, that Mr. Barnum engaged Charles S. Stratton, whom he christened Tom Thumb. With him he traveled and made large sums of money in different parts of the world. Later in life he saw him married to a dwarf like himself.

Regarding a visit which he made with Tom Thumb to the Queen of England, Mr. Barnum in after years wrote: "We were conducted through a long corridor to a broad flight of marble steps, which led to the Queen's magnificent picture gallery, where her Majesty and Prince Albert, the Duchess of Kent, and twenty or thirty of the nobility were awaiting our arrival. They were standing at the further end of the room when the doors were thrown open, and the General walked in looking like a wax doll gifted with the power of locomotion. Surprise and pleasure were depicted on the countenances of the royal circle on beholding this remarkable specimen of humanity so much smaller than they had evidently expected to find him. The General advanced with a firm step, and as he came within hailing distance made a very graceful bow and exclaimed, 'Good evening, ladies and gentlemen.' A burst of laughter followed this salutation. The Queen then took him by the hand, led him about the gallery, and asked him many questions, the answers to which kept the party in an uninterrupted strain of merriment. The General familiarly informed the Queen that her pictures were 'first-rate,' and told her he should like to see the Prince of Wales. The Queen replied that the Prince had retired to rest, but that he should see him on some future occasion. The General then gave his songs, dances, and imitations, and after a conversation with Prince Albert and all present, which continued for more than an hour, we were permitted to depart." After this visit the General and his manager visited the rulers of France and Belgium and many other notable persons in Europe, and were everywhere well received and entertained.

As has already been stated, Mr. Barnum very justly regarded his engagement of Jenny Lind as one of the great events in his career. That engagement was entered into in 1850. It resulted in a fortune for Mr. Barnum, and in the payment to Jenny Lind for ninety-five concerts of the sum of $176,675.09. Besides this sum all the expenses of herself and suite were paid by the manager. As high as $650 was paid at auction for a single ticket of admission to one of her concerts. During the tour which resulted so profitably, Miss Lind stopped for a day at Iranistan, Mr. Barnum's beautiful country seat near Bridgeport, which was afterward burned. While there she said to her manager:

"Do you know, Mr. Barnum, that if you had not built Iranistan I should never have come to America for you?"

"Pray explain," said Mr. Barnum, much surprised, and she went on: "Well, I had received several applications to visit the United States, but I did not much like the appearance of the applicants, nor did I relish the idea of crossing 3,000 miles of water, so I declined them all. But the first letter which your agent, Mr. Wilton, addressed to me was written upon a sheet headed with a beautiful engraving of Iranistan. It attracted my attention. I said to myself a gentleman who has been so successful in his business as to be able to build and reside in such a palace cannot be a mere adventurer. So I wrote to your agent and consented to an interview, which I should have declined if I had not seen the picture of Iranistan."

To which the manager gallantly replied: "Then I am fully repaid for building it."

After his successful engagement with Jenny Lind Mr. Barnum was everywhere regarded as being "a made man" and at the head of his business. So he continued for a time, engaging in many new enterprises.

But, as the years went on, trouble fell upon him, and by unwise speculation with what was known as the Jerome Clock Company of East Bridgeport he lost every penny he had in the world. Still he did not give up the fight, but by the help of friends, the increase in value of certain real estate owned by him, and the great energy which was ever one of his chief traits, he again commenced in a small way; subsequently took Tom Thumb to Europe for a second visit, and by degrees repaired his broken fortunes. Later on he again undertook the management of the museum in New York, and upon its destruction by fire established "the new museum" further up Broadway. It was also burned, and he lost much money. So also was his great world's fair building, built in Fourteenth Street in 1873. But after a time fortune again smiled upon him, and as a manager of monster circuses and traveling shows and as a public lecturer he met with much success in all parts of the country.

During all his life Mr. Barnum was a great believer in the power of advertising. Indeed, to such an extent did he carry this belief that he spent the entire receipts of his first year in the old museum in making the attractions of that place known to the public. The result proved the wisdom of his course. Still, much as he coveted the good offices of the newspapers, he was bold enough to stand out against them when he believed that the occasion required it. This fact was fully proved by his quarrel with the New York *Herald* and the elder Bennett, a quarrel which grew out of differences regarding the lease of the museum site, and which resulted, first, in Mr. Bennett's refusal to take Barnum's advertisements, and subsequently in the refusal of the Theatrical Managers' Association, headed by Mr. Barnum, to advertise in the *Herald*. The war was continued for two years.

Mr. Barnum had natural genius as an advertiser. No man knew better than he the value of printer's ink. He made it part of his business to be talked about. The more attention he got in that way the better he liked it. He had learned the advertising art when a New York showman, for that was practically what he was until his Fourteenth Street Museum burned down. Jenny Lind and Tom Thumb were cards too great to be kept within one city, however large. Excepting the years when they were his attractions he confined his efforts principally to pleasing the New York public. His show in its present extent and character was put in operation within twenty years. When he branched out on this grand scale his ideas kept pace with his opportunities. Nothing was too ambitious for him to undertake.

One of the greatest chances of his life came with Jumbo. He had often gazed on that monster with a showman's eyes in the Zoological Gardens at London, but it had never occurred to him as possible to possess the English pet. It was reserved for one of his agents to induce the manager of the garden to offer the animal for £2,000. Mr. Barnum snapped up the offer at once. There was a cry of protest from all England. The newspapers, royalty, the clergy, statesmen, and men high in the arts and professions led the outcry. It was taken up by the masses. The ladies and children became hysterical over the prospective loss. England ran mad over Jumbo. Pictures of Jumbo, Jumbo's life, Jumbo stories and poetry, Jumbo collars, neckties, cigars, fans, polkas, and hats were put on the market and worn, sung, smoked, and danced by the entire English nation. The funny papers took up the cry and published coats-of-arms with Jumbo in the lion's place and labeled "Dieu et mon Jumbo." Jumbo became nearly an international question.

Mr. Barnum was importuned to name the price at which he would relinquish his contract and permit Jumbo to remain in London. People crowded the Zoo day after day to see Jumbo. Between November, 1881, and March, 1882—the dates of purchase and removal—the receipts at the Zoo, because of this craze, increased about $15,000, a sum that might justly be added to the purchase price of $10,000 as the total revenue to the sellers from this transaction. Mr. Barnum reminded the English people of this when they wanted him to let Jumbo alone. He said he had promised to show the animal in America and had advertised him extensively. Therefore, £100,000 would not induce him to cancel the purchase.

An animal so heralded was bound to make a sensation here. The English craze had been so much advertising for Barnum. When Jumbo and his movements became a matter of deep public interest the newspapers printed all they could get about him as a matter of news.

As an advertising attraction alone Jumbo was worth to Barnum more than his price. He also became a favorite here, and his untimely death was mourned practically by two nations. Jumbo's mate, Alice, never awoke anything like the popular enthusiasm or affection that Jumbo enjoyed. The bones of Jumbo went to the Smithsonian Institution, and his stuffed hide to the Barnum Museum of Natural History at Tufts College.

When Jumbo became an old story, Mr. Barnum secured as his next startling novelty the white elephant. If this animal was not white and if people had their opinion about the search for such an exhibit having involved an outlay of $250,000, this acquisition proved another great advertisement for the show. Mr. Barnum spared no effort to let every one understand that this was one of the world's wonders. He got up a prize poem competition over the animal, to which Joaquin Miller was a contributor.

Mr. Barnum's gift of a museum to Tufts College was announced at Commencement in June, 1884. A handsome and well-appointed stone building was the result, which cost him $55,000. Afterward he contributed largely of exhibits for the museum. A gift equally notable was that which he made in June, 1888, to the Fairfield Historical Society and Bridgeport Scientific Society of Bridgeport. The land was a corner plot 100 feet square, and he contributed also $200,000 for a ten-story building to be erected upon it. Although this gift had been contemplated by him for some time, he had thought of making it on his birthday in July, 1888, when he would be seventy-eight years old. It was made a month in advance. This is the way he explained the change of date:

> "I awoke about 5 o'clock that morning, and when I looked over at Nancy, still sleeping, I said to myself: 'I am getting old. At my age a man may drop off any moment. Nancy, poor girl, will have enough to bother her when I go without looking after the business of the estate. I had better attend to this thing myself.' I rose and sent word to the Trustees to come to my house after breakfast. Before 9 o'clock the whole thing was done."

Mr. Barnum's solicitude that no business cares should devolve upon his wife at his death had led him to make and publish his will in 1883. He had three physicians with him at the time, who subscribed to affidavits that he was of sound and disposing mind and memory. His estate was then valued at $10,000,000. The will named twenty-seven heirs and was generous in charitable bequests. He valued his share in the show at $3,500,000. His executors were empowered to renew contracts to carry on the show for the estate at the expiration of the present contract in 1899. The Children's Aid Society was specifically named as a beneficiary of a certain percentage of each season's profits.

"I don't know anybody connected with that society," the great showman explained, "but I believe in the society. To me there is no picture so beautiful as smiling, bright-eyed, happy children; no music so sweet as their clear and ringing laughter. That I have had power to provide innocent amusement for the little ones, to create such pictures, to evoke such music, is my proudest reflection. I believe this society to be the most practical Christian institution in America. I have catered to four generations of children. I want children to remember me."

Other codicils were afterward added to the will to include the Tufts and Bridgeport institutions within its provisions. In April, 1889, he arranged that the management of his interests in the show after his death should devolve upon his grandson, Clinton Barnum Seeley.

Mr. Barnum's latest great personal triumph was won during his visit to England in the Fall of 1889 and Winter of 1890. The feat of carrying across the ocean his enormous show compelled the admiration of the English people. They forgot the Jumbo incident and received him with popular enthusiasm. All classes extended to him every possible honor, and his London season was a most wonderful and satisfying success.

No notice of Mr. Barnum would be complete without at least a passing reference to his services in the field of politics. He was originally a Democrat, but when the war broke out was one of the most outspoken defenders of the Union, and subsequently acted enthusiastically with the Republicans. He was four times elected to the General Assembly of Connecticut, and made his mark by advocating the rights of individuals as against railway monopolies. He also served with credit as Mayor of Bridgeport, a city in the improvement and beautifying of which he spent much time and money.

Such in brief has been the career of one of the remarkable men of this country. Phineas Taylor Barnum was a good father, a faithful husband, a true friend, and an honest public servant. He was a shrewd manager, and in his business made money when he could. From the smallest of beginnings he won notoriety, if not fame, in two continents. His life was filled with the most striking examples of what may be accomplished by that peculiar quality known as "Yankee push." His name will long be remembered in his native land. He was twice married, his second wife being an English lady. He engaged in live stock enterprises with Vanderbilt, the Eastmans, and others.

Bridgeport's Great Benefactor

Mr. Barnum's Home Life and His Many Philanthropic Works

BRIDGEPORT, Conn., April 7.—From the time Mr. Barnum decided upon Bridgeport as his home his interest was centered in what would best benefit the city. He invested largely in real estate, induced manufacturing concerns to locate here, and did much to beautify the city. He gave part of the land comprising Seaside Park, one of the most beautiful spots in the country. No charitable object was ever refused assistance by Mr. Barnum, and his name can be found as a Director and stockholder in many of the enterprises that came to this city with struggling concerns and are now rich and prosperous. When he had, by the accumulation of wealth, passed all question of financial trouble, he used what his foresight had secured to him for the benefit of the poor people. He established the system of building houses and selling them to the working people on long payments and low rates of interest, and hundreds of pretty residences now owned by the working class here were secured through Mr. Barnum's generosity.

For the past few years Mr. Barnum's home life was passed quietly at Marina. His household consisted of his wife and servants, including W. D. Roberts, for many years his faithful colored valet. He was always very happy to see his fellow-townsmen, and to call and chat a few minutes with Mr. Barnum was a pleasure many availed themselves of. Marina, his residence, although small compared to Iranistan and Waldemere, the two mammoth structures he had occupied in this city, is most pleasantly situated at Seaside Park, overlooking the Sound, and is perfect from an architectural point of view. His reason for tearing down the stately Waldemere and building the smaller residence at the park was, according to Mr. Barnum's own statement, to have his wife in a house before he died where he thought she would be contented to live the rest of her days. Up to the time he was taken sick, with the exception of the time occupied in his trip to Denver a few months ago that he might see the Rocky Mountains once more before he died, he had been a familiar figure on the streets of this city. He always had a pleasant nod for his acquaintances, and oftentimes stopped them to relate some pleasing story.

Mr. Barnum was very liberal-minded. When the question of giving the Sunday sacred concerts at the park for the benefit of the working people was advanced last Summer, there was a great howl of indignation on the part of many of the residents at the park. Mr. Barnum, however, took a different view of the matter. He was in favor of it. He advocated it through the local papers, and Sunday afternoon, when the first concert was in progress, drove through the park in his carriage, and was cheered by thousands. There was talk of police interference, and Mr. Barnum told the leader of the band to come up to Marina and play all day, and the grounds would be free to all who wished to hear the music.

The Barnum prize medals in the public schools of this city and the many prizes offered to the scholars came from Mr. Barnum. He invariably attended the prize speaking of the scholars, and took great pleasure in the contests. When in his eightieth year, he contracted for the filling in of a portion of his land near Seaside Park. The work cost $100,000, and was finished but a short time ago. It was his intention to erect a large Summer hotel on the land, calling it Ozone Hotel.

Next to Brighton, England, and some other resorts in Europe, he considered Bridgeport the most healthy place in the world, and the atmosphere as having the most ozone, and the building of the great Summer hotel was what he most wished to do before he died. He made statements that he had made arrangements to have his wishes carried out in this respect.

His most recent gift to Bridgeport was that of $150,000 for a new building for the historical and scientific societies of this city, a description of which has already been printed in *The Times*. He expressed a wish a few days ago that he might live to see the dedication of the building that is now in process of construction.

Mr. Barnum at the time of his death was paying taxes on about $1,000,000 worth of real estate in this city, and some volumes of the records of the city are almost completely filled with his real estate transactions.

Appreciated Abroad

LONDON, April 8.—The *Times,* in speaking of the death of P. T. Barnum, says: "The octogenarian showman was unique. The death of Mr. Barnum removes a noteworthy and almost classical figure, typical of the age of transparent puffing through which the modern democracies are passing. His name is a proverb already, and will continue to be a proverb until mankind has ceased to find pleasure in the comedy of a harmless deceiver and the willingly deceived."

All the newspapers contain long obituaries and eulogies of Mr. Barnum.

The Show Went On As Usual
But It Will Be Closed on the Day of the Funeral

The show at the Madison Square Garden went on just the same last night, although the news of the old showman's death reached his partner at 6:30 o'clock, and was being hawked about by evening newspaper vendors as the audience arrived. Mr. Fish, one of Mr. Barnum's secretaries, came down from Bridgeport in the afternoon, when the physicians decided that death was but a few hours off, and said that Mr. Barnum and all the members of his family wished the show to continue in any event and to be closed only on the day of the funeral.

Mr. Bailey said last night that it would have been almost impossible to do anything else. He could not turn away an audience of 10,000 people last night and could not get word out in time to stop hundreds of people coming in from out of town for today's performances. He will announce, however, as soon as the day of the funeral is decided upon, that the show will be closed for both performances that day, and all tickets for these performances will either be exchanged or the money therefor refunded.

Everybody in the company, down to the ring attendants, seemed to be greatly affected at the death of Mr. Barnum and every one had his bit to add to the story of the dead man's kindliness and worth. Mr. Bailey said that his partner's death would make no difference in the show, as by articles of agreement entered into several years ago the company will be held together for many years. The heirs and assigns of both men are directed by the agreement to keep the $3,500,000 capital intact and to continue the present aims and policy of the organization.

WHERE BLUE IS BLUE

Mark Richard

—This stunningly beautiful short story by Mark Richard from the 1998 collection Charity *concerns the emotional and psychological unraveling that occurs in a group of beach town locals when the butchered remains of a carnival contortionist wash ashore.*

THIS LAST TIME THE carnival came to our town we had the contortionist in the inlet. Not exactly all of the contortionist. Somehow she had been sucked into the dredge boom that sweeps back and forth chewing sand underwater to keep the inlet open. Pieces of our contortionist were funneled along the spillway pipeline and were pumped in spume to nourish a washaway beach. What all morning a lifeguard at Fifth Street had thought was a big red jellyfish turned out to be something better identified by a doctor from Dayton, Ohio, out beachcombing with his son. The largest piece anyone had found so far by the time Cecil of our police got down there was a leg with a knot of intestine hung to it. A colored man was holding it against the current next to the dredge with a long-handled crab net. There were so many crabs all over that leg you could hardly make out the tattoos. Us we all who saw it lost our taste for crabmeat the rest of that summer.

There was no certain idea at the time how the contortionist came to be in the inlet, whether she had jumped the inlet bridge or had been pushed or if there was something else to it altogether. We all knew it was her, though, by what remained of the leg tattoos the crabs hadn't eaten off. You would be surprised how deep tattoos get into the skin. Cecil had his notebook, looking; the rest of us hired ourselves out for the job no one else wanted, breaking down the dredge teeth to search for more evidence. You could tell by the way Cecil watched us, sketching in his notebook, that he thought there was something else to this thing altogether.

Cecil, our one friend in the police, the deck-shoe detective with his sketch pad and paint book. All our oceanfront crime, all our oceanfront criminals. Coked-up busboys with steak knives, strangulation games by tourists taken a tightness too far. Seamy little deeds on vacation with evidence slipping away with every turn of the tide. The unidentified dead, homicides away from home, sometimes solvable by Cecil with just a postcard sketch and a drink with the linen maid.

Yes, Cecil, we had all seen the contortionist. *Seen* is an easy word for men like us. In her stuffy tent we saw more of her at once in one angle than we could ever see even of ourselves or the people we get to sleep with us. Like in a painting where everything is shown at once, everything unfolded and flat and impossible. We all stepped close to see more, and her stare kept us back, something in her eyes steady beyond the flicker of lamplight across her face. The more she showed us the more we saw there was no approach to her, nothing to touch that wasn't something else. Her tattooed legs became draping snakes around her neck, her hands kicking feet, her tongue a finger from her mouth pulling through narrows of flesh. Her eyes always on yours until you had to turn away and feel them still burn where they bore into your neck, her eyes we paid to conjure until we couldn't bear it and the tent canvas would bellows in and out about us, men coughing and lighting cigarettes coming out, shaking trouser legs, taking quick steps away from where we had been in this thing together.

Yes, everyone had seen her the last night when she disappeared, even Cecil, Cecil in the back of the tent, once when I had to look away from what the girl was showing. There was Cecil standing next to the carny bouncer where the canvas was knotted against the night, Cecil with his notebook open and sketching. We had also seen the contortionist when we didn't know it was her, us skulking around the carnival for the odd job, taking her for a man in long-sleeve khaki and long khaki pants, a man's hat pulled low over her face, not a scratch of tattoo to show. We saw her when we hustled her boyfriend to buy the scraps from around the docks we worked, things to feed the reptiles he wrestled, big fish guts, shark livers, yellow, and bags of fins. We would hang around to watch the boyfriend feed the big lizards, sissing them out of the low cages and scuffed wooden boxes, kicking open latches with his cowboy boots, the big lizards pressing through the burnt-up grass of the old town lot. They would press around the boyfriend as he fed them from the bags of guts we had brought, the girl in a magic trance watching, cooing them closer to angle their cold eyes to her, fish guts hung in their throats until they scrambled and gaped for more, us jumping the fence to get out of their way.

We had stood there next to the girl in khaki never knowing it was her until the day we showed up with a bottle of scotch and a bag of glue fumes we wanted to share with the boyfriend, and a long sleeve of khaki shot its cuffs into the circle where we were and a spider-sketched hand at the end of a serpent-stained wrist knocked what we offered away. Please don't, she said, and we saw it was her taking the boyfriend away for him to feed something else for her to watch. A carny came by and wrapped the paper sack around his face and lung-sucked the boyfriend's share of fumes. The carny told us that when the boyfriend gets high he tries to erase the girl's tattoos with forks and broken glass. We passed the bag and watched the girl make her rounds, laying out feed and filling water; the toothless lions gummed and licked her, the rainbow animal snatched her against its cage to make another kiss.

These were the ways we had seen the contortionist until this day when we put what we could of her into plastic bags with numbers, packages of her we laid in an ice chest on the deck of the barge. Cecil shuffled through them, looking. There were some parts we didn't find, some parts no one wanted to find. We all thought we had seen more of the contortionist at her last show than we would ever see but the bags in the ice chest proved us wrong, bags full of us working in dark, waist-deep water inside the muddy conveyor boom, flashlights stuck in our teeth with sick suspense.

Cecil shuffled through the plastic packets, a housewife at market, laying a flat piece on the hot steel deck, sketching. Cecil. His off-duty art he entered every year in the Boardwalk Art Show. Pieces that every year we would help him load home unsold. Last year the judge said that there was a disturbing incompleteness about Cecil's work. The portrait Cecil had done of his girlfriend, Veronica, her in purples and blacks, sitting cross-legged, naked, and headless. Cecil could have just been protecting her modesty or maybe he had not yet mastered faces. Sometimes it seemed Cecil had looked at the wrong thing in a roomful of things to paint. A tennis shoe with a ripped-out tongue. A chair like a step to an open window. Sometimes you would wonder what clues to what crimes we had missed were these things that bubbled up in Cecil's brain. Sometimes somebody who knew Cecil would ask him at the art show if his police work affected his artwork and Cecil would say he didn't really think about it all that much. Cecil would say that the best thing about having his art on display on the boardwalk was that he could sit there all day drinking beer and cultivate snitches from amongst the petty thieves who picked the pockets of the crowds.

Shark parties coming in the inlet from the tournament kicked up wakes where we worked, so Cecil and the police pulled us up for the day. They gave us all who had been in the water with what was left of the girl shots against tetanus and some whiffs of gas-soaked rags for the stench. By the bait shack we hosed ourselves down and waited for the cash handout. Forty dollars a head to flush out the dead girl of our dreams. Later, when some of us drank our money, we had to pick pieces of stenciled flesh we thought we saw from the folds of our clothes. There was nothing they could give us against that. Or against Cecil's suspicion. Empty your pockets before you leave the area, he told us.

Jesus Christ, we said.

Across the inlet boats were flying fin flags, jagged-mouth carcasses bled and lolled across aft decks and were bent over sterns. An Instamatic crowd of tourists in the way of us hustling tips from the beer-drunk fishermen and sunburned mates, us springing lines and running hose. Cecil followed us over, leaning on a gas pump, his sketchbook furled in a back pocket, him just watching.

They had brought in hammerheads and browns, some duskies. Some were cleanly gaffed and dull-eyed, others were beat all to hell, their skin peeled back in places like weather-blistered vinyl. Brain cavities caved in under the gusto of softball bats and lead pipes, shark hunting the thuggery of sport fishing.

All of the boats were in except for our friend Royce and his boat, the *Risky Business,* Royce still outside the inlet dragging a tiger shark backward by the tail to drown it, five miles now and still the shark fought them as they tried to bring it aboard. From the dock you could hear them work the fish over once more, first a shotgun then a service revolver.

A commotion at the weigh-in, the official water people in blue shirts with clipboards and fillet knives were there to gut open shark bellies, part of some research, they said, it was all spelled out in the print at the bottom of the shark-hunt tickets. There were some spit words from the trophy-conscious and a thrown can of beer. Somebody said Cecil ought to step in but Cecil did not.

Royce was finally coming in the inlet, still the occasional gunshot to the head of the monster lashed to his boat. When hoisted up it split a shackled block and broke one of our wrists. Then we winched the shark up on a frame lashed to a telephone pole and nobody could believe it, the fish too large to weigh. The official water people came out of the crowd with all their clipboards and knives and the commotion came up again.

Royce sat up in his flying bridge chewing the strand of monofilament his sunglasses were strung from. Shank, his mate, picked up a gaff off the stern coming around the carcass toward a blue-shirt girl. She had her knife hard into his shark's belly, salt-smelling syrup leaking everywhere.

You had to be careful with Shank, in his mind a bounty hunter of these big fish that he and Royce always won these contests with. His red face eaten up with little skin barnacles, his brain broiled under years of white glare. You could knock Shank down but Shank would get up, and you could knock Shank down again, and again he would get up, until after a while of this you had to pick up something handily substantial like a folding chair to hit him with so he would stay down. You could see this drinking in the Grey Gull afternoons after coming in.

Shank shoved over the official water girl and drew the knife from the shark, spinning it into the telephone pole. Cecil eased out of the crowd and stood close to Shank; whistling admiration at the size of his shark until Shank tapped his gaff, eyes down, against one of his rough raw feet.

What about it, Cecil? said Royce. Royce wanted to know didn't they need a search warrant or something like that to butcher up a trophy fish.

Cecil said it didn't seem so and the water girl went to pull the knife out of the pole but Cecil was there first handing the blade over to Shank, and in that way, everything was all right.

You are always surprised at what is in a shark, some of it still alive coming out, pushing eager flips to show that it is not dead, you looking down thinking, Yeah, right, you've been *eaten!*

In the contest sharks there was the usual, the bluefish, the chunks of tuna heads in onionskin bags that hunters use to work up their slicks of chum. In the tigers you find the bottom dwellers and the sunken throwaway, skates and rays the sharks snuffle off the bottom where they have hidden in the sand. They'll eat rocks, shells, junk. Royce and Shank's shark had other things in it, things like we knew when we saw them spill out would be things that Cecil would want to sketch.

First was the wad of stench that cleared the dock. Then there was a Dixie cup, a beer can, some sheets of undigested skate wings that fanned themselves out like pages in a thumbed-through book. They raked more of the muck until somebody yelled, There's a hand! a scream and a laugh. Cecil stared hard over shoulders while a knife coaxed out the hand. Aw, they said, it's just a rubber glove, faded that water-flesh gray and full of sand. A dog-food can stuck with holes on a string was explained away as what crabbers use to bait their traps. The last was a shark-size bite of plywood and a shotgunned seagull.

It is against our laws to shoot down seagulls to freshen up the chum-slick blood, and that dead bird hurt the way having the winning fish looked, everyone always watching Royce and Shank.

We finished cleaning Royce's boat and helped Shank lug away the shark. Cecil was already drinking beers at the Grey Gull, sketching on a paper sheet torn from his book. He said he was working on getting mouths right. Every time you said anything, Cecil would stare at your mouth as you spoke, making strokes on his page. Having someone stare at your mouth while you talk makes you feel that they do not believe whatever it is you are saying. Cecil had all our mouths down on his paper, working them one by one in little strokes of disbelief.

Royce bought us our beers and picked at Cecil about the dead girl, wasn't she the one twisted up in the tent show, and Cecil said hadn't Royce seen her there himself? Royce said he'd ever deny being there, and Cecil said, I saw you there that last night with Shank, and Royce said he'd ever deny being there to his wife, and Cecil kept sketching Royce's mouth, saying, Well, I am certainly not your wife.

We all took our turns in disbelief. We had all been to the carnival that last night and we all told our stories. I finally said I didn't like Cecil asking any more dispersions on us and Cecil turned to me saying, Right, and it wasn't you in the bus station that time trying to pick up those runaways with a pocketful of tokens from the video arcade.

I said, That had all been a misundertanding. It had only happened once.

Cecil left us at the Grey Gull, us all sitting around staring at his beer-soggy sketch page, a small wet canvas of little blue kisses.

No more dead girl washed our beach. The inlet was closed for a day while they back-flushed the dredge, not finding anything else, not even a fingernail. There was a short thing in the paper about the girl but the carnival closed and people seemed to forget. The old town lot was empty for a few days except for flattened popcorn boxes and the white crusts of lizard shit, then came the rolling in of the antique cars for our festival. We swept the boardwalk for the art show, stopping on our brooms to watch overhead the flying jets practicing stunts for Sunday.

On Sunday they had the sand-castle contests and the free beer, lifeguard races and the stunt pilots. There were sailors there because the fleet was in, and in the bars there were rounds and rounds of drinks on the houses.

Locals on the boardwalk browsed, the better off from out of town came to buy a certain kind of art for the summer houses. Seascapes, seagulls, sea horses, shipwrecks, sand dunes, and sunsets, all the kind of art you see in the sweep of your flashlight on their walls those nights off-season.

Cecil's work was not what they wanted, wasn't enough sand in it, they said. The boardwalk judge said that Cecil had a hardware-store palette, that when Cecil wanted to do blue sky or blue ocean Cecil just squeezed a tube of blue paint and said Here's blue! The judge said that the best he could say about Cecil's work was that although the paintings were just a menace of fragments, they seemed to have in them a primitive, dreamlike quality. Then the judge looked ahead to the exhibit of seashell wind chimes and sad clown faces on velvet he was to speak on next, Cecil thanking him very much.

By evening we had all dirtied our pockets with money. The light was gone, the beer stands stood empty, spigots blowing foam. Trash drifted along the boardwalk, and on the beach drunks were getting knocked down by knee-high surf.

Cecil. Sitting alone, staring across the boardwalk at his unsold art, beer can adrip from his hand. The last other artist loading a case of turquoise jewelry into a van.

Cecil said that he was glad to see us. I said we had come back over to see if maybe he needed some help taking the exhibition home. I also in secret meant that we might borrow Cecil's car to run an errand to a girl's house by midnight with. You could borrow Cecil's car if you would leave him a note to where it was.

Cecil pointed out to his, the only artwork left on the boardwalk.

These are so new I only painted them last night, he said. He said after he had gone to sleep he got up and went into the garage and painted all night. The paint still isn't dry and this morning I got it all over the seats of my car, he said.

You know, when I paint, I don't have any idea what I'm going to paint, Cecil said. Sometimes I see things like Veronica naked or the sun coming up and I want to paint to capture, and then sometimes I see some piece of something that hangs on the edge of my mind and won't go over and I paint for release. Maybe I should just get myself a camera, Cecil said, and drank his beer.

How much have you had to drink this day? somebody asks Cecil, but Cecil goes on saying into his second six-pack he started to see something *going on* in this new work, a *welling up* on the edge of his mind of a larger picture, something bigger, something all in a series. We all looked to where the paintings were hanging but the sun gone down had emptied them out of everything but the dark.

Cecil stood up and said to allow him to give us a tour of his exhibition. Standing close we looked at the first painting by cigarette-lighter light. Cecil said that the painting was called *S Designs on Gray, What Boat Propeller Looks Like Going Through Skin,* and we all stepped back, Cecil saying he saw it the other day in one of those plastic bags we collected with a number. He said at the police lab downtown that they had told him the girl was still alive when she got the propeller blades across her back. Cecil asked us wasn't it a wonder of modern science?

What made all this well up, said Cecil, is that nobody had a boat out the inlet when the girl disappeared. He had asked us all, hadn't he, Cecil said. *S Designs on Gray,* and it is not for sale.

Cecil showed us next the second picture he said he worked off a sketch he had made shark-hunt day. He said he had liked the look of all the lines and shadows of the workboats tied up near the fuel dock. They cut an angle that caught my eye, Cecil said.

We all took turns holding the lighter to see by until it got too hot to hold and we had to drop it in the sand.

See how this one boat in particular is choked against the dock at low tide? Cecil asked us. We looked but couldn't see, could not have seen that he meant Shank's boat.

Cecil said he had to wonder where the girl got her propeller bites if not in the inlet. He said he also had to wonder why a familiar hand at boats like Shank would cinch his lines too tight in the first place, what, was he in a hurry when he tied up? Cecil said these were the things that hung on the edge of his mind.

Cecil's next work we remembered from seeing in daylight. Cecil had painted a wagon wheel on a piece of raw plywood, then nailed a beaten-flat dog-food can to its hub. He was calling it *Shark Strike!* In the day, pieces of dog food still in the can had attracted flies and people had pointed. Cecil said he thought the flies added a dimension of motion to the piece.

Cecil said that the key to the work was the monofilament string tied to the dog-food can, like the string that was tied to the can in Royce and Shank's tiger. That fact had hung on his mind, Cecil said, why a crabber would tie string onto a dog-food can he was just going to drop into a crab pot-bait pocket. Cecil said he had never seen that done before.

I was getting anxious about this welling up of Cecil's thought and I wanted to see that girl on an errand by midnight, so I said, Come on, Cecil, do you want us to help take this exhibition home or what?

Cecil said to me that I and all of us were going to sit tight and answer some questions. Cecil said he was going to find out all there was about who killed that girl.

Aw, she drownt in the inlet, somebody said.

Yeah, she fell in, couldn't swim, somebody said.

Likely drunk, fell in and drownt, somebody said.

Dead now, in pieces too, said somebody.

On and on, through and through, dead, over, us we all said.

Cecil said even though she didn't drink and the boyfriend said she could swim he would grant us there was an invitation of death about the girl, the deadness already in her eyes when she danced. Didn't you all see that is what it really was? I saw it, said Cecil. Just like I've seen in so many faces on this beach. I wish I could paint that face. When I see it I know there will be trouble later. That would have rounded out this little exhibition of mine, Cecil said, a painting of the fear on your faces from her invitation. I saw all of you feeding off her that last night and I knew there would be trouble. I wish I could paint that hunger for the fear but I haven't mastered faces yet. Your hunger! Your fear! said Cecil suddenly, staggering up toward us. You all know I'm right, he said.

Steady, Cecil, we said. You've been drinking.

Yes, I have, said Cecil and he sat down.

But I've seen something here, he said, something welling up in the edges of these paintings. I don't have anything on any one of you specific but I got it all in general. Somebody coaxed her out on the ocean then ran over her with his boat. Her body just came through the inlet on the tide.

Nobody could have got that woman to do nothing she didn't want to do, we said, and Cecil said, Somebody made her an unusual offer, something she had never heard before to do. It wouldn't have been for a man or a drink or anything else. Somebody with a load of chum offered to take her out in the ocean and feed the animals. Somebody asked her would she like to feed the biggest fishes ever.

That's crazy, we said. Nobody goes out in the ocean in the middle of the night to feed fish.

Oh, but Cecil said, feeding the animals was the only thing she had ever seemed to like to do.

Cecil rapped his knuckles on his plywood painting. Digging out the plywood like the piece they found in Royce and Shank's shark, Cecil said he finally found an old piece to paint on in his garage. Holding it he remembered a trick he had seen fishing one time, a man opening the Sunday paper page by page and laying it out over the ocean, the man saying the fish liked the shade when it was hot and would congregate. Cecil said the man told him professionals sometimes used baited plywood but it was a lot of trouble.

So what, we said.

So what does Shank do off-season, Cecil asked us and we all knew, us all during hurricane season for a few dollars each riding crew with

Shank in his truck nailing plywood over cottage windows on the south of the beach.

So what, we said.

So the night before the shark hunt Shank goes out to rig the contest laying out plywood baited with dog-food cans and chum. All he would have to do then is figure out the current the next day to find all the big fish congregating in the shade.

Your figuring sounds fishy, somebody said.

Fishy, Cecil said, is Shank's workboat snugged too tight to the dock shark-hunt day. It means to me that when Shank tied up his boat there was something big on his sunburnt mind, something so big that after all these years tying up tide in and tide out, something made him forget to rightly rig his rig.

Rig his rig? You're drunk, Cecil, we said.

I think this is more asking dispersions, I said to Cecil. I said that since he was leaning so hard on Shank why didn't he ask Shank about all of this instead of fouling us up in it, and Cecil said that nobody can seem to find Shank, wherever he has conveniently disappeared off to, from Panama to New Brunswick. I'll tell you why you are all fouled up in this, is because I asked you all, Did any boats go in or out the night before we found the girl, and everybody said, Oh no, nobody went out at all, and the only reason beside my sketch of the lines I figured it was Shank was by checking all the gas receipts at the pump house and I saw he'd had to top off his tanks to lay bait and rig the contest. But none of you all saw fit to help me out because you all are so tight with Royce and Shank, everybody wanting Royce and Shank to be able to bring in the biggest shark no matter how they get it so you all can clean up Royce's boat and gut Shank's shark to put in your pockets a little extra spending money. Nobody is going to worry if somehow this girl they saw in the way they saw her got herself out in the ocean with Shank and into some trouble she couldn't handle where something happened, she was pushed or jumped and Shank ran over her with his boat. That's still murder. That is still murder. That's you helping decide to write that girl out of the life book and you all can hardly make the decision of whether to bathe or not, much less that one. You all keep quiet because everybody here likes to feed off Royce and Shank, never mind there was murder.

And I'll tell you something else. I think it takes more than one man to handle those plywood and dog-food rigs over the side of a work-boat, and I don't think Shank was by himself, especially if he could get a little help for cheap, a little help maybe for a little pocket money for somebody to go off and drink on and run around to get their god-damn errands done by midnight!

I said, That does it. We said we didn't want to borrow his goddamn car anymore. We said we just wanted to help him move his goddamn no-sale exhibit home. And Cecil said we were all going to help him move the exhibition all right. He said he was going to give us all a little piece of it to take home whatever rat-hole or sewer pipe we slept in calling home was. He said he wanted us to get us a hammer and get us a nail, and to nail up on the walls of our rat-holes and sewer pipes the piece he was going to give to each of us, he wanted each of us every time we woke up from our cheap-help-drinking sleep to think about being in on writing somebody out of the life book, that if we thought we could sanely think about hiding fear by helping hide the man who killed the girl, well then we ought to have some lovely artwork of our own of the whole thing to help us contemplate with.

Cecil ripped down all his art and pushed it on us, a piece to us all.

Cecil, we said.

Go on with it, get out of here, Cecil said. Each of you gets a piece. Any more than one piece, I can tell you, is too much for one man to bear.

Cecil, we said.

Go, said Cecil. Scurry to your rat-holes and sewer pipes. I don't ever want to see your faces. And don't leave town, ever!

We all took our art. There wasn't the best of us there who could tell Cecil what we knew, how wrong he was about us. Men like us can never tell a man like Cecil all we know. We could never tell him of a place we knew, a place where finally the ocean is blue blue, the eel-grass is green green, where a man like Shank might rest forever, wrapped in chains to keep him down, his flesh feeding the fishes and no more murder in his crab-eaten eyes. We could never tell a man like Cecil about a pretty place like that. But maybe we hoped as we scattered with what he had given us in our arms, maybe someday somebody could paint him a picture.

EPILOGUE

Gwendoline Riley

TWO CLOWNS FALL IN love on April Fool's Day. Two painted mouths. Four red-rimmed eyes. What's in their pockets? What's up their sleeves? They're throwing buckets of glitter; taking a tumble, now taking a bow. Their eyes are crossed out. The greasepaint's stubborn. Here comes the fire truck. The klaxon siren hees and haws. Get up you two. *Hee Haw.* Get up. *Hee Haw.* The blue light blinks on two empty costumes in the sawdust.

PERMISSIONS

"Circus Music: for clowns, lions, and solo trapeze" by Edward Hoagland. Copyright © 2002 by *Harper's* magazine. All rights reserved. Reproduced from the February issue by special permission.

Excerpt from *Something Wicked This Way Comes* by Ray Bradbury. Copyright © 1962, renewed 1990 by Ray Bradbury. Reprinted by permission of Don Congdon Associates, Inc.

Excerpt from *Suite for Calliope* by Ellen Hunnicutt. Copyright © 1987 by Ellen Hunnicutt. Reprinted by arrangement with Walker & Co.

Excerpt from *Blood and Grits* by Harry Crews. Copyright © 1988 by Harry Crews. Reprinted by permissions of John Hawkins & Associates, Inc.

"The Frog Prince" by Johnny Meah. Copyright © 1996, 1998 by Johnny Meah. Reprinted by permission of the author. Originally appeared in *Shocked and Amazed!*, Vol. 5, 1998.

Excerpt from *Up in the Old Hotel* by Joseph Mitchell. Copyright © 1992 by Joseph Mitchell. Used by permission of Pantheon Books, a division of Random House, Inc.

"The Passing of Philomena Marker" by James Taylor. Copyright © 1995 by James Taylor. Reprinted by permission of the author. Originally appeared in *Shocked and Amazed!*, Vol. 1, 1995.

Excerpt from *Geek Love* by Katherine Dunn. Copyright © 1989 by Katherine Dunn. Used by permission of Alfred A. Knopf, a division of Random House, Inc.

Excerpt from *Lobster Boy* by Fred Rosen. Copyright © 1995 by Fred Rosen. Reprinted by permission of Citadel Press/Kensington Publishing Corp. www.kensingtonbooks.com. All rights reserved.